SCHOLASTIC

D0488333

Terms and conditions

IMPORTANT – PERMITTED USE AND WARNINGS – READ CAREFULLY BEFORE USING

IF YOU ACCEPT THE ABOVE CONDITIONS YOU MAY PROCEED TO USE THE CD-ROM.

Recommended system requirements:

- Windows: XP (Service Pack 3), Vista (Service Pack 2), Windows 7 or Windows 8 with 2.33GHz processor
- Mac: OS 10.6 to 10.8 with Intel Core™ Duo processor
- 1GB RAM (recommended)
- 1024 x 768 Screen resolution
- CD-ROM drive (24x speed recommended)
- 16-bit sound card
- Adobe Reader (version 9 recommended for Mac users)
- Broadband internet connections (for installation and updates)

For all technical support queries, ple███████████████s on 0845 6039091.

■■SCHOLASTIC

Book End, Range Road, Witney, Oxfordshire, OX29 0YD
www.scholastic.co.uk

© 2014, Scholastic Ltd

1 2 3 4 5 6 7 8 9   4 5 6 7 8 9 0 1 2 3

British Library Cataloguing-in-Publication Data
A catalogue record for this book is available from the
British Library.

ISBN 978-1407-12767-5
Printed by Bell & Bain Ltd, Glasgow

Author
Malcolm Anderson

Consultant
Juliet Gladston

Series Editor
Peter Riley

Editorial team
Rachel Morgan, Melissa Somers, Pollyanna Poulter,
Louise Titley, Kate Redmond

Cover Design
Andrea Lewis

Design Team
Sarah Garbett, Shelley Best and Andrea Lewis

CD-ROM development
Hannah Barnett, Phil Crothers, MWA Technologies
Private Ltd

Typesetting
Tracey Camden

Illustrations
Tomek.gr

Every effort has been made to trace copyright
holders for the works reproduced in this book,
and the publishers apologise for any inadvertent
omissions.

Contents

Introduction

About the series

The *100 Science Lessons* series is designed to meet the requirements of the 2014 Curriculum, Science Programmes of Study. There are six books in the series, Years 1–6, and each book contains lesson plans, resources and ideas matched to the new curriculum. It can be a complex task to ensure that a progressive and appropriate curriculum is followed in all year groups; this series has been carefully structured to ensure that a progressive and appropriate curriculum is followed throughout.

About the new curriculum

The curriculum documentation for Science provides a single-year programme of study for each year in Key Stage 1 and 2. However schools are only required to teach the relevant programmes of study by the end of the key stage and can approach their curriculum planning with greater flexibility than ever before in the following ways. Within each key stage they can introduce content earlier or later than set out in the programme of study and they can introduce key stage content during an earlier key stage if appropriate. Whatever plan is used the school curriculum for science must be set out on a year-by-year basis and made available online.

Knowledge and conceptual understanding

The national curriculum for science aims to ensure that all children develop scientific knowledge and conceptual understanding through the specific disciplines of Biology (Plants, Animals including humans, Seasonal changes, Living things and their habitats, Evolution and inheritance), Chemistry (Everyday materials, Uses of everyday materials, Rocks, States of matter, Properties and changes of materials) and Physics (Seasonal changes, Light, Forces and magnets, Sound, Electricity, Earth and space). It is vitally important that the children develop a secure understanding of each key block of knowledge and its concepts in order to progress to the next stage. As they do so they should also be familiar with and use technical terminology accurately and precisely and build up an extended specialist vocabulary. Equally they should also apply their mathematical knowledge to their understanding of science including collecting, presenting and analysing data.

The nature, processes and methods of science

The requirements needed for the understanding of the nature, processes and methods of science are set out at the beginning of Key Stage 1, Lower Key Stage 2 and Upper Key Stage 2 in a section called Working scientifically. This section of the curriculum replaces the Science enquiry section of the previous science curriculum. It is important that Working scientifically is not taught as a separate strand and guidance is given in the non-statutory notes to help embed it in the scientific content of each area of the programme of study. In the working scientifically section the children are introduced to a range of types of scientific enquiry. These include observing over time, classifying and grouping, identifying, comparative and fair testing (making controlled investigations), pattern seeking and researching using secondary sources. The questions used to stimulate the enquiry should be answered by the children through collecting, presenting and analysing data and drawing conclusions from their findings.

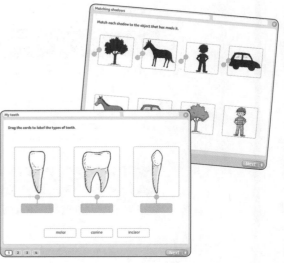

■SCHOLASTIC

About the book

This book is divided into six chapters; each chapter contains a half-term's work and is based around one of the content areas in the programme of study. Each chapter follows the same structure:

Chapter introduction

At the start of each chapter there is an introduction with the following features. This includes:

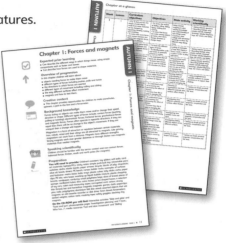

- **Expected prior learning:** What the children are expected to know before starting the work in the chapter.
- **Overview of progression:** A brief explanation of how the children progress through the chapter.
- **Creative context:** How the chapter could link to other curriculum areas.
- **Background knowledge:** A section explaining scientific terms and suchlike to enhance your subject knowledge, where required.
- **Speaking scientifically:** A section highlighting some of the key words featured in the chapter for building up the children's scientific vocabulary. This is also a feature of every lesson (see below).
- **Preparation:** Any resources required for the teaching of the chapter, including things that need to be sourced or prepared and the content that can be located on the CD-ROM. As part of the preparation of all practical work you should consult your school's policies on practical work and select activities for which you are confident to take responsibility. The ASE *Be Safe Forth Edition* gives very useful guidance on health and safety issues in primary science.
- **Chapter at a glance:** This is a table that summarises the content of each lesson, including: the curriculum objectives, lesson objectives, the main activity or activities and the working scientifically statutory requirements that are featured in each lesson.

Lessons

Each chapter contains six weeks' of lessons, each week contains three lessons. At the start of each half term there is an introductory lesson revisiting relevant content from work in previous years then introducing the new area of study. There is also a checkpoint section to check on the children's knowledge before proceeding to the next lesson.

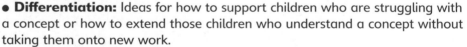

All lessons including the introductory lesson have lesson plans that include the relevant combination of headings from below.

- **Lesson objectives:** A list of objectives for the lesson.
- **Resources:** What you require to teach the lesson.
- **Speaking scientifically:** A list of words to use in the lesson. The children should learn to spell them, understand their meanings and use them when talking about their activities, particularly when working scientifically.
- **Introduction:** A short and engaging activity to begin the lesson.
- **Whole-class work:** Working together as a class.

- **Group/Paired/Independent work:** Children working independently of the teacher in pairs, groups or alone.
- **Differentiation:** Ideas for how to support children who are struggling with a concept or how to extend those children who understand a concept without taking them onto new work.
- **Science in the wider world:** The information in this section may develop some of the content and concepts in the lesson and show how they relate to the wider world in their implications for humanity (such as health care) or impact on the environment (such as initiating conservation strategies).
- **Review:** A chance to review the children's learning and ensure the outcomes of the lesson have been achieved.

Assess and review

At the end of each chapter are activities for assessing and reviewing the children's understanding. These can be conducted during the course of the chapter's work, saved until the end of the chapter or done at a later date.

All assessment and review activities follow the same format:

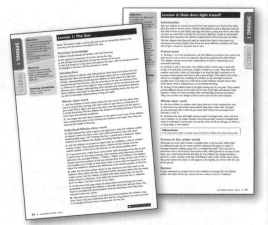

- **Curriculum objectives:** These are the areas of focus for the assess and review activity. There may be one focus or more than one depending on the activity.
- **Resources:** What you require to conduct the activities.
- **Working scientifically:** Each activity features one or more of the Working scientifically objectives for assessment.
- **Revise:** A series of short activities or one longer activity to revise and consolidate the children's learning and ensure they understand the concept(s).
- **Assess:** An assessment activity to provide a chance for the children to demonstrate their understanding and for you to check this.
- **Further practice:** Ideas for further practice on the focus, whether children are insecure in their learning or you want to provide extra practice or challenge.

Photocopiable pages

At the end of each chapter are some photocopiable pages that will have been referred to in the lesson plans.

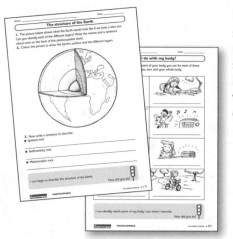

These sheets are for the children to use; there is generally a title, an instruction, an activity and an 'I can' statement at the bottom. These sheets are also provided on the CD-ROM alongside additional pages as referenced in the lessons (see page 7 About the CD-ROM). The children should be encouraged to complete the 'I can' statements by colouring in the traffic lights to say how they think they have done (red – not very well, amber – ok, green – very well).

■SCHOLASTIC

About the CD-ROM

The CD-ROM contains:

- Printable versions of the photocopiable sheets from the book and additional photocopiable sheets as referenced in the lesson plans.
- Interactive activities for children to complete or to use on the whiteboard.
- Media resources to display.
- Printable versions of the lesson plans.
- Digital versions of the lesson plans with the relevant resources linked to them.

Getting started

- Put the CD-ROM into your CD-ROM drive.
  - For Windows users, the install wizard should autorun, if it fails to do so then navigate to your CD-ROM drive. Then follow the installation process.
  - For Mac users, copy the disk image file to your hard drive. After it has finished copying double-click it to mount the disk image. Navigate to the mounted disk image and run the installer. After installation the disk image can be unmounted and the DMG can be deleted from the hard drive.
- To complete the installation of the program you need to open the program and click 'Update' in the pop-up. Please note – this CD-ROM is web-enabled and the content will be downloaded from the internet to your hard-drive to populate the CD-ROM with the relevant resources. This only needs to be done on first use, after this you will be able to use the CD-ROM without an internet connection. If at any point any content is updated you will receive another pop-up upon start up with an internet connection.

Navigating the CD-ROM

There are two options to navigate the CD-ROM either as a Child or as a Teacher.

Child

- Click on the 'Child' button on the first menu screen.
- In the second menu click on the relevant class (please note only the books installed on the machine or network will be accessible. You can also rename year groups to match your school's naming conventions via the Teacher > Settings > Rename books area).
- A list of interactive activities will be displayed, children need to locate the correct one and click 'Go' to launch it.
- There is the opportunity to print or save a PDF of the activity at the end.

Teacher

- Click on the 'Teacher' button on the first menu screen and you will be taken to a screen showing which of the *100 English* books you have purchased. From here, you can also access information about getting started and the credits.
- To enter the product click 'Next' in the bottom right.
- You then need to enter a password (the password is: login).
- On first use:
  - Enter as a Guest by clicking on the 'Guest' button.
  - If desired, create a profile for yourself by adding your name to the list of users. Profiles allow you to save favourites and to specify which year group(s) you wish to be able to view.
  - Go to 'Settings' to create a profile for yourself – click 'Add user' and enter your name. Then choose the year groups you wish to have access to (you can return to this screen to change this at any time). Click on 'Login' at the top of the screen to re-enter the disk under your new profile.

- On subsequent uses you can choose your name from the drop-down list. The 'Guest' option will always be available if you, or a colleague, wish to use this.
- You can search the CD-ROM using the tools or save favourites.

For more information about how to use the CD-ROM, please refer to the help file which can be found in the teacher area of the CD-ROM. It is a red button with a question mark on it on the right-hand side of the screen just underneath the 'Settings' tab.

Curriculum grid

The tables below show the weekly curriculum coverage for each chapter.

Curriculum objectives	Autumn 1						Autumn 2					
	W1	W2	W3	W4	W5	W6	W1	W2	W3	W4	W5	W6
Plants												
To identify and describe the functions of different parts of flowering plants												
To explore the requirements of plants for life and growth and how they vary from plant to plant												
To investigate the way in which water is transported within plants												
To explore the part that flowers play in the life cycle of flowering plants												
Animals, including humans												
To identify that animals need the right types and amount of nutrition, and that they cannot make their own food							✓	✓	✓			✓
To identify that humans and some animals have skeletons and muscles for support, protection and movement										✓	✓	
Rocks												
To compare and group together different kinds of rocks on the basis of their appearance and simple physical properties												
To describe in simple terms how fossils are formed when things that have lived are trapped within a rock												
To recognise that soils are made from rocks and organic matter												
Light												
To recognise that they need light to see things and that dark is the absence of light												
To notice that light reflects from surfaces												
To recognise that shadows are formed when the light from a light source is blocked by a solid object												
To recognise that shadows are formed when the light from a light source is blocked by a solid object												
To find patterns in the way that the size of shadows change												
Forces and magnets												
To compare how things move on different surfaces			✓	✓								
To notice that some forces need contact between two objects, but magnetic forces can act at a distance	✓	✓				✓						
To observe how magnets attract or repel each other and attract some materials					✓	✓						
To compare and group together a variety of everyday materials on the basis of whether they are magnetic					✓	✓						
To describe magnets as having two poles												
To predict whether two magnets will attract or repel each other					✓							

Curriculum objectives	Spring 1						Spring 2					
	W1	W2	W3	W4	W5	W6	W1	W2	W3	W4	W5	W6
Plants												
To identify and describe the functions of different parts of flowering plants							✓	✓				
To explore the requirements of plants for life and growth and how they vary from plant to plant								✓	✓	✓		✓
To investigate the way in which water is transported within plants							✓					
To explore the part that flowers play in the life cycle of flowering plants										✓	✓	✓
Animals, including humans												
To identify that animals need the right types and amount of nutrition, and that they cannot make their own food.												
To identify that humans and some animals have skeletons and muscles for support, protection and movement												
Rocks												
To compare and group together different kinds of rocks on the basis of their appearance and simple physical properties												
To describe in simple terms how fossils are formed when things that have lived are trapped within a rock												
To recognise that soils are made from rocks and organic matter												
Light												
To recognise that they need light to see things and that dark is the absence of light	✓				✓							
To notice that light reflects from surfaces		✓										
To recognise that shadows are formed when the light from a light source is blocked by a solid object	✓											
To recognise that shadows are formed when the light from a light source is blocked by a solid object		✓	✓	✓								
To find patterns in the way that the size of shadows change			✓	✓	✓							
Forces and magnets												
To compare how things move on different surfaces												
To notice that some forces need contact between two objects, but magnetic forces can act at a distance												
To observe how magnets attract or repel each other and attract some materials												
To compare and group together a variety of everyday materials on the basis of whether they are magnetic												
To describe magnets as having two poles												
To predict whether two magnets will attract or repel each other												

Curriculum objectives	Summer 1						Summer 2					
	W1	W2	W3	W4	W5	W6	W1	W2	W3	W4	W5	W6
Plants												
To identify and describe the functions of different parts of flowering plants												
To explore the requirements of plants for life and growth and how they vary from plant to plant												
To investigate the way in which water is transported within plants												
To explore the part that flowers play in the life cycle of flowering plants												
Animals, including humans												
To identify that animals need the right types and amount of nutrition, and that they cannot make their own food												
To identify that humans and some animals have skeletons and muscles for support, protection and movement							✓	✓	✓	✓	✓	✓
Rocks												
To compare and group together different kinds of rocks on the basis of their appearance and simple physical properties	✓	✓		✓		✓						
To describe in simple terms how fossils are formed when things that have lived are trapped within a rock			✓									
To recognise that soils are made from rocks and organic matter					✓							
Light												
To recognise that they need light to see things and that dark is the absence of light												
To notice that light reflects from surfaces												
To recognise that shadows are formed when the light from a light source is blocked by a solid object												
To recognise that shadows are formed when the light from a light source is blocked by a solid object												
To find patterns in the way that the size of shadows change												
Forces and magnets												
To compare how things move on different surfaces												
To notice that some forces need contact between two objects, but magnetic forces can act at a distance												
To observe how magnets attract or repel each other and attract some materials												
To compare and group together a variety of everyday materials on the basis of whether they are magnetic												
To describe magnets as having two poles												
To predict whether two magnets will attract or repel each other												

Forces and magnets

Expected prior learning
● Can describe the different ways in which things move, using simple comparisons such as faster and slower.
● Can describe how forces are used to shape materials.

Overview of progression
In this chapter children will learn about:
● objects needing forces to make them move
● different types of forces including pushes, pulls and twists
● the directions in which forces are exerted
● different types of movement including rolling and sliding
● the way different surfaces effect movement
● magnets and how to test them.

Creative context
● This chapter provides opportunities for children to build ramps and design posters about magnets.

Background knowledge
Forces acting on objects can make them move and/or change their speed, direction or shape. Different types of forces include: contact forces (pushing, pulling or twisting); electrostatic forces; frictional forces; gravitational forces and magnetic forces. Forces often operate in opposite directions. If they are equal then there will be no change in the object's movement. If they are unequal then a change will happen.

Magnetism is a force of attraction or repulsion between certain materials. Iron, cobalt, nickel and their alloys are all attracted to magnets. Like gravity, magnetism can work from a distance. Magnets have different strengths. Strong magnets work over greater distances or through thicker non-magnetic materials than weaker magnets.

Speaking scientifically
Children should be familiar with the terms: contact and non-contact forces, balanced forces, friction, south and north poles (for magnets).

Preparation
You will need to provide: Children's scooters; toy gliders; soft balls; card; art materials; laptops/PCs; sticky notes; simple push/pull toy; retractable pens; switches; cloths; elastic bands; paper arrows; bicycle; blocks of jelly; chopsticks; olive oil; bowls; timers; PE bench; ramps; ladder racks; examples of surfaces and footwear; metre sticks; balls; trays; plastic cubes; lolly sticks; corks; paper clips; PE kits; wire loops; washing-up liquid; bubble mixture; plastic chopping boards; sandpaper; corduroy; small polythene bags; slices of bread; pieces of sponge; cardboard tubes; dice; coins; boxes; prism-shaped boxes; a selection of toy cars; rulers and measuring tapes; corrugated card; cotton; strong thin thread; bar and horseshoe magnets; magnetic games; cloth; paperclips; pins; nails; polystyrene; aluminium foil; thin wood; assorted objects that use magnets; an old cassette recorder or disk drive; 5mm dowel; forcemeters; slotted weights; cotton reels; masking tape; safety goggles; stacking ring magnets.

On the CD-ROM you will find: Interactive activities 'Slide and glide' and 'Twist and turn'; photocopiable pages 'Investigation planning' and 'I have... Who has...?'; media resources 'Fast and slow movement' and 'Sliding'

Chapter at a glance

Week	Lesson	Curriculum objectives	Objectives	Main activity	Working scientifically
1	1	• (Y2) To find out how the shapes of solid objects made from some materials can be changed by squashing, bending, twisting and stretching. • To notice that some forces need contact between two objects, but magnetic forces can act at a distance.	• To review the actions of sliding, rolling, falling, flying, walking and running. • To know that forces can make moving objects go faster, slow down, change direction or change shape.	Using concept mapping to elicit existing knowledge and understanding of how things move. Creating a class collage with annotated drawings to show the different ways things move.	• Asking relevant questions. • Recording findings using simple scientific language, drawings, labelled diagrams, keys, bar charts, and tables.
	2	• To notice that some forces need contact between two objects, but magnetic forces can act at a distance.	• To know the different types of forces. • To identify pushes, pulls and twists as examples of forces in action.	Looking at examples of toys that require a force, a push, a pull or a twist in order to play with them.	• Asking relevant questions. • Recording findings using simple scientific language, drawings, labelled diagrams, keys, bar charts, and tables.
	3	• To notice that some forces need contact between two objects, but magnetic forces can act at a distance.	• To understand that all forces are directional. • To learn how arrows can be used to indicate the direction of a force.	Using practical work to experience and feel how forces are exerted. Introducing how to use an arrow to represent the direction of a force.	• Asking relevant questions. • Recording findings using simple scientific language, drawings, labelled diagrams, keys, bar charts, and tables.
2	1	• To notice that some forces need contact between two objects, but magnetic forces can act at a distance.	• To know that there is a force called friction and that it acts between the surfaces of objects.	Revising children's understanding of frictional forces and surveying how friction is used in everyday life.	• Using straightforward scientific evidence to answer questions or to support their findings.
	2	• To notice that some forces need contact between two objects, but magnetic forces can act at a distance.	• To understand ways of increasing and decreasing the effect of friction. • To know how this is used in everyday life.	Planning an investigation into how different materials and surfaces affect friction.	• Setting up simple practical enquiries, comparative and fair tests.
	3	• To notice that some forces need contact between two objects, but magnetic forces can act at a distance.	• To understand ways of increasing and decreasing the effect of friction. • To know how this is used in everyday life.	Investigating how different materials and surfaces affect friction.	• Setting up simple practical enquiries, comparative and fair tests.
3	1	• To compare how things move on different surfaces.	• To explore things that move quickly and slowly.	Investigating how bubbles move and float.	• Setting up simple practical enquiries, comparative and fair tests.
	2	• To compare how things move on different surfaces.	• To understand that certain things move by sliding. • To understand that certain materials slide better than others.	Investigating sliding different objects across different surfaces.	• Setting up simple practical enquiries, comparative and fair tests.
	3	• To compare how things move on different surfaces.	• To undertand that some objects move by rolling. • To understand that some shapes roll better than others.	Looking at which shapes roll the best.	• Setting up simple practical enquiries, comparative and fair tests.

Chapter at a glance

Week	Lesson	Curriculum objectives	Objectives	Main activity	Working scientifically
4	1	• To compare how things move on different surfaces.	• To begin to understand how different types of car move across a flat surface.	Concept mapping knowledge of springs.	• Setting up simple practical enquiries, comparative and fair tests.
	2	• To compare how things move on different surfaces.	• To understand how toy cars move down different slopes.	Investigating how the slope of a ramp effects a toy car.	• Setting up simple practical enquiries, comparative and fair tests.
	3	• To compare how things move on different surfaces.	• To understand how toy cars move down different surfaces.	Investigating how different surfaces can speed up or slow down a toy car.	• Gathering, recording, classifying and presenting data in a variety of ways to help in answering questions.
5	1	• To observe how magnets attract or repel each other and attract some materials and not others. • To describe magnets as having two poles. • To predict whether two magnets will attract or repel each other, depending on which poles are facing.	• To know that a magnet is attracted and repelled by another magnet.	Using magnets to experience the forces of repulsion and attraction. Discovering what happens when like and unlike poles are brought together.	• Using straightforward scientific evidence to answer questions or to support their findings. • Making decisions about what observations to make.
	2	• To notice that some forces need contact between two objects, but magnetic forces can act at a distance. • To observe how magnets attract or repel each other and attract some materials and not others.	• To know that magnets can be tested for strength.	Planning an investigation to test the strength of magnets.	• Setting up simple practical enquiries, comparative and fair tests. • Making decisions about what observations to make.
	3	• To observe how magnets attract or repel each other and attract some materials and not others. • To compare and group a variety of everyday materials on the basis of whether they are attracted to a magnet, and identify some magnetic materials.	• To know that some materials are magnetic and some are non-magnetic.	Testing materials for attraction by magnets.	• Setting up simple practical enquiries, comparative and fair tests. • Using straightforward scientific evidence to answer questions or to support their findings.
6	1	• To observe how magnets attract or repel each other and attract some materials and not others. • To compare and group a variety of everyday materials on the basis of whether they are attracted to a magnet, and identify some magnetic materials.	• To investigate whether magnets will work through a range of materials.	Planning an investigation to test which materials magnets will work through.	• Gathering, recording, classifying and presenting data in a variety of ways to help answer questions. • Recording findings using simple scientific language, drawings, labelled diagrams, bar charts, and tables.
	2	• To observe how magnets attract or repel each other and attract some materials and not others.	• To know that magnets have uses.	Using secondary sources to look at the uses of magnets.	• Identifying differences, similarities or changes related to simple scientific ideas and processes. • Making accurate measurements using standard units, using a range of equipment. • Recognising when and how secondary sources might help to answer questions.
	3	• To notice that some forces need contact between two objects, but magnetic forces can act at a distance.	• To know how to use a forcemeter and how to read the scale on a forcemeter. • To have a 'feel' for a force of 1N and a force of 10N.	Demonstrating how to use Newton meters, including how to read the scale. Making simple forcemeters to measure forces.	• Making accurate measurements using standard units, using a range of equipment.
Assess and review					

Objectives
● To review the actions of sliding, rolling, falling, flying, walking and running.
● To know that forces can make moving objects go faster, slow down, change direction or change shape.

Resources
Three children's scooters; a selection of toy gliders; some small soft balls; paper and drawing equipment; access to laptops/PCs; sticky notes; interactive activities 'Slide and glide' and 'Twist and turn' on the CD-ROM

Speaking scientifically
falling, flying, movement, pull, push, rolling, running, sliding, twist, walking

Lesson 1: Movement all around us

Previous knowledge
Children should already be familiar with how movement is involved in changing the shape of objects by squashing, bending, twisting or stretching them through their work on the properties of materials. They may have also observed, identified and classified the way in which different materials are impacted and recorded these observations. The children may have used this and other information in carrying out simple investigations related to the use of particular materials.

Introduction
Begin the lesson by asking the children to think about all the things they have done during the day. Ask them to think particularly about the movements they have made while carrying out these activities. Using talk partners, ask the children to talk about some other things they have noticed that have involved movement. This might include not only vehicles and other people but also objects.

Paired work
1. Allow the children to try out a selection of resources such as the scooters, the toy gliders and the small balls to demonstrate movement. (They may need to rotate in their pairs around the different resources to allow all children to experience each resource.)

2. Encourage the children to discuss examples of movement as they use the resources. Promote use of the correct scientific vocabulary such as *sliding, rolling, falling, flying, walking* and *running*.

3. Ask the children to draw an annotated drawing showing the resources being used and describing what is happening. These annotated drawings could form the basis for a class collage that can be displayed as part of the topic. Ask the children about the different words we could use to describe the movement of the different resources. Is it fast or slow? How do we make something move faster or slower?

Whole-class/Paired work
4. Use the interactive activity 'Slide and glide' on the CD-ROM to introduce the children to the topic. You could use this activity with the whole class before letting the children try it in pairs, or they can simply complete it independently in their pairs. This may depend on your access to school laptops, PCs or tablets.

5. Introduce the idea of concept mapping to the children. Talk about concept maps being lots of thoughts, ideas and words that can be linked together in some way.

6. Model this elicitation strategy by writing the topic title 'Forces and magnets' on the board. Ask the children for suggestions of words and phrases that might be related to forces and magnets.

7. Write just a few of these suggestions on sticky notes and place them around the title. Use lines and arrows to link these words and phrases in such a way that they form concepts.

8. Having modelled this for the children, they can now work in pairs to create the start of their own concept map. This can be added to and updated throughout the topic.

Checkpoint
● If you push something, what will happen to it?
● If you put your bicycle brakes on, what will happen to your bicycle?
● Tell me some of the ways in which things move.

Introducing the new area of study

Bring the children back together and ask some pairs to briefly share their concept maps. This will begin to show the level of understanding the children have based on their prior experience of the topic.

Talk about the movements that they considered earlier in the lesson. Ask the children how we start a movement. What do we do to make something roll or slide? Encourage them to think about how we might push, pull or twist something in order to make movement happen.

Use the interactive activity 'Twist and turn' on the CD-ROM as an additional activity to help children consolidate their prior learning and to introduce some of the new concepts. This would work well with the children working collaboratively in pairs.

> **Differentiation**
> ● Support children who may find the concept mapping activity difficult. You could encourage them to create their concept maps using pictures. Alternatively you could prepare some words for the children to use as a starter for their own thinking.
> ● Challenge confident learners to develop a more complex concept map and to make links that demonstrate the extent of their scientific understanding.

Science in the wider world

Movement is all around us and we tend to take most of it for granted. But everything that moves requires a force to make it do so. This means that forces also exist all around us. Even if they are not always obvious, their effects are observable.

Review

Use the children's annotated drawings and concept maps as a means of determining their levels of prior learning. Look out for any gaps in their understanding or misconceptions they may hold.

Objectives
● To know the different types of forces.
● To identify pushes, pulls and twists as examples of forces in action.

Resources
Toys and games brought by the children from home that require a force in order to work; your own example of a suitable toy or game; secondary sources such as books and the internet about the history of toys; laptops/PCs/tablets with internet access

Speaking scientifically
force, pull, push, twist

Lesson 2: The Great Toy Rally

Introduction
Prior to the lesson, ask the children to bring to school one toy or game that uses forces; examples might include pull-along or push-along vehicles, wind-up or pull-back vehicles, magnetic games, spinning tops or any mechanical devices. It would also be a good idea to bring a suitable item that you yourself have found, as a stimulus to start the lesson.

Share the toy that you have brought in with the children. Encourage them to formulate questions in order to ascertain how the toy uses forces.

Paired work
1. Ask the children to share the toys that they have brought in with a talk partner. They should discuss with their partner the movement involved in their toy or game and/or how it uses forces.

Group work
2. Working in groups of three or four, encourage the children to take turns sharing their toys with their group. The children should work together to explore the range of ways that each toy moves and/or uses forces.

3. Ask the children to consider ways of grouping the toys using identifiable features, such as how they move. For example, do they need a push or a pull to make them move? Do they roll, spin, slide or float? The children could also test each toy to see how far it moves.

4. Ask the children to examine the toys and decide how they are made to move or work. Is it mechanical or electrical? Do they use magnetism?

5. Encourage the children to record their findings by preparing a description card to sit alongside each toy in a display.

Independent work
6. Ask the children to find out more about how moving toys have changed over the years. They should use secondary sources to extend their thinking. For example, the children could use books or the internet to learn more about the transition from clockwork toy trains to electric toy trains.

> ### Differentiation
> ● Some children will need support to consider these questions. You could narrow the range of questions and toys for these less confident learners.
> ● Challenge confident learners can begin to ask their own more open-ended questions.

Science in the wider world
An understanding of the different ways in which things move and use forces enables us to build devices that operate effectively and move freely.

Review
Consider the range of movements and forces looked at. Assess the children's understanding through observation, discussion and examining their written work.

Objectives
● To understand that all forces are directional.
● To learn how arrows can be used to indicate the direction of a force.

Resources
A collection of objects that can be manipulated with a pull, a push or a twist (such as springs, elastic bands, retractable pens, taps, switches and cloths); straight and curved paper arrows (most word processing packages have these as images); photocopiable page 36 'Push, pull and twist'

Speaking scientifically
direction, exert, force, pull, push, twist

Lesson 3: Push, pull and twist

Introduction

At the start of the lesson, display the words 'push', 'pull' and 'twist'. Ask the children to discuss with a talk partner what is meant by each of these words and to think of examples. Ask some of the children to come to the front of the class to demonstrate different body movements that include pushes, pulls and twists. For example, they could simply twist their torso or wrists, or push against each other. Remind the children that these are examples of forces.

Group work

1. Ask the children to work in groups of three or four. Give each group a selection of the objects listed in Resources above. Ask them to identify those that require pushes, pulls or twists. Encourage them to consider the direction in which they are applying the force.

2. Ask the children to group these objects according to the force that is applied to them. There may be some objects where more than one directional force is usually applied.

3. Encourage the children to think about how some other objects can be pushed, pulled or twisted in normal use.

Independent work

4. The children can work independently to complete photocopiable page 36 'Push, pull and twist'.

Whole-class/Group work

5. Bring the children back together to share and discuss their understanding of pushes, pulls and twists as a whole class.

6. Ask them to look at some of their own drawings, which they should have produced as part of the independent work. Encourage them to talk about which direction the force is being exerted in.

7. Make explicit the idea of a force being exerted in a particular direction, and how this might be shown using arrows. Use examples to model the use of arrows. You could have two children exerting forces on each other at the front of the class, and show the directions using paper arrows.

8. Ask the children to return to their original groups. They should now use paper arrows to show the direction of the forces on the different objects.

9. Now ask the children to look again at their photocopiable sheets. They should add directional arrows to the illustrations and their own drawings.

Differentiation
● Some children may require additional support in identifying the forces and the directions they are applied in. Support them by using additional and simpler practical examples.
● Challenge others to draw more complex examples of pushes, pulls and twists and use objects that are subject to all of these forces.

Science in the wider world

Many mechanical and electrical devices are operated by pushes, pulls and twists, for example light switches, door handles and screw tops on bottles.

Review

The children can be assessed by their understanding and awareness of what is happening in terms of identifying pushes, pulls and twists. Have they been able to correctly identify the type of directional force and the direction in which it is being exerted? Look at their drawings to see if they are using arrows accurately to represent the direction of the forces.

Objectives
● To know that there is a force called friction and that it acts between the surfaces of objects.

Resources
A bicycle; blocks of jelly separated into small cubes; chopsticks (or something similar); olive oil; bowls; timers

Speaking scientifically
force, friction, grip, slip, surface

Lesson 1: Frictional surfaces

Introduction

Briefly recap the previous lessons about how to make objects move by exerting a force on them. Ask the children to think about the different ways there are to *stop* something from moving. Lead the discussion towards the idea of applying another force to counteract the original pull, push or twist.

Show the children an up-turned bicycle. Spin the wheel and ask how this can be safely stopped. Demonstrate the use of the brakes and the coming together of the two surfaces. Ask the children if they know the correct scientific word to describe why the wheel has stopped spinning, and reinforce the use of the word *friction*. Ask the children to rub their hands together to experience something similar to what happens between the bicycle brake blocks and the wheel.

Independent work

1. Ask the children to draw a series of four annotated drawings to show examples of how friction is used in everyday life. Some examples might include gripping objects, brakes working, skiing and walking up a hill.

Paired work

2. Ask the children to work in pairs. Give each pair two bowls, some cubes of jelly, a pair of chopsticks and a timer.

3. Ask them to take turns in timing how long it takes them to move the cubes of jelly from one bowl to the other using only the chopsticks. Ask the children to devise a table to record their times, and see who can be the fastest.

4. Now add the olive oil to the jelly so that it coats the cubes. The children should take turns to use the chopsticks to move the cubes of jelly between the bowls in the same way as before, recording the time taken.

5. Encourage the children to compare the times and explain what the differences might be and why. How was friction being demonstrated in this activity?

Differentiation
● Some learners might have some difficulty in devising a table and accurately recording the times, so you could let them use a simpler timer. They could also choose to record their findings using annotated drawings.
● Challenge confident learners by encouraging them to consider the wider practical applications and implications of what they have learned.

Science in the wider world

Without the lubrication provided by the olive oil, the chopsticks use static friction to grip the cubes of jelly. When the cubes are coated in oil there is a barrier between the two surfaces that allows greater freedom of movement. This means that it becomes very difficult to grip the oily jelly cubes with what will now be oily chopsticks.

Review

Check that the children understand that when two surfaces come together there is a frictional force between them. The children could rub their hands together and share what they feel. Using some soap or baby oil to provide simple lubrication will help assess the children's awareness that creating a lubricated barrier overcomes some of the frictional force.

Objectives
● To understand ways of increasing and decreasing the effect of friction.
● To know how this is used in everyday life.

Resources
The school hall or gym; a PE bench and a safe means of inclining it; ramps; free-standing ladder racks; timers; metre sticks or tape measures; a range of different surfaces (from smooth to rough) such as smooth, shiny plastic and a rough carpet; a range of footwear with differing grips; photocopiable page 'Investigation planning' on the CD-ROM

Speaking scientifically
fair test, friction, investigate, slide, slip

Lesson 2: Increasing and decreasing friction (1)

Introduction
Take the children into the hall or gym where they have PE. Look at the apparatus and talk about what the children wear when they are using it. Focus their thinking onto footwear and discuss their ideas about why they use a particular type of footwear (trainers or gym shoes) when exercising.

Whole-class work
1. Ask three children to walk along a PE bench in turn. One will be wearing their socks, another a pair of trainers or gym shoes, and the third will have bare feet. Make sure you use all necessary safety precautions.

2. Ask each of the three children to describe how easy or difficult it was to walk along the bench.

3. Next incline the bench and then, safely and with your guidance, ask each of the three to walk up the bench. Again, it is important that you use all necessary safety precautions.

4. Ask the children to describe how easy or difficult it was to walk up the bench this time. Ask questions to elicit the desired responses.

5. Continue your discussion with the class about the reasons for wearing certain footwear in the context of safety and the practical application of friction and frictional surfaces.

6. Back in the classroom, set up a model of the inclined bench using a ramp and free-standing ladder rack. Have a range of different soled footwear and different surfaces available.

7. Challenge the children to devise an investigation to find out which surface and footwear combination would have the least friction between them and which combination would have the most.

8. Question the children to gather some ideas and initial thoughts about:
   ● how this might be achieved
   ● what data they will record, for example distance that a shoe slips or time taken for it to slide down the ramp
   ● the idea of a fair test. (In your modelling you might like to purposely push one of the items of footwear down the ramp to encourage the children to think about how to keep their investigation fair.)

Group work
9. Ask groups to start writing simple plans of how they will carry out their investigation. The investigation itself will be carried out in lesson 3 (or you can combine the lessons into one longer lesson if you prefer).

Differentiation
● Some children may need additional support to understand the idea of a fair test. You may want to use some starter sentences such as 'To make my investigation a fair test I will...' or 'To make my investigation a fair test I will change...' to get the children thinking about fair testing. You could also use photocopiable page 'Investigation planning' from the CD-ROM.

Science in the wider world
The relationship between surfaces is key to increasing or reducing friction. Where two rough surfaces come together there is increased friction. Where both surfaces are smooth, friction is reduced.

Review
Assess the children's ability to identify the properties of the two surfaces when the result is that friction is reduced (more slip) and increased (less slip).

Objectives
● To understand ways of increasing and decreasing the effect of friction.
● To know how this is used in everyday life.

Resources
Ramps; free-standing ladder racks; timers; metre sticks or tape measures; a range of different surfaces (from smooth to rough) such as smooth, shiny plastic and a rough carpet; a range of footwear with differing grips

Speaking scientifically
fair test, friction, investigate, slide, slip

Lesson 3: Increasing and decreasing friction (2)

Introduction

Ask the children to review their investigation plans from the previous lesson by sharing them with another group. This is part of the scientific way of working. Emphasise this as you introduce the activity, stressing that science is a collaborative process and that it is fine for groups to investigate the same question in different ways.

Group work

1. Encourage the children to make predictions about which pairing they think will have the most and least grip. These predictions can be recorded informally by the children on sticky notes. The predictions can then be shared as a class by combining the notes in a shared display on the board.

2. The children should work in their groups to devise a simple table to record their findings before they start the tests.

3. Working in their groups, the children can carry out their tests according to their plans. You might like to use some digital technology to record images of their findings; this could be either as still images or video.

4. Ask the children to share their findings by drawing a safety poster to show the two extremes of grip and slip. Children often want their predictions and conclusions to be the same and for their predictions to be seen as having been 'correct'. Encourage them to compare their predictions and conclusions in a way that allows them to feel that it is 'OK' for these to be different. As you do so, you can reinforce their understanding of the way that scientists work.

Independent work

5. In bringing these lessons together, ask the children to think of occasions when we want to reduce the effects of friction, such as when ice skating or skiing, or in simple machines such as bicycles. They could draw some annotated drawings to show these examples.

Differentiation
● Some children may need additional support to carry out their fair test and encouragement to make predictions. Some will also need support in devising a table and identifying exactly what they might record.

Science in the wider world

Carrying out a fair test is an important way of investigating an answer to a question or problem. Fair testing involves controlling variables in such a way that you can measure or observe the impact of one variable at a time. However, depending on the question you are investigating, this may not always be possible. There are other ways of carrying out scientific enquiries and children should be aware of this.

Review

Assess the children's ability to carry out a fair test and to record data in a table by observing their practical work and analysing the tables produced.

Objectives
● To explore things that move quickly and slowly.

Resources
PE kits; use of the hall; wire that can be shaped into loops; containers for a mixture of washing-up liquid and water; bought bubble mixture (enough for one to be shared between four children); media resource 'Fast and slow movement' on the CD-ROM

Speaking scientifically
fast, slow, streamlined, floating

Lesson 1: Fast and slow movement

Introduction
Take the children into the hall. Ask them to move quickly, then slowly, without using their feet. Ask them to move quickly, then slowly, now using their feet. They will be able to run or walk in slow motion with larger exaggerated steps. Ask them to crawl, hop, skip and roll slowly and then quickly.

Whole-class work
1. Ask: *Which animals move quickly/slowly?* Show the children the media resource 'Fast and slow movement' on the CD-ROM and use the cheetah and tortoise as examples. Ask: *Why does the cheetah have to be fast?* Ask: *Why is a tortoise slow?* (A tortoise has a heavy shell to carry around; a cheetah has a streamlined body and powerful legs so it can catch its prey.)

2. Talk to the children about things that move quickly, include racing cars, rockets and aeroplanes. Introduce the idea that being 'streamlined' helps an object to cut through the air more easily.

3. Ask: *What objects move slowly?* Make sure that they include feathers, parachutes, bubbles and smoke in their answers. Introduce the idea that certain things move by floating in the air.

Individual/Group work
4. Ask the children to write down two things that can move quickly and two things that move slowly.

5. Tell the children that bubbles float slowly through the air. Give each child a piece of wire and show them how to make a loop in one end a little bigger than a £2 coin. Give each small group of four a container with a mixture of washing-up liquid and water that is big enough and deep enough to dip the looped wire into. Take them outside to blow bubbles. (This works best on a still day.) After they have tried with the small loop ask them to try making a larger loop. Do the bubbles float more slowly? Do big bubbles float more slowly than larger ones?

6. Give out the bought bubble mixture that may or may not be better than the washing-up liquid mix. Use the loop provided but then try larger wire loops. If the children blow through the loop quickly they should notice a fast stream of small bubbles that float and drop quickly; if they blow slowly the bubbles should be larger and slower.

7. Ask the children to draw some of their bubbles and describe what they saw. Ask them to use the words 'fast', 'slow', 'float' and 'sink'.

Differentiation
● Support children who need help in making the wire loops and describing what they saw when they were making bubbles.
● Challenge children to find different-size feathers and to use a stopwatch to time how long it takes for them to float from a fixed height.

Science in the wider world
Moving through the air and flying are important ideas and the children need to begin to understand such concepts as streamlined and floating.

Review
The children could be assessed on their ability to describe what they see when their bubbles are floating and their knowledge of objects that move quickly or slowly.

Objectives
● To understand that certain things move by sliding.
● To understand that certain materials slide better than others.

Resources
Photocopiable page 37 'My investigation: sliding'; a flat surface (a plastic chopping board or other smooth surface that you don't mind sandpaper being pushed across); materials for each group of four children (a sheet of paper, a piece of rough sandpaper, a small sample of corduroy, a small polythene bag, a slice of bread, a small piece of sponge); pencils; media resource 'Sliding' on the CD-ROM

Speaking scientifically
fast, slow, joint, parts of the human body, floating, sliding, surfaces, smooth, rough

Lesson 2: Sliding

Introduction
Discuss bicycles, cars and aeroplanes and the fact that they can take people further and faster by using wheels to travel along the ground and wings to move through the air. Remind the children how bubbles and feathers float and explain this lesson is about sliding as a movement.

Whole-class work
1. Show the children the media resource 'Sliding' from the CD-ROM, or other pictures or DVDs of people skiing, sledging or bobsleigh racing. Ask: *How are these people moving?* Use the word 'sliding'.

2. Talk to them about how sliding works and explore the idea that skis and ice are both smooth surfaces. Ask: *What would happen if one of the surfaces was rough – or if both were rough?* Don't use the term 'friction' at this stage but explain that sliding quickly depends on both surfaces being smooth.

Group work
3. Each child needs photocopiable page 37 'My investigation: sliding'. Each group needs a smooth surface (like a plastic chopping board, or something else you don't mind sandpaper being pushed across!) and one of each of the six materials: paper, sandpaper, corduroy, plastic, bread and sponge. Tell the children that they must work together in their groups and try to slide each of the materials, rough side down, across the smooth surface. They must discuss which one they think is the easiest to slide, which is slightly less easy and which one is the hardest. There are six spaces on the photocopiable sheet and six things to slide. Each child should complete their own photocopiable sheet.

Whole-class work
4. Talk to the children about what they have observed from their tests. Ask: *Why are the plastic bag or the piece of paper the easiest to slide?* The children should understand that both the paper and polythene are smooth and are sliding on a smooth surface. There may be differences of opinion as to which one is the hardest to slide. The rest of the materials are all either rough or much less smooth. The bread and the sponge are both soft so the children may also understand that both rough and soft materials are quite difficult to slide.

5. Explain to the children that they have to write answers in the spaces at the bottom of their photocopiable sheet. Tell them that they have been trying to find out which materials are easiest to slide.

Differentiation
● Support children when they are completing their photocopiable sheet. They may know what to say but might find it difficult to write it down.
● Challenge children to explain how water skiers slide across the water or how they might make a drawer slide more smoothly.

Science in the wider world
Sliding is another way that materials move and this word can be added to their vocabulary to enable them to explain movement with more accuracy and in more detail. Sliding well and not so well will also help when they explore friction in later lessons.

Review
Children can be assessed on how well they complete the photocopiable sheet.

Lesson 3: Rolling

Introduction
During a PE lesson show the children how to do a forward roll and ask them what shape they have to make their bodies. They should suggest that they have to curl up like a ball. Ask them to roll across the floor or mats in different ways and ask them what shape they have to make their bodies. (They have to be round or cylindrical and they should know that they can't stick out parts of their bodies, like their arms or legs, or it will stop them rolling.)

Whole-class work
1. Remind the children of their body shapes when they were rolling during their PE lesson. Ask them to tell you some of the shapes that they could make that wouldn't roll: for example, standing on one leg, or lying on their side with their arm stretched out.

2. Show them each of the objects they will be testing in the lesson and ask them what their shapes are. They should have a sphere (the ball), two cylinders (the cardboard tube and the coin), two cubes (the dice and the box) and a triangular prism.

Group work
3. Give each child photocopiable page 38 'My investigation: rolling' and give each group of four a set of the six objects. Explain to them that they have to try rolling each of the objects on the smooth floor. When they have tried rolling each one and talked about which one is the easiest to roll and which is the hardest, they should complete the boxes on the photocopiable sheet.

4. Talk to them about their experiment, which was to find out about rolling. They should have found out that the only shapes that actually roll properly are the cylinders and the sphere. We do say 'roll the dice' but although a dice does move over a smooth surface if we throw it, it doesn't actually roll. Ask the children to complete the statements on the photocopiable sheet.

Differentiation
● Support children who have difficulty recording their experiment in writing. The names of some of the shapes are difficult and some children will need help when they are completing their sheets.
● Challenge children to roll the same six objects over a rough surface. Ask them whether the same object was the easiest to roll? (It should have been.) They may start to explore the idea of rough surfaces slowing things down, which will lead to them understanding friction later on.

Science in the wider world
Rolling is another way to explain how things move and can be added to their vocabulary.

Doing simple experiments and observing what happens as well as recording their findings will be an important part of science lessons.

Review
Children can be assessed on their knowledge of the names of the shapes that rolled easily and how well they complete the photocopiable sheet.

Objectives
● To begin to understand how different types of car move across a flat surface.

Resources
A selection of cars and wheeled toys (if possible each child should have brought one in); a scooter and a bicycle or large pictures instead; a large flat surface; sticky notes; pencils

Speaking scientifically
round, smooth, wheels, cogs, axle

Introduction
Ask the children to describe some of the ways they have travelled recently. This should include by bicycle, scooter, car and so on. Ask them how these vehicles move. They may say that a bicycle moves when they push with their legs, or that a car moves because it has an engine, but what the children need to understand is that they all use wheels.

Whole-class work
1. Show the children the scooter and allow someone to ride it. Ask: *How does it move across the ground?* Look at the size of the wheels and what they are made of. Look at one of the axles. Ask: *What shape is it?* It has to be cylindrical, in order to roll.

2. Show the children the bicycle and look at the differences between the bicycle and the scooter. The bicycle will have larger wheels, rubber tyres and lots more moving parts. Look at the moving parts, such as the chain wheel, and remind them that it is wheel shaped and it turns, but it also has teeth. Use the word 'cog'.

3. Take the children outside to look at parked cars. Explain that they have four wheels instead of two. Discuss the shape and size of the wheels and remind them that cars also have cylindrical axles.

Group work
4. Ask the children, in groups of four, to examine their toy cars. Look at the wheels and axles carefully. Ask: *Do they vary in size? Do some move more smoothly than others? Are they made of different materials?*

5. Tell the children that they will be going to the hall to push the cars along a flat surface to see how far they will go. Ask them to decide which toy car they think will travel the furthest. They should put a sticky note on each car and number them: '1' for the one that they think will travel the furthest, '2' for the next, and so on.

6. Allow each group to take it in turns to push each of their cars from a line marked on the floor. Tell the children to push each car in the same way so that the test is as fair as possible. When they have finished, they should change round the sticky notes so that the cars are now numbered in the correct order. Ask: *Why do you think you got these results? Were the wheels bigger or softer? Did they move more smoothly?*

7. Ask them to complete the sentences below, based on their observations:
● Car Number 1 went the furthest because _____.
● Car number 4 went the least far because _____.

> ### Differentiation
> ● Support groups who have difficulty pushing their cars in a reasonably fair way. Support children who might need help in completing their sentences.
> ● Challenge children to look for wheels and cylinders around the school and to write down how many they see.

Science in the wider world
Wheels, gears, cogs and axles turn as they move and this movement is an important scientific concept because it means that machines such as cars and even bicycles can move quickly and slowly and in different directions.

Review
Children can be assessed on their understanding of wheels turning and moving on cylindrical axles.

Objectives
● To understand how toy cars move down different slopes.

Resources
The toy cars from lesson 1 that travelled the furthest (if the cars all performed poorly, each group of four will need to have another car that moves smoothly); photocopiable page 39 'My investigation: ramps'; a large flat space; a length of wood for a ramp for each group; books to support the ramps; rulers; measuring tapes; pencils; adult volunteers or more teaching assistants than usual (or Year 6 children)

Speaking scientifically
height, distance, push, measure, movement, speed, smooth

Lesson 2: Faster and slower slopes

Introduction
Talk to the children about the different wheels on bicycles, scooters and cars and remind them what they did with their four cars in the previous lesson. Ask them why they thought their number 1 car went the furthest. Demonstrate what they did by pushing a car along the classroom floor. Push it hard and then gently to make it move. Ask them what they notice. They should see that the harder it is pushed the further it goes.

Whole-class work
1. Give each child photocopiable page 39 'My investigation: ramps'. Give each group of four all the equipment they need: a car, a ramp, a ruler, books and a measuring tape. Show them how to set up the ramp by piling up the books and setting the height to 10cm, 15cm, 20cm and 30cm using the ruler. Set up a ramp 10cm high to demonstrate what to do in the investigation they are about to carry out. Place a car at the top and let it go without pushing it. Show the children how to measure the distance from the bottom of the ramp to where the car stops. Ask them what they think will happen as the ramp is raised.

Group work
2. Using the photocopiable sheet, the children can investigate the effects of raising the height of the ramp. They should work in groups when they are using the ramp but each child has to complete their own photocopiable sheet.

3. The more adult/older-child help you have for the group work the better: measuring the distance using a measuring tape might be difficult and needs to be reasonably accurate.

4. When the children have completed the test ask them what happened to the distance each time. What observations can they make? Ask: *Which ramp made the car roll the furthest? Why?*

Differentiation
● Support children who might find completing the photocopiable sheet difficult. Support children who find setting the ramp to the right height and measuring the distance the car travels difficult.
● Challenge children to try different cars on the ramps. Ask: *Do cars with larger wheels travel the furthest?*

Science in the wider world
Movement, speed and size of wheels are all related. These three concepts can also be related to the smoothness of the slope and the smoothness of the tyres. Machines that need to go over very rough ground often have large soft wheels, but racing cars that have to travel quickly often have large, smooth tyres.

Review
Assess the children in their understanding of the relationship between the height of the ramp and the distance travelled.

Resources
Ramps, books, rulers and measuring tapes (from the previous lesson); materials to cover the ramp (sandpaper, corduroy or corrugated cardboard, cotton, a polythene sheet); adult volunteers or more teaching assistants than usual (or Year 6 children); pencils

Speaking scientifically
ramp, roll, measure, distance, speed, materials

Lesson 3: Faster and slower surfaces

Introduction
Talk to the children about the previous lesson. Ask them which ramp height made the cars go faster and further and why they think this happened. Remind them about the lesson on sliding and how different surfaces made it easier or harder to slide across the surface. Ask them whether they can remember which materials made it easier and which was the hardest to slide.

Whole-class work
I. Tell the children that they will be using the same car and the same ramps as they used in the previous lesson. They will need to work with the same group of four children and set up the ramp at 30cm. The ramp should stay at this height. The children will be changing the material each time not the height. Explain that this time they will be letting the car roll down the ramp over different materials. Show them the ramp not covered by anything – call this 'normal' – then show them the materials they will be using to cover it: sandpaper, corduroy or corrugated cardboard, cotton and polythene. Which materials do they think will make the car go fastest and furthest, and slower and least far?

2. Show them how to make a table on their piece of paper using a column for the materials and a column for distances. Start with the word 'normal' for the ramp not covered by anything and then write down each of the materials they will be using.

Group work
3. Each group of four should do each of the tests using the different materials.

4. Each child should complete their own materials/distance travelled table.

5. When they have finished the test, they should discuss their data and why they think they got these results.

6. Each child should complete the following sentences:
  ● The material that made the car go the slowest and the least far was the
    _____ .
  ● I think that this happened because _____ .

Differentiation
● Support children who need help making their ramp and measuring the distances. Support children who need help with written work.
● Challenge children to find materials that slow down their cars. This will mean using the ramp 30cm high and rolling the cars down the 'normal' slope. Each material that was used can be placed in turn on the floor close to the ramp. Ask: *Which material slows the car down the most and why?*

Science in the wider world
The link between friction and real cars stopping being dependent on materials slowing them down is an important one and can be seen on steep hills with lorry escape routes that are made of deep rutted sand that will slow the lorries down in an emergency.

Review
The children can be assessed on how accurately they link the materials to the speed and distance travelled by their cars.

Objectives
● To know that a magnet is attracted and repelled by another magnet.

Resources
A magnetic travel game; a selection of bar magnets of different strengths; photocopiable page 41 'Magnets'; strong thin thread; pieces of polystyrene (for example from packing materials) cut into pieces big enough to sit a magnet on; trays of water; coloured pens or pencils
(Check that the magnets are sufficiently magnetic to repel and attract one another. School magnets often become demagnetised!)

Speaking scientifically
attract, magnet, magnetism, north, poles, repel, south

Lesson 1: Magnets

Introduction
Begin the lesson by using a magnetic travel game or magnetic letters and numbers as a visual aid to encourage the children to begin thinking about magnets. Ask them why the letters and numbers stick to the board, or why the pieces of the travel game do not fall off. Most should be able to tell you that they are magnets or magnetic. Ask the children if they can think of the words we use when a magnet 'sticks'. Introduce the words 'attract' and 'repel' (although we shall see that repel in magnetic terms has a more active effect than simply 'not sticking').

Whole-class/Paired work
1. Distribute magnets to the children and ask them to tell you about the magnets they have. Introduce the idea that there are two ends to a magnet called poles. These poles, indicated by the letters N and S, are the north and south poles of the magnet.

2. Ask the children to work in pairs to see what happens when these poles are brought together. Ask them to try like poles and unlike poles. Discuss the outcomes.

Independent/Group work
3. Distribute photocopiable page 41 'Magnets'. Ask the children to read through the photocopiable sheet with you, and then to complete it by exploring with the magnets. If resources are short, let the children work in pairs or fours with two magnets per group.

4. Let the children investigate repulsion and attraction further. They could try suspending a magnet on a thread so that it spins freely. They can then bring another magnet towards it and observe what happens. They can repeat this at each end of the magnet.

5. They could also try floating a magnet on a small piece of polystyrene in a tray of water. Again, they should use a second magnet, bring the poles together in different combinations, and see what happens.

6. In each case, ask: *Which direction does the magnet point in when allowed to move freely?* Encourage them to make up a general rule based on what they have found out about magnets repelling and attracting.

Differentiation
● Some learners could choose to record their findings diagrammatically.
● Challenge confident learners to record their findings in writing.

Science in the wider world
Magnetic materials have a number of 'miniature magnets' called domains, each of which themselves have a north and a south pole. In a non-magnetised piece of metal, these domains are all jumbled up and their magnetic effects cancel each other out. If the domains are aligned, either by using another magnet or by using an electric current, the material becomes magnetised.

Review
Mark the children's work for evidence of understanding. Their diagrams or written notes should indicate that like poles repel and unlike poles attract.

● To know that magnets can be tested for strength.

Resources
Bar magnets; horseshoe magnets; paper clips; pieces of paper, card and cloth; steel pins or nails; photocopiable page 'Investigation planning' from the CD-ROM

Speaking scientifically
attract, bar magnet, fair test, horseshoe magnet, repel

Lesson 2: Magnet strength test

Introduction
Remind the children that in the last lesson they were looking at how magnets attract and repel one another. Ask the children if they think that all magnets are the same. Talk about magnets being of varying sizes and strengths. Ask the children if they can think of a fair way to test a magnet to find out how strong it is. Collect their suggestions and record these on the board.

Whole-class/Group work
1. Together as a class, discuss an investigation to test the strength of the magnets you have. The children could look at:
- the number of paper clips that can be attracted in a line
- whether the size of the magnet affects its strength
- which are stronger – horseshoe or bar magnets
- how close something needs to be to a magnet before it is attracted to it
- the thickness of materials (for example, layers of paper, card or cloth) through which a magnet can attract objects.

2. The class could then work in groups of three or four to plan their investigations into one of these different factors. On the board or a flipchart, provide a writing frame to help the children with the format and to direct their thinking (see photocopiable page 'Investigation planning' from the CD-ROM). Use the following headings:
- Our question
- What we will do to find the answer
- What we will need
- What we think will happen

The children should record appropriate details below each heading.

3. Highlight the importance of making this a fair test.

Group work
4. In their groups, the children should carry out their investigation. They should record their work as they go along under headings such as:
- 'This is what we did' – where they record how they carried out their tests
- 'This is what we found out' – where they draw up and complete a table of their results
- 'This is what we now know' – where they write down what they have learned from this investigation.

Write these headings on the board or flipchart for the children to copy.

5. Ask the children to use a bar magnet and a steel nail or needle to create a new magnet. They should make at least 20 strokes in the same direction with the magnet to magnetise the nail. The group can then test the new magnet's strength.

Differentiation
● In this lesson the children could support each other in mixed-ability groups.

Science in the wider world
Larger magnets are not always the strongest. Relatively small magnets can sometimes exert a greater magnetic force than larger ones.

Review
Assess the children's understanding that magnets have varying strengths. They should know that magnets can be tested to see how strong a force they exert and over how wide an area.

Objectives
● To know that some materials are magnetic and some are non-magnetic.

Resources
A collection of different magnetic and non-magnetic materials (in trays); magnets; large sheets of paper; secondary sources of information on magnetic materials

Speaking scientifically
attract, magnet, magnetised, magnetism, north, poles, repel, south

Lesson 3: Magnetic materials

Introduction
Revise magnets repelling and attracting. Ask the children if they can tell you what sort of materials (or objects, such as the fridge) magnets are attracted to. Compile a list of suggestions on the board. Talk about the difference between 'repulsion' (a push away) and 'non-attraction' (no reaction). Tell the children that in this lesson they will be finding out about materials that are magnetic and those that are not.

Group/Independent work
1. Write the headings 'Attracted by magnets' and 'Not attracted by magnets' on the board or flipchart.

2. Distribute large sheets of paper, the magnets and selections of various materials/objects on trays. These trays could each contain different materials and could be passed on to another child/group after a given time.

3. Ask the children to test each item in their tray to see if it is attracted to the magnet or not. This could be done in groups, as a circus, or individually with each child's results collated onto a large sheet of paper using the headings you have written.

4. If this is done as group work, each child in a group could have a responsibility, such as object selector, material identifier, predictor, tester, and recorder. The children could change responsibilities each time, so that each gets a 'turn' at them all.

Group/Independent work
5. Distribute more large sheets of paper. The children should now investigate some more items found in the classroom and around the school. This time, however, they should concentrate specifically on items that are metal (or appear to be metal). The children should record their thoughts about the objects that are and are not attracted by the magnet.

6. The children could use secondary sources to try to research which metals are attracted by magnets and which are not. (For example, materials such as iron and steel are magnetic, whilst aluminium, copper and gold are non-magnetic.)

Differentiation
● Some learners can concentrate on testing materials for attraction to magnets.
● Challenge confident learners to extend their work to include further research into magnetic and non-magnetic metals.

Science in the wider world
The effects of magnets can be felt without materials coming into contact with them (depending on the magnet's strength), making magnetism a non-contact force. Magnetic materials have many uses, including recording data on magnetic strips on cash cards, as catches, and also in burglar alarms. Magnets are also very important parts of electric motors.

Review
Looking at the children's work will give a good indication of whether they have learned that some materials are attracted by magnets and others are not. Discussion during the activities will help to support this judgement.

Objectives
● To investigate whether magnets will work through a range of materials.

Resources
Magnets; paper clips; a variety of materials to test such as card, paper, fabrics, aluminium foil, thin wood, water, iron (sufficient for group work); a selection of magnetic games (such as face disguises, table football, magnetic draughts or chess)

Speaking scientifically
attract, magnet, magnetism

Lesson 1: Do magnets work through materials?

Introduction

Begin the lesson by recapping on how some materials are attracted by magnets and others are not. Ask the children to share their thoughts and ideas about this by making a list of 'Materials that are attracted by magnets'.

Introduce the idea of using magnets in games. Share with the children a selection of magnetic games. Encourage them to consider how the magnets are used and the materials that the game is made from. Elicit from the children some understanding that, for these games to work, some of the materials must be attracted by the magnets and others must not. Talk about these materials and make a second comparative list of 'Materials that are not attracted by magnets'.

Whole-class work

1. Introduce the children to a challenge. The manufacturers of the magnetic games would like them to test a range of materials that could be used in the games, to see if the magnets will work through them.

2. Show the children the selection of materials to be tested that you have gathered together. Encourage them to share their ideas about how they could carry out the test, and which materials they think would pass the test and which would not. Reassure the children that there is no right or wrong answer when they are making these predictions. At this stage it is only what they think that is important.

3. Having discussed a number of different ways that this investigation could be carried out, tell the children that they are going to work in groups and decide for themselves how to test each material. Stress that they must ensure they carry out the tests in a fair way.

Group work

4. Distribute samples of the materials to be tested together with a magnet and a few paper clips to each group. Tell the children that they have to predict a result for each of the materials and then test them.

5. Ask the children to devise a simple table to record their predictions and results. Allow them to carry out their tests and record their results in their tables.

6. To report their findings to the rest of the class, the children should work together to write a simple poem or rap. This does not need to rhyme but it should enable the children to report on what they have found out about the materials.

Differentiation
● Some less confident learners may need support to compile a results table. You may want to give these children a pre-prepared table to complete. They may also need some assistance in writing their poems. You could provide them with some starter phrases, lines to complete or a model to follow.
● More confident learners could test a wider range of materials and should be able to work independently in devising the table and writing their poem.

Science in the wider world

Magnetic window cleaners that work through double-glazed windows use the science considered in this lesson.

Review

Through discussion and questioning, together with scrutiny of their written work, assess whether the children were able to identify which materials allowed magnets to be used through them and which did not.

Objectives
● To know that magnets have uses.

Resources
Magnetic games; examples of other objects that use magnetism to work (and preferably that can be taken apart to expose the magnet, such as electric bells, motors and loudspeakers); an old cassette recorder and/or computer disk drive (try car boot sales); secondary sources of information on the uses of magnets such as books, videos, CD-ROMs or the internet

Speaking scientifically
burglar alarms, compasses, door latches, metal detectors, telephones, vending machines

Lesson 2: Uses of magnets

Introduction
Reinforce the concepts covered so far in the magnetism topic. Ask the children if they can think of any uses of magnets. If they have difficulty, show them again your selection of magnetic games.

Whole-class work
1. Show the children any of the objects you have collected together, such as an electric bell, a (classroom) motor, or an old loudspeaker.

2. Show the children that these objects all have magnets in them to make them work.

3. Talk about cassette tapes and how they use magnets to record data. Highlight the dangers of putting magnets near such items. (You will lose the data stored on the tape.)

4. As a class, begin to compile a list of uses of magnets.

Group work
5. Ask the children to write down all the uses of magnets that you have discussed as a class. Then challenge them to add more uses of magnets to their lists by using any available secondary sources of information.

6. Tell the children to go on to use the secondary sources provided to investigate one or two uses of magnets in more detail, according to their abilities.

7. They could present their findings as an information sheet or poster providing a 'Guide to...' the different uses of magnets.

Differentiation
● Some children may need support in making their lists.
● Challenge others to undertake some independent research, which could be presented with annotated diagrams.

Science in the wider world
With the increasing use of digital technology, the use of magnetic recording tape is diminishing. However, the use of magnetism is still significant. The generation of electricity is intrinsically linked with magnets, and researchers are still developing maglev trains, which produce an electromagnetic force to levitate the train away from its track system, thus reducing friction and allowing for faster rail travel.

Review
The children's posters can be used to assess the level of understanding they have about how magnets are used. All should identify some uses, with the more confident learners being able to identify increasingly sophisticated uses.

Objectives
● To know how to use a forcemeter and how to read the scale on a forcemeter.
● To have a 'feel' for a force of 1N and a force of 10N.

Resources
Commercially available forcemeters (these are available in a range of calibrations, such as 2.5N, 5N and 10N); 100g slotted masses up to 1kg; one 15cm length of 5mm dowel per forcemeter; a cotton reel; a long elastic band; a paper clip; masking tape; safety goggles

Speaking scientifically
forcemeter, mass, newton

Lesson 3: Measuring forces

Introduction
Recap some of the previous experiences in this topic. Ask the children to recall some of the investigations and activities they have carried out. Talk about the different forces they have experienced and ask them to think about which forces might have been the strongest and how they might be measured. Introduce to the children the idea of forcemeters. Show them some commercially-made forcemeters but explain that they are going to make their own. Demonstrate how to measure a force using the forcemeter, including how to read the scale to give numerical data.

Whole-class work
1. Model for the children how to make a forcemeter:
● Open up the paper clip into an S-shaped hook, loop the elastic band over one end of the hook and tape the hook onto the dowel so that the other end of the hook is at the end of the dowel.
● Loop the other end of the elastic band over the cotton reel and secure it in place by taping round the sides of the reel where the cotton would have been.
2. Holding the forcemeter around the barrel of the cotton reel, a load can now be placed on the hook end and the dowel will be pulled through the centre of the cotton reel.

Independent/Paired work
3. Give the children time and practical support to make their own forcemeters.
● To calibrate a forcemeter, hang 100g weights on the hook one at a time and then mark the dowel where it rests in the cotton reel.
4. If you wish to measure larger masses/forces, you may need to use a stronger elastic band. The children could try using different elastic bands. Challenge them to make their forcemeter carry 1kg.

5. The children can now test their forcemeters by measuring the forces needed to move some relatively small classroom objects. They can use the scales they marked earlier to record the force numerically.

Differentiation
● The children may need some practical support to make their forcemeters. For some children it may be more appropriate to have prepared some of the components for them in advance.

Science in the wider world
The newton is the unit of force. It is named after Sir Isaac Newton. He formulated the laws of motion and explained gravity. A newton is described as the force that gives a mass of 1kg an acceleration of 1m/s2.

Review
Assess the children's understanding of how a forcemeter works through observation of their use and consideration of the data they gather.

Objectives

● To know that a magnet has two poles and is attracted and repelled by another magnet.
● To know that some materials are magnetic and some are non-magnetic.
● To know that magnets have uses.

Resources

A selection of magnets; a selection of magnetic and non-magnetic materials; a selection of magnetic games such as table football, disguise kits, apparent floating paper clip illusions and stacking ring magnets; photocopiable page 42 'Understanding magnets'

Working scientifically

● Gathering, recording, classifying and presenting data in a variety of ways to help in answering questions.
● Recording findings using simple scientific language, drawings, labelled diagrams, bar charts, and tables.

Understanding magnets

Revise

● Let the children have an opportunity to explore magnets by simply 'playing' with them in a semi-structured way. This should help them to understand what happens when like and unlike poles are brought together.
● Again, further opportunity to informally explore magnets and materials through structured 'play' will enable children to quickly realise that only metallic objects are attracted by the magnets.

Assess

● Assess the children's understanding of how magnets attract and repel each other by asking them to complete the photocopiable page 42 'Understanding magnets'. This photocopiable sheet will enable you to identify any misconceptions associated with the presence of north and south poles and any misunderstanding of the way in which like and unlike poles behave.

Further practice

● Some children may have the misconception that all metals are attracted to magnets and not just those containing iron, nickel and cobalt. Further understanding can be gained of the metals that can be attracted by a magnet through exploring simple games and toys that use the principles of magnetic attraction and repulsion. These might include things like table football, disguise kits, apparent floating paperclip illusions and stacking ring magnets. Many of these are available commercially from science resources suppliers.
● The children could also carry out further enquiries to find a range of metallic objects in school and use secondary sources to identify whether the metal might contain iron, nickel or cobalt.

Objectives
● To know that there is a force called friction and that it acts between objects
● To be able to identify situations where friction is effective
● To know when friction is useful and when it is not useful

Resources
Examples of frictional surfaces and situations for the children to survey (many will be readily identifiable around school although you may want to add some examples or illustrations such as skiing, skating, braking and so on); photocopiable page 43 'Friction survey'

Speaking scientifically
Force, friction, grip, slide, slip

Understanding friction

Revise

● Understanding of the concept that friction is a force that acts between the surfaces of objects
● Understanding of the ways in which friction can be increased or decreased
● Knowledge of the ways in which we use friction and how that sometimes we need the effects of friction (such as in brakes) and other times we try to reduce the effects (such as when skiing or skating).

Assess

Assess the children's understanding of friction by asking them to complete the photocopiable page 43 'Friction survey'. This sheet will enable you to identify if the children have an understanding of the concept of friction through their ability to identify different situations where friction or the lack of it comes into effect. You will also be able to assess their understanding of the uses of friction and identify those times when we want to increase and make use of friction together with those times when we want to reduce friction between surfaces. You will also be able to assess the children's ability to give explanations for their choices which are based on their understanding of these scientific concepts.

Further practice

Some children may have the misconception that friction is either useful or not and therefore not understand the circumstances where there are advantages or disadvantages to friction. Children's understanding can be developed by further practical experiences of increasing and decreasing friction, considering the impact and whether this is useful or not. Children may also think that friction is only effective between solid surfaces, whilst a difficult concept some experience of the frictional impact of water and air (water resistance/air resistance and streamlining).

Objectives
- To know the different types of forces.
- To identify pushes, pulls and twists as examples of forces in action.
- To learn how arrows can be used to indicate the direction of a force.
- To know that there is a force called friction and that it acts between the surfaces of objects.

Resources
Photocopiable page 'I have... Who has...?' from the CD-ROM

Working scientifically
- Gathering, recording, classifying and presenting data in a variety of ways to help in answering questions.
- Recording findings using simple scientific language, drawings, labelled diagrams, bar charts, and tables.

Understanding forces

Revise
- Ability to use the key scientific vocabulary associated with forces, such as push, pull and twist.
- Understanding contact and non-contact forces and the difference between them.
- Awareness that forces can be pushes, pulls and twists.
- Understanding that forces are exerted on objects in a particular direction, and that objects usually have more than one force being exerted on them. Know that sometimes these forces work in opposition.
- Understanding that friction is a force opposing movement.

Assess
- Assess the children's understanding using the loop game template on the photocopiable page 'I have... Who has...?' from the CD-ROM. This can be done in different ways to suit your particular class. You can either complete the cards yourself, or for a higher level assessment the children can complete the cards.
- The loop game works through asking questions ('Who has...?') about some of the key ideas in the topic of forces, and then seeing if the right child can answer the question ('I have...') before asking the next question. If the children answer all the questions correctly, the child starting will also finish the game. For example, if the game starts with 'Who has the name we give to pushes, pulls and twists?' the child with the answer says 'I have forces' before reading out the question on their card.

Further practice
- Develop the loop game idea further. The children can find out more about forces and add their own information to make a more complex and longer version of the game.

Push, pull and twist

- Describe what is happening in each picture.
- Include the words "push", "pull" or "twist".

_____   _____

_____   _____

_____   _____

_____   _____

_____   _____

_____   _____

- Now make up some of your own on the back of this photocopiable sheet.

I can identify pushes, pulls and twists.

How did you do?

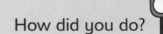

SCHOLASTIC
www.scholastic.co.uk

Name: _____

Date: _____

My investigation: sliding

■ Draw the objects in order of easiest to hardest to slide across the floor.

Easiest to slide ──────────→ **Hardest to slide**

■ We wanted to find _____

■ To investigate this we _____

■ It was the easiest to slide _____ because _____ .

■ It was the most difficult to slide _____ because _____ .

I can carry out an investigation on sliding.

How did you do?

Name: _____

Date: _____

My investigation: rolling

■ Draw the objects in order of easiest to hardest to roll across the floor.

Easiest to roll → **Hardest to roll**

■ We wanted to find _____.

■ To investigate this we _____.

■ It was the easiest to roll _____ because _____.

■ It was the most difficult to roll _____ because _____.

I can carry out an investigation on rolling.

How did you do?

PHOTOCOPIABLE

■SCHOLASTIC
www.scholastic.co.uk

Name: _____

My investigation: ramps

- Place a piece of wood on some books to make a slope that is 10cm high.
- Place a toy car at the top of the ramp and let it go.
- Measure how far the car has rolled and record the distance in the table below.
- Do the same thing for ramps that are 15cm, 20cm and 30cm high.

Height of ramp	Distance travelled
10cm	
15cm	
20cm	
30cm	

- Which car rolled the furthest? _____

I can carry out an investigation on ramps.

How did you do?

Investigation planning

■ Plan your investigation using the headings below.

Our question: _____

_____

What we will do to find the answer:

What we will need:

What we think will happen:

I can plan an investigation.

How did you do?

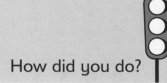

PHOTOCOPIABLE

SCHOLASTIC
www.scholastic.co.uk

Magnets

- Draw and colour a diagram of a bar magnet.
- Colour one end red and the other end blue.
- Mark N at the red end and S at the blue end.

[   ]

- Complete these sentences

N stands for _____. S stands for _____.

The ends of the magnet are called the _____.

- Bring the ends of two bar magnets close together.

Bring N to N.   What do you notice? _____

Bring S to S.   What do you notice? _____

Bring N to S.   What do you notice? _____

- Draw a diagram to show what happens each time.

Magnets	Diagram	What happened?
N to N		
S to S		
N to S		

I can observe closely.

How did you do?

Understanding magnets

1. Draw a picture of a bar magnet. Show what is usually written at the ends.

What happens when two magnets are brought together?
Draw sketches to help explain your answers.

2. a) When the poles are the same:

_____

_____

_____

b) When the poles are different:

_____

_____

_____

3. Write down six uses of magnets.

_____

_____

I can gather and record data.

How did you do?

PHOTOCOPIABLE   **SCHOLASTIC** www.scholastic.co.uk

Friction survey

■ Carry out a survey to find examples of friction in your classroom or around school. Record your findings in the space below.

■ Think about the things you have found, sometimes friction is useful and sometimes it is not. Group the things you have found and explain your answers

Things where friction is useful	Why

Things where friction is not useful	Why

I can carry out a survey on friction.

How did you do?

Animals including humans: nutrition

Expected prior learning
- Know some of the basic needs of animals, including humans.
- Understand the importance of exercise and diet.
- Understand that animals, including humans, grow from babies into adults and have some awareness of the stages in between.

Overview of progression
In this chapter children will learn:

- about the importance of exercise
- about the need to eat the right amounts of different types of food
- that animals cannot make their own food
- that some animals eat only animals, some only plants, and some eat both
- how nutrients and water are transported around animals.

Creative context
- This chapter provides opportunities for children to use visual representations, models and drama. There are links to D&T.

Background knowledge
- It is important to eat a diet containing a range of different foods, as they serve different purposes. There are five main food groups:
  - proteins: for the growth and repair of the body
  - fats and oils: for energy and insulation
  - carbohydrates: for energy (and fibre to help move food through the gut)
  - minerals: to build bones and teeth and help the nervous system and red blood cells function properly
  - vitamins: to help control chemical reactions and prevent deficiency diseases.
- These five groups are often combined into three groups: energy-giving foods (carbohydrates and fats/oils), body-building foods (proteins) and maintenance foods (vitamins and minerals). We also need water and fibre. A balanced diet consists mainly of carbohydrates, fats and proteins. Vitamins and minerals are needed in much smaller quantities.

Speaking scientifically

Children should be familiar with the terms: carnivore, herbivore, omnivore, food chain, food web, digestive system, gullet, liver, pancreas, large intestine, small intestine, bile, enzymes, circulatory system.

Preparation

You will need to provide: pictures,recipes and menus from different countries; local cooks; school nurse/community health visitor; secondary reference sources on animals, human teeth, the body and digestion; laptops/PCs; data-handling software; sorting rings; thread; red and white card; art materials; hole punch; examples or pictures of food from the major food groups; food packets; healthy and unhealthy menus; illustrations/models of teeth; apples/pears; mirrors; sweet, salty and sour/bitter food samples; sandwich box; sandwich; knife; plate; potato masher; plastic bag; food colouring; vinegar; *The Magic School Bus Inside the Human Body*; junk modelling materials; tabard/pictures of major body organs; stethoscopes/tubing and funnels; timers; train sets; digital/video cameras; pictures of people.

On the CD-ROM you will find: Interactive activities 'Going shopping' and 'My teeth'; photocopiable pages 'Food (2)', 'Food groups (3) ', 'Food groups (4)', 'My teeth (2)', 'My teeth (3)' and 'Healthy eating'; media resource 'Athlete'

Chapter at a glance

Week	Lesson	Curriculum objectives	Objectives	Main activity	Working scientifically
1	1	• (Y2) To describe the importance for humans of exercise, eating the right amounts of different types of food, and hygiene. • To identify that animals, including humans, need the right types and amount of nutrition.	• To review the importance of exercise and eating the right amounts of food in staying healthy. • To consider what is meant by a balanced diet.	Visit by the school nurse or heath visitor to talk about staying healthy. Drawing a series of annotated pictures (cartoon strip) to show how to stay healthy both in what they eat and the exercise they get. (This can be repeated as an assessment task in week 6.)	• Asking relevant questions. • Gathering, recording, classifying and presenting data in a variety of ways to help in answering questions.
	2	• To identify that animals, including humans, need the right types and amount of nutrition and that they cannot make their own food; they get nutrition from what they eat.	• To know that animals have different diets.	Comparing foods eaten by humans and other animals.	• Using straightforward scientific evidence to answer questions or to support their findings.
	3	• To identify that animals, including humans, need the right types and amount of nutrition and that they cannot make their own food; they get nutrition from what they eat.	• To know that different sorts of food are eaten by animals.	Survey of pet owners to determine foods eaten by pets.	• Reporting on findings from enquiries, including oral and written explanations, displays or presentations of results and conclusions.
2	1	• To identify that animals, including humans, need the right types and amount of nutrition and that they cannot make their own food; they get nutrition from what they eat.	• To know the meaning of the terms carnivore, herbivore and omnivore. • To be able to classify animals as carnivores, herbivores or omnivores.	Classifying animals as carnivores, herbivores or omnivores.	• Gathering, recording, classifying and presenting data in a variety of ways to help in answering questions.
	2	• To identify that animals, including humans, need the right types and amount of nutrition and that they cannot make their own food; they get nutrition from what they eat.	• To know the meaning of the terms carnivore, herbivore and omnivore. • To be able to classify animals as carnivores, herbivores or omnivores.	Designing menus for 'animal cafes' that will cater for herbivores, carnivores and omnivores. Using simple classification devices.	• Gathering, recording, classifying and presenting data in a variety of ways to help in answering questions.
	3	• To identify that animals, including humans, need the right types and amount of nutrition and that they cannot make their own food; they get nutrition from what they eat.	• To know that feeding relationships can be shown using food chains. • To be able to classify living things as producers or consumers.	Creating simple food chain mobiles. Identifying the producers and consumers in the food chains.	• Gathering, recording, classifying and presenting data in a variety of ways to help in answering questions.
3	1	• To identify that animals, including humans, need the right types and amount of nutrition and that they cannot make their own food; they get nutrition from what they eat.	• To know that foods can be grouped into those needed for growth, activity and keeping healthy.	Sorting a bag of shopping into three food groups.	• Gathering, recording, classifying and presenting data in a variety of ways to help in answering questions.
	2	• To identify that animals, including humans, need the right types and amount of nutrition and that they cannot make their own food; they get nutrition from what they eat.	• To group the foods in their meals into those needed for growth, activity and keeping healthy.	Looking at the contents of packed lunches. Keeping a food diary.	• Gathering, recording, classifying and presenting data in a variety of ways to help in answering questions.
	3	• To identify that animals, including humans, need the right types and amount of nutrition and that they cannot make their own food; they get nutrition from what they eat.	• To know what a healthy meal is like. • To understand how knowledge of food groups can help build a healthy diet.	Assessing menus and creating a balanced diet.	• Using straightforward scientific evidence to answer questions or to support their findings.

Chapter at a glance

Week	Lesson	Curriculum objectives	Objectives	Main activity	Working scientifically
4	1	• *To find out how different parts of the body have special functions.*	• To recognise different types of teeth. • To describe the functions of different types of teeth.	Looking at and naming types of teeth in relation to the range of foods eaten.	• Using straightforward scientific evidence to answer questions or to support their findings.
	2	• *To find out how different parts of the body have special functions.*	• To know that the senses, including taste, make us aware of our surroundings.	Classifying foods by taste: sweet, salty and sour/bitter.	• Reporting on findings from enquiries, including oral and written explanations, displays or presentations of results and conclusions.
	3	• *To find out how different parts of the body have special functions.*	• To know how food is digested within the digestive system.	Practical demonstration of how the digestive system works. Making a model to illustrate the digestive system.	• Reporting on findings from enquiries, including oral and written explanations, displays or presentations of results and conclusions.
5	1	• *To find out how different parts of the body have special functions.*	• To know how food is digested within the digestive system.	Modelling digestion in creative ways, such as through an illustrated story, a 3D model or a dramatisation.	• Gathering, recording, classifying and presenting data in a variety of ways to help in answering questions.
	2	• *To find out how different parts of the body have special functions.*	• To know how nutrients and water are transported through the body.	Using models and analogies to illustrate the body transportation systems.	• Reporting on findings from enquiries, including oral and written explanations, displays or presentations of results and conclusions.
	3	• *To find out how different parts of the body have special functions.*	• To know how the blood system transports nutrients around the body.	Modelling the blood system using wooden train sets.	• Reporting on findings from enquiries, including oral and written explanations, displays or presentations of results and conclusions.
6	1	• To identify that animals, including humans, need the right types and amount of nutrition and that they cannot make their own food; they get nutrition from what they eat.	• To know that different people need different amounts of food to stay healthy.	Examining food packaging for food information.	• Recording findings using simple scientific language, drawings, labelled diagrams, bar charts, and tables.
	2	• To identify that animals, including humans, need the right types and amount of nutrition and that they cannot make their own food; they get nutrition from what they eat.	• To know that food gives us energy. • To know that there is a relationship between activity and the amount of food required.	Using secondary sources to find out what athletes eat. Designing a meal for a famous sports personality.	• Using straightforward scientific evidence to answer questions or to support their findings.
	3	• To identify that animals, including humans, need the right types and amount of nutrition and that they cannot make their own food; they get nutrition from what they eat.	• To know that foods from different cultures contain healthy combinations of nutrients.	Looking at food from different cultures around the world to compare and contrast similarities and differences. Invite cooks from the community to bring samples of dishes from their cultures to share with the children.	• Using straightforward scientific evidence to answer questions or to support their findings.
Assess and review					

■SCHOLASTIC

Objectives
● To review the importance of exercise and eating the right amounts of food in staying healthy.
● To consider what is meant by a balanced diet.

Resources
A school nurse or community health visitor who will give a talk to the children; slips of paper; 'question box'

Speaking scientifically
balanced diet, exercise, health

Lesson 1: Staying healthy

Previous knowledge
Children should already be familiar with the following:
- the basic needs of animals that must be fulfilled if they are to survive
- the important role that exercise and nutrition play in living a healthy life
- the importance of eating the right amounts of different types of food
- the importance of hygiene
- how animals obtain their food from plants and from other animals
- simple food chains
- different sources of foods.

Introduction
Begin the lesson by telling the children that there will be a special visitor coming to speak to them later – the school nurse or community health visitor.

Whole-class work
1. Ask the children to write on slips of paper any questions that they may have about health, exercise and diet. These can then be placed in a 'question box'. Whilst the children are working independently, look through the slips of paper and identify some appropriate questions that can be asked later in the lesson.

2. Tell the children that all food is important. Explain to them that no food is 'bad for you' as such, but rather that too much of the wrong food or not enough of the right food can lead to an unhealthy diet.

3. Talk about the need to have a balanced diet. Ask the children to tell you what sort of foods might be part of a balanced diet. Introduce the idea that foods can be placed in the following groups: those that give us energy (carbohydrates and fats), such as bread, potatoes, pasta, rice, sugar, and fatty and oily foods; those that help to build our bodies (proteins), such as meat, fish, dairy, seeds and nuts; and those that help to maintain our bodies (vitamins and minerals), found in red meat, milk, fruits and vegetables. On the board, classify each of their suggestions as 'Energy foods', 'Body-building foods' or 'Maintenance foods'.

4. Make a list of foods that should be eaten only in moderation, such as sweet and salty foods.

Independent work
5. Ask the children to draw cartoon strips to show a typical day for them. Their illustrations should show them getting up, the meals they eat, how they get to and from school, the exercise they take and going to bed. Make sure they include close-up pictures of a typical breakfast, lunch and dinner showing the foods they eat. Encourage them to make this a typical day and to include the things that they already do, rather than those they might like to do in future or think they should do. This is important, as you are trying to assess the children's current level of understanding and awareness of these concepts and issues.

Whole-class work
6. Bring the children back together to share their cartoons and discuss their ideas about diets and exercise. Identify any misconceptions the children may have.

7. Introduce the school nurse or community health visitor. Let the school nurse or community health visitor comment on some of the children's answers to the checkpoint questions on page 48.

8. The school nurse or community health visitor should give their talk to the children, explaining about their work and how they help people to eat a healthy diet and get sufficient exercise.

Checkpoints
● What does it mean to be healthy?
● How do we stay healthy?
● What types of food should we eat in order to stay healthy?
● What types of food should we avoid in order to stay healthy?
● Is exercise important?
● What sorts of exercise could you take part in?
● Can food be bad for you?

9. Use the children's health and exercise questions from the question box to have a question and answer session with the school nurse or community health visitor.

Introducing the new area of study

Introduce the new topic to the class. Outline that they will be learning about eating healthy diets, how our bodies break down and transport the foods we eat, and the idea that we cannot make our own food. They will also be learning about the foods that animals eat – that some animals only eat other animals, some only eat plants, and some eat both. They will look at the ways in which our bodies use food and the system we have for transporting the nutrients we get from our food around our bodies.

> **Differentiation**
> ● Some of the children may need support in asking appropriate questions and in correctly ordering their daily activities. These children might find a pre-prepared and timed grid useful, with the different mealtimes and activity times already identified.

Science in the wider world

Exercise and diet are becoming increasingly important issues for people in many parts of the world. The increase in obesity levels amongst both adults and children in the UK has raised concerns about the amount of fat, salt and sugar in our diets. Changes in lifestyle have also resulted in people getting less daily exercise through their everyday routines.

Review

Through their engagement in the discussion with the health visitor, assess the children's understanding of the importance of exercise and eating a balanced diet, together with their understanding of the links between these things and living a healthy life.

Objectives
● To know that animals have different diets.

Resources
Photocopiable page 69 'Food (1)'; photocopiable page 'Food (2)' from the CD-ROM; secondary reference sources about animals such as books, videos, CD-ROMs and internet access

Speaking scientifically
processed

Lesson 2: Food

Introduction

Begin by talking to the children about the foods that animals eat. Ask them a few silly questions such as: *Does an elephant eat jam sandwiches? Does a fish have a boiled egg for breakfast?* Talk about how animals and plants are food for other animals (including humans), using examples. Encourage the children to suggest further examples of their own.

Whole-class work

1. Ask the children to think about the different foods that they themselves eat. Compile a list of their suggestions on the board or flipchart.

2. Now ask them to think about the foods that are eaten by animals and list these separately.

3. Compare the lists. In general, the foods eaten by animals will be different (though there may be some foods that appear in both lists).

4. Encourage the children to think about the ways in which an animal's food may differ from a human's food. For example, human food is often cooked or processed, whereas food for wild animals is usually raw and unprocessed.

Independent work

5. Give out photocopiable page 69 'Food (1)' for the children to complete.

6. Encourage them to think about how our food may be eaten raw, cooked or otherwise processed.

7. The children should use various secondary sources to find out about the range of foods eaten by one particular animal, with each child focusing on a different animal. Encourage them to relate what is eaten by the animal to where it lives.

8. They can use the 'Animal diet factfile' at the bottom of the photocopiable sheet to record their findings.

> **Differentiation**
> ● For children who need support, use 'Food (2)' from the CD-ROM. This version of the photocopiable sheet asks the children to draw the foods rather than writing their names.

Science in the wider world

Many children will have experience of animals, either as pets or through the media. This will help them to see that the diets of animals vary and may depend on where they live and the conditions in that area, such as climate, the physical environment and the other organisms that live there.

Review

Share the findings of the children's research into animal diets and assess their ability to identify the foods eaten by animals. Look for evidence of an understanding of the different diets eaten by humans and animals, and also that different animals have different diets.

Objectives
● To know that different sorts of food are eaten by animals.

Resources
Computer and data-handling software

Speaking scientifically
behaviour, discomfort, disease, distress, hunger, thirst

Lesson 3: Pet food survey

Introduction
Begin the lesson by asking the children to think about what they need to stay safe and healthy. Allow some paired talk time before collecting together all their ideas. Some children may identify wants and desires rather than needs.

Whole-class work
1. Begin to focus the children's thinking towards the 'five freedoms' commonly associated with animal welfare, which are:
   - freedom from hunger or thirst (access to suitable food and water)
   - freedom from discomfort (a comfortable place to live)
   - freedom from pain, injury or disease (good health)
   - freedom to express normal behaviour
   - freedom from fear and distress.

2. Ask the children to share with the rest of the class information about any pet animals they may have. Encourage them to explain how they look after their pets.

3. Focus the discussion on the need for food. Relate this back to the previous lesson, when the children compared the foods they themselves eat with those eaten by animals.

Paired work
4. Tell the children that they are going to carry out a survey to find out more about the types of food that we feed to domestic pets.

5. Ask them to think of a way to carry out a survey of the pets owned by children in the class and the foods eaten by these pets. They should try to answer questions such as: *What are the most popular pets? What is the favourite food they eat? What is the most unusual pet and the most unusual diet or food eaten?*

6. Talk to the children about how they might gather and record the information and then how they might present it. Encourage them to think creatively about how they might share their findings. Could they design a poster, write a newspaper report, or record a TV or radio news item? If appropriate, they could use data-handling software to record, interpret and present their findings.

7. Ask the children to work in their pairs to design and carry out their surveys and present the results.

Differentiation
● Some children may need support with the data collection.
● Challenge children to ask and answer additional questions about the data they have collected, such as: *What is the most popular food eaten by rabbits?*

Science in the wider world
In the same way that humans need to eat a good balanced diet in order to stay healthy, so too do animals (though of course their needs will differ depending on the type of animal). Children should be aware that animals experience similar feelings to humans in terms of their health and wellbeing and that having access to appropriate food is an important part of this.

Review
Assess the children's ability to identify the different types of food eaten by animals, through scrutiny of their work and discussion.

Objectives
● To know the meaning of the terms carnivore, herbivore and omnivore.
● To be able to classify animals as carnivores, herbivores or omnivores.

Resources
Pictures of animals, including herbivores, carnivores and omnivores (choose an interesting range of different types); photocopiable page 70 'Animal I spy'; secondary sources of information about animals such as books, videos, CD-ROMs and internet access

Speaking scientifically
carnivore, herbivore, omnivore

Lesson 1: Animal diets

Introduction
Look at the results of the pet food survey with the children and together make a list on the board of all the foods that the pets eat. Continue the discussion by broadening it out to discuss the different foods eaten by animals that live in the wild. Have a set of pictures of different animals ready to share with the children. Ask them if they know what each of these animals usually eats. Record the different foods eaten against the animal pictures.

Whole-class work
1. Ask the children if they can think of some ways to group the animals in the pictures according to what they eat.

2. Elicit the idea that some of these animals eat only plants (herbivores), some eat only other animals (carnivores) and some eat both (omnivores). Use the correct scientific vocabulary for these three groups of animals and encourage the children to practise using the terms too.

Independent work
3. Distribute photocopiable page 70 'Animal I spy'. Explain to the children that they are going to imagine they are on a visit to an animal park where there are animals whose names begin with each letter of the alphabet.

4. The children need to think of one animal for each letter and use their own knowledge and secondary sources to decide what sort of diet each would require. They should fill in the photocopiable sheet and classify each animal as a herbivore, a carnivore or an omnivore.

Differentiation
● Some children may need support in sourcing and using appropriate secondary sources of information. You may want to prepare some simplified secondary sources ahead of the lesson for these children.

Science in the wider world
The definition of a diet is not related to slimming and losing weight but to an animal's complete food intake. Some animals have very varied diets and select from a wide range of foods; this includes humans. Other animals are restricted to a much narrower diet, often due to evolutionary and environmental factors.

Review
Assess the children's understanding of and ability to compare and contrast herbivores, carnivores and omnivores through the whole-class activity and by checking the photocopiable sheets.

Objectives
● To know the meaning of the terms carnivore, herbivore and omnivore.
● To be able to classify animals as carnivores, herbivores or omnivores.

Resources
Examples of simple Venn diagrams; pictures of animals; sorting rings; restaurant menus; secondary sources relating to animal diets such as books, videos, CD-ROMs and internet access

Speaking scientifically
carnivore, herbivore, omnivore, Venn diagram

Lesson 2: Animal cafe

Introduction

Show the children some examples of simple Venn diagrams. Then demonstrate a classification exercise to the children by using some pictures of animals to create your own Venn diagram on the board. A suitable example could be animals that live in water only, animals that live on land only, and animals that live on both. (Avoid using an example that involves food so that the children can do this themselves later.) Encourage the children to offer suggestions to help sort the animals correctly into the different sections of the Venn diagram.

Group work

1. Give the children copies of various animal pictures and sorting rings. Ask them to work in groups to sort the images in any way they like.

2. The children may want to sort the pictures in many different ways. Ask them to discuss the different ways in which they could be grouped. This can be unrelated to feeding at this stage. They could choose to sort them according to features such as size, shape, movement, colour, number of legs, habitat and so on.

3. Ask the children to settle on one classification and complete their Venn diagrams by copying the pictures onto their diagrams. Then ask each group to share their Venn diagram with the class, giving the class a short time to look at and discuss the ways in which others have classified their animals.

4. Now ask the children to re-classify their animals according to the foods they eat. Make sure you reinforce the use of the correct scientific vocabulary for herbivores, carnivores and omnivores. The Venn diagrams will therefore have one set of animals that are carnivores, one set that are herbivores and an overlapping set that are omnivores.

Independent work

5. Children should use the Venn diagrams and secondary sources to devise suitable menus for:

- Harriet's Herbivore Bistro
- Colin's Carnivore cafe
- Ollie's Omnivore Take Away

These can be presented in the same style as a restaurant menu, so you could provide some examples to help model this activity.

> **Differentiation**
> ● Some children may need extra support in using the sorting rings and with the idea of the Venn diagram. They may also need some help in identifying and using suitable secondary sources of information.

Science in the wider world

Unlike in the human world, where most of our food is produced by farming, in the natural world animals spend much of their time finding and eating their food. Herbivores do not usually have to search very far for their food but often need to consume a lot of it, whereas carnivores usually spend a lot of time finding or hunting their food.

Review

Assess the children's understanding of different animal diets through scrutiny of their diagrams and menus. Do their menus include a range of different types of food eaten by herbivores, carnivores and omnivores?

SCHOLASTIC

Objectives
● To know that feeding relationships can be shown using food chains.
● To be able to classify living things as producers or consumers.

Resources
Thread; card; art materials; sticky tape; hole punch

Speaking scientifically
consumers, food chain, producers

Introduction

Ask the children to think about all the animals and plants that live in or visit the school grounds. Make a list of the suggestions and talk about why some of the animals named might live in or visit the school grounds. Ideas might include finding shelter, living in an environment with the conditions that they prefer, or the availability of food.

Whole-class work

1. Discuss as a class how the animals on the list eat other animals or plants that are present in the school grounds.

2. Show the children how to create a very simple food chain using organisms from your list, such as: dandelion plant → caterpillar → robin.

Independent work

3. Ask the children to look at the list of animals and plants that you have compiled together and use it to make a food chain of their own. These could be created as simple vertical hanging mobiles, with the feeding relationship being from plants at the bottom to top consumer at the top.

4. The children can draw and colour pictures of their chosen plants and animals on card. These can then be cut out and the picture repeated on the back. The pictures can then be hole-punched and joined together with thread to create the food chain.

5. Look at each other's food chains and discuss whether there are links between them that would enable a simple food web to be created.

6. Ask the children to talk briefly to the class about the plants and animals in their food chain and to give some reasons for their choices.

7. Introduce the idea that as you go up the food chain, the animals eating either plants or other animals are called consumers (in the same way that humans are consumers). Explain that the plants in the food chains are called producers.

8. Ask the children to look at their food chains and to identify the producer and consumers. Ask: *Where are most of the producers to be found?* (The food chains should always begin with the producer (plant).)

9. Finally, as an element of challenge, ask the children to think about why their food chains exist. (Elicit the idea that each organism gets its energy from the things it eats). Ask the children if they can explain where the producers get their energy from, given that they don't eat other things. Encourage them to identify that the Sun is the source of energy for the producers in their food chain.

> **Differentiation**
> ● Some children might need to be given a selection of simple outline pictures that they can select to create a food chain before colouring and ordering the images.
> ● Challenge confident learners to leave the reverse of the shapes blank so that they can carry out some research and then record additional information about each animal or plant there.

Science in the wider world

The idea of interdependence begins to emerge from work on food chains. The intricate web of life shows how dependent animals are on the other animals and plants in the ecosystem in which they live. Any factor that affects a living thing in an ecosystem can have an impact on many other organisms in that ecosystem.

Review

Look at the food chains to assess the children's ability to identify the relationships between different consumers and between consumers and producers.

Objectives
● To know that foods can be grouped into those needed for growth, activity and keeping healthy.

Resources
Stand-up labels with the words 'Meat, fish and eggs', 'Dairy products', 'Cereals, fruit and vegetables' and 'Processed foods' written on them; carrier bags of food including examples of energy-giving foods (carbohydrates and fats), body-building foods (proteins) and maintenance foods (vitamins and minerals), or alternatively just pictures of these foods; empty food packets and containers; large sheets of paper; art materials

Speaking scientifically
activity, body-building foods, energy-giving foods, growth, healthy, maintenance foods

Lesson 1: Sorting foods

Introduction
Ask the children to think about the different types of food they may see on a visit to the supermarket. Ask: *How are foods grouped together in the supermarket?*

Use a carrier bag of food (or pictures) to show the children examples from the food groups: meat, fish and eggs; dairy products; cereals, fruit and vegetables; and processed foods. The children can help with this by coming to the front and having a 'lucky dip' into the bag. They then have to place the food by a card labelled with the appropriate category.

Whole-class work
1. Ask the children if they can think of any other ways of grouping the foods.

2. Lead them into suggesting that we could group them by their functions and uses in the body. Introduce the idea that some foods give us energy, some foods help us to grow and some foods keep us healthy.

3. Tell the children that each food belongs in one of these groups. Write three column headings on the board: 'Energy-giving foods', 'Body-building foods', and 'Maintenance foods'.

4. Talk about each of these food groups and tell the children about the types of food in each group and their functions. Stress that energy-giving foods are good for fuelling activity, body-building foods are good for growth and repair, and maintenance foods keep us healthy.

Group work
5. Distribute the other bags of food (one per group) and sheets of paper.

6. Ask the children to work in groups of three or four to arrange their shopping into the three groups you have written on the board.

7. When they have sorted the food, the children should record their work on a large sheet of paper using the column headings from the board: 'Energy-giving foods', 'Body-building foods', and 'Maintenance foods'.

8. Ask the children to design symbols that could be used to identify the three food groups. You may like to compare them to computer icons. The designs should be based on the benefits to the body. For example, suitable symbols could be: an athlete for energy-giving foods; a weightlifter for body-building foods; and a toolkit for maintenance foods.

Differentiation
● Some children may need support in order to sort the foods correctly.
● To challenge confident learners, ask them to write a sentence about each of the different food types on their chart.

Science in the wider world
All living things, including humans, need nutrients in order to stay alive and healthy. Nutrition is a process in which animals use food and the body's digestive system to get the nutrients they need. If a diet is lacking in any particular type of nutrient then the animal or human is said to be malnourished. The children may be aware of parts of the world where humans are short of the correct types of food needed to keep them healthy and well nourished.

Review
Monitor the children's ability to sort the foods into groups correctly through observation.

Objectives
● To group the foods in their meals into those needed for growth, activity and keeping healthy.

Resources
Prepared word cards: 'Energy-giving foods', 'Body-building foods', 'Maintenance foods', 'apples', 'bread', 'butter', 'carrots', 'cheese', 'cream', 'fish', 'ice cream', 'meat', 'oil', 'oranges', 'pasta', 'potatoes', 'rice'; Blu-Tack®; the children's packed lunches (and possibly some sample lunches for those who have school meals); photocopiable page 71 'Food groups (1)'; photocopiable page 72 'Food groups (2)'; photocopiable pages 'Food groups (3)' and 'Food groups (4)' from the CD-ROM

Speaking scientifically
balanced diet, bones, healthy diet, teeth

Lesson 2: Food groups

Introduction
Reinforce the three food groups introduced in the previous lesson. Remind the children that the foods in each of these groups carry out a particular function in the body: energy-giving foods are good for activity; body-building foods are good for growth; and maintenance foods help to keep us healthy, especially our teeth and bones.

Stick the prepared word cards 'Energy-giving foods', 'Body-building foods', and 'Maintenance foods' on the board as column headings. Then hold up the word cards with food names written on them, one by one. Ask the children to help you put these in the correct food groups and stick them in the right columns using their suggestions.

Whole-class work
1. Ask the children to think about how they could investigate the foods they eat.

2. Tell them to open up their own packed lunch and try to sort the contents into the three food groups. If some children have school meals you might provide some sample lunches for them.

3. Remind the children of the importance of food hygiene. Ensure that they wash their hands before handling their packed lunch. They should not take the food out of the wrappings and put it down on their desk.

Group work
4. Ask the children to use the contents of their packed lunch to complete the photocopiable page 71 'Food groups (1)'.

5. Now encourage the children to think about other meals they have eaten recently, for example, breakfast or the previous day's evening meal. Ask them to complete photocopiable 72 'Food groups (2)' by writing down the foods they ate at each meal and then putting a tick in the appropriate column depending on whether the food's function is growth or activity.

6. You could then set up a database into which each child can input their findings to give a class view of the foods eaten. Alternatively, this activity could be used as homework and photocopiable sheet 'Food groups (2)' could be filled in as a food diary over the next few days.

Differentiation
● To extend more confident learners, use photocopiable page 'Food groups (3)' from the CD-ROM, which challenges them to select the correct food group name for each item in their lunch box. More confident learners can also use 'Food groups (4)', which asks them to write the name of the food group that each item belongs to.

Science in the wider world
Food contains seven different kinds of nutrient. Proteins, fats and carbohydrates are the most important, although smaller quantities of minerals, vitamins, fibre and water are also needed in order to maintain health.

Review
Discuss with the children the foods they have eaten, in order to gauge their ability to sort their meals into food groups. Analysis of the photocopiable sheets will support this assessment.

Objectives
● To know what a healthy meal is like.
● To understand how knowledge of food groups can help build a healthy diet.

Resources
Sample menus (enlarged for class discussion), one healthy and one unhealthy; photocopiable page 73 'Going shopping'; interactive activity 'Going shopping' on the CD-ROM; laptops/PCs

Speaking scientifically
carbohydrates, fats, fibre, minerals, proteins, vitamins, water

Lesson 3: Going shopping

Introduction
Begin the lesson by asking the children to share with the class their 'favourite meal'. You can share yours too! Continue by asking them to think about what life would be like if they were to *always* eat their favourite meal – how long would it be before they became bored with it?

Whole-class work
1. Ask the children if they can think of any other, more 'scientific' reasons why we do not always eat the same foods. Encourage them to think about the importance of eating a variety of different foods.

2. Explain to the children that because different foods help our bodies to perform different functions, it is important to eat a balanced diet.

3. Ask the children if they can remember the names they gave to the different food groups in previous lessons ('energy-giving foods', 'body-building foods', and 'maintenance foods'). Reinforce their understanding of some of the foods in these groups, before introducing the following new words: *carbohydrates*, *fats and oils* as being energy-giving foods; *proteins* as being body-building foods; and *vitamins and minerals* as being maintenance foods.

4. Provide the sample menus for the children to look at. Ask them to consider each menu and to decide if the menu seems to provide a balanced diet. Ask: *What is 'good' about each of them? What is 'bad'? Is the 'unhealthy' meal necessarily 'bad'?* (No, not if it is an occasional treat – no food is 'bad' as such.)

Independent work
5. Distribute photocopiable page 73 'Going shopping'. Ask the children to consider the diets of the two people and to assess them for balance and health. They will then write a shopping list of their own, which should represent a healthy, balanced diet.

6. Ask the children to write a letter to a friend that explains the foods people should eat as part of a healthy diet.

7. Let the children explore the interactive activity 'Going shopping' on the CD-ROM as a consolidation activity.

Science in the wider world
Eating a balanced diet is essential to maintaining a healthy lifestyle. It is important to understand that the quantities and types of food needed by a person depend on their age, sex, height, weight, health and activity levels. In addition to eating a range of healthy foods, we also need to drink plenty of water every day. We could survive without food for several weeks, but only for a few days without water.

Review
Using the photocopiable sheets, look for evidence of the children's understanding through their ability to appreciate the differences between the two lists. Look also for evidence that they can write their own shopping list that includes other healthy food ideas not already used.

▲■ SCHOLASTIC

Objectives
- To recognise different types of teeth.
- To describe the functions of different types of teeth.

Resources
Illustrations or models of teeth; hard fruits such as apples and pears; mirrors; photocopiable page 74 'My teeth (1)'; photocopiable pages 'My teeth (2)' and 'My teeth (3)' from the CD-ROM); secondary sources of information about human teeth (such as books, videos, CD-ROMs, the internet); red and white card; scissors; glue; laptops/PCs; interactive activity 'My teeth' on the CD-ROM

Speaking scientifically
biting, canines, cutting, grinding, incisors, molars, premolars, tearing

Lesson 1: My teeth

Introduction
Ask the children to think about what they use when they are eating. Bring the discussion around to how they use their teeth.

Share your illustrations or models of teeth. Introduce ideas about how we use our teeth when eating, the different types of teeth we have, their names and their different functions.

Paired work
1. Hand out the pieces of fruit so that the children can watch each other eat and observe the functions of the different teeth. These include: incisors to bite; canines to hold and tear; and molars and premolars to grind the food up. (The children will not have permanent molars yet.)

Whole-class work
2. Encourage the children to discuss the different types of teeth we have and the jobs they do.

3. Develop the idea of the first teeth (milk teeth) being replaced by permanent teeth. Discuss how, as our teeth change and develop, so do the range and types of foods we eat.

4. Distribute mirrors to enable the children to look at their own teeth to assess their permanent and milk teeth.

Independent work
5. Give each child photocopiable page 74 'My teeth (1)'. Tell them to complete it by drawing each tooth type and then writing about its function. They can use the mirrors to help them to see their own teeth.

6. Ask the children to use secondary sources of information to find out how many teeth children and adults should have. They can use their research to make an information leaflet about teeth to be given out at a dentist's surgery.

7. The children can make models of gums and teeth using red paper for the gums and white paper for the teeth. They can stick the teeth onto the gums to create a replica of their own mouth.

8. Let the children explore the interactive activity 'My teeth' on the CD-ROM as a consolidation activity.

Differentiation
- For children who need support, use photocopiable page 'My teeth (2)' from the CD-ROM, which allows them to choose the function of each tooth from a list of options.
- To challenge confident learners, use photocopiable page 'My teeth (3)' from the CD-ROM, which asks them to provide examples to support their explanations of how the teeth work.

Science in the wider world
Human babies are generally born without teeth but by the age of one their milk teeth will have appeared. Between the ages of six and twelve these milk teeth are replaced by permanent teeth. We lose our milk teeth as we grow, but we can also lose our permanent teeth for a variety of reasons – through injury, gum disease or tooth decay. Most adults have 32 teeth in their second, or permanent, set. These consist of: eight incisors, four canines, eight premolars and twelve molars.

Review
Through observation and discussion with the children, assess their ability to recognise different types of teeth. The photocopiable sheet will provide documentary evidence.

Objectives
● To know that the senses, including taste, make us aware of our surroundings.

Resources
A variety of foods (sweet, salty and sour/bitter) in bite-sized samples for children to try

Speaking scientifically
sweet, salty, sour, taste

Lesson 2: Different tastes

Introduction
Begin the lesson by talking again about favourite foods. Be ready to share with the children some of your own favourites before asking them to contribute theirs. Some of these could be recorded on the board. Then ask the children to suggest foods that they definitely do not like; the ones they would never choose. Again, these can be recorded on the board.

Whole-class work
1. Ask the children to think about their favourite and least favourite foods and why they chose them. What is it about the foods that they really love to eat that make them their first choice? Similarly, why do they dislike certain other foods so much?

2. Some of the reasons might be to do with the look of the food, strange and unfamiliar foods, having never tried them, allergies, textures and smells.

3. Bring the discussion round to the taste of the food. Ask the children to think of some words to describe the taste of different foods. Record some of their suggestions on the board.

Paired work
4. Provide a variety of foods (in small, bite-sized samples) that the children can classify into one of these tastes: sweet, salty or sour. You will need to check whether any children have food allergies before starting the activity. Examples of suitable foods to use include:
- sweet: iced cake, jelly sweets, most fruits, biscuits
- salty: ready-salted crisps, standard baked beans, cheese
- sour: lemons, rhubarb, grapefruit.

5. Explain to the children that they are going to see how good they are at grouping different tastes according to whether they are sweet, salty or sour. Tell them that all the foods provided are quite safe, but if they do not want to taste any particular food then that is OK. (Ideally each of the samples should be tried by at least one child within each pair.)

6. Ask the children to record their results in a table with three simple headings: 'Sweet', 'Salty' and 'Sour'.

Whole-class work
7. Bring the children back together and talk about what they have found out and which foods they have put in each group.

8. Ask them to talk about how they determined the type of taste that each food had. Elicit the idea that their tongue is used to help them identify the taste of foods.

Differentiation
● Most children should be able to work on this task without difficulty, since the different tastes are usually quite distinctive.

Science in the wider world
Humans have a sensory system that keeps us in touch with our environment by processing information received from our surroundings and sent to our brain. In common with other mammals, we have a number of sensory organs that help us to monitor and make sense of our environment.

Review
Through discussion with the children, identify whether they demonstrate an understanding of what senses such as taste tell us.

Objectives
● To know how food is digested within the digestive system.

Resources
A sandwich box containing a jam sandwich (or your preferred alternative); knife; plate; potato masher; plastic bag; food colouring; water; vinegar; secondary sources of information about the body and digestion

Speaking scientifically
bile, digestion, digestive system, incisors, liver, molars, saliva, stomach acid

Lesson 3: Modelling digestion

Introduction

Begin by asking the children what they have eaten recently. Ask them to discuss in pairs what happens to the food when they eat it.

Tell the children that they are going to learn about how the food we eat passes through our bodies. Ask them if anyone knows the name of the process in which our food is broken down into the things we need for energy, health and growth. Use the word digestion and tell the children that they will be learning about the digestive system.

Whole-class work

1. Use the jam sandwich to model some of the stages involved in digestion, as outlined below .

   ● Using a knife, chop the jam sandwich into small pieces. Ask: *What do we use to cut up our food in our mouths?* (The knife represents our incisors, which cut up the food.)

   ● Place the pieces into a bowl and use the potato masher to mash them. Ask: *What part of the mouth is the potato masher like?* (It works like our molars to grind the food.)

   ● Add some water and continue to mash. Ask: *What happens to the food when this is added? What does it represent?* (The mashed sandwich gets sloppier. The water represents saliva, which begins to break the food down.)

   ● Now place the mashed-up sandwich into a plastic bag. Ask: *What might this bag represent?* (The bag represents the stomach.)

   ● Add some vinegar. Ask: *What does the vinegar represent?* (The vinegar represents stomach acids.)

   ● Add some food colouring and say it represents an enzyme: a chemical that breaks down food.

   ● Squeeze and churn the contents of the bag. Ask: *What action does squeezing the bag represent?* (The squeezing action shows the working of the stomach muscles as they mix up the contents to aid digestion.)

2. As with all models, there are limitations to how useful this model is. It is worth pointing out to the children that this is simply a representation.

Independent work

3. Based on the above model, ask the children to draw a storyboard of illustrations that describe the digestive process. They can use some secondary sources of information to extend and develop their ideas.

Differentiation
● Challenge confident learners to examine some more advanced scientific vocabulary and concepts through the secondary sources provided. An example might be the use of the word 'enzymes', which are involved in the chemical breakdown of food during digestion.

Science in the wider world

The digestive system is responsible for breaking down food into small particles and absorbing these into the body, ready for transportation around the body in the circulatory system. Digestion consists of both physical and chemical processes.

Review

Look at the children's storyboards to assess their understanding of the process of digestion.

 SCHOLASTIC

Objectives
● To know how food is digested within the digestive system.

Resources
Storyboards from the previous lesson; *The Magic School Bus Inside the Human Body* (published by Scholastic); junk modelling materials; art materials

Speaking scientifically
bile, digestion, digestive system, incisors, liver, molars, saliva, stomach acid

Lesson 1: Digestion

Introduction
Recap on the previous lesson and ask the children to share their understanding through explaining their storyboards to each other.

Read the book *The Magic School Bus Inside the Human Body* to the children. Use this as a stimulus to encourage them to think about how they could develop their own storyboard into something that is similarly creative. You could either choose one or more of the following activities, or allow the children to choose for themselves which they will do. They should use their own storyboard from the previous lesson to help plan their work.

Independent work
1. The children could write their own illustrated stories that show what happened when they ate their last meal. Encourage them to use appropriate scientific vocabulary and to ensure that the sequence of events is correct.

Paired work
2. The children could use junk modelling materials to build a 3D model that represents the digestive system. This does not need to be a realistic representation, just a model that shows the process of digestion, the parts of the body involved, and the order of events.

Group work
3. Working in groups of four or five, the children could try to dramatise the processes involved in digestion. Again, this just needs to follow the process through and enable them to demonstrate their understanding of the functions of the body parts involved at each stage. The children may need to make some props from junk materials. One of the children could act as narrator and describe what is happening as food passes through the system.

Whole-class work
4. Towards the end of the lesson, bring all the different groups and activities together and allow the children to share their work and explain their understanding.

Differentiation
● Some learners might make greater use of pictures and require some support in using the appropriate scientific terminology.
● Challenge confident learners to develop a more complex explanation and use more advanced terminology.

Science in the wider world
Children often hold misconceptions about the process of digestion – what happens to the food they eat and how it is used by the body – because it is something they are unable to see for themselves. For example, some children think that the body is just one big container that holds blood and food together with the waste that is passing out of the body. Practical experience and modelling can help to overcome some of these misconceptions.

Review
Analyse the children's work as they share it with the class in order to assess their understanding of the process of digestion.

Objectives
● To know how nutrients and water are transported through the body.

Resources
Tabard of the major body organs or illustrations to show these; photocopiable page 75 'The digestive system'; secondary sources of information such as books, CD-ROMs and the internet

Speaking scientifically
gullet, large intestine, liver, mouth, nutrients, pancreas, small intestine, stomach

Lesson 2: Transport of nutrients around the body

Introduction

Ask the children to talk with a partner about their journey from home to school – not particularly focusing on the mode of transport, but on the route that they take. Have some simple maps of the local area available so that they are able to see the route they take.

Talk about journeys and transport before returning to the previous lesson and the journey that food takes around the body. Ask the children to tell you what they think happens after the food has been through the small intestine, where digested food is absorbed into the blood system.

Paired work

1. Ask the children to talk about what journey they think food makes through the body as a means of identifying their misconceptions. You can contribute to the discussion through asking them to explain their ideas and to tell you what they think is happening.

Whole-class/Independent work

2. Using a tunic or tabard showing the major body organs, a model torso, or another illustration, let the children see the journey that food and water makes through the digestive system.

3. Identify the main parts in the process as mouth, gullet, stomach, liver, pancreas, small intestine and large intestine.

4. Using photocopiable page 75 'The digestive system', the children can draw an annotated illustration of the digestive system using the outline of the body. The children can use the tabards or illustrations to help with the order, shape and size of the parts of the digestive system. It is recommended that you enlarge the photocopiable sheet to A3.

5. Bring the children back together for a few minutes. Tell them that we have seen how food and nutrients enter the body and are digested, but ask if they know how these nutrients then travel around the body. What system do we have to carry nutrients and water around the body? (Blood.)

6. In preparation for the next lesson and as a means of gauging understanding and misconceptions, ask the children to also draw on their outline body their ideas about our blood system.

Differentiation
● Some children will need to work much more with the tabards and illustrations in order to develop their understanding of the digestive system. Their illustrations may be only simply annotated and you may wish to provide a word bank of key words from the 'Speaking scientifically' section above for them.
● Challenge confident learners to write more complex annotations and to use secondary sources to develop their understanding further.

Science in the wider world

By the time the colon is reached in the digestive system, all the digestible food has been broken down and absorbed into the body. What is left is indigestible and consists mainly of roughage and water. In the colon much of the water is absorbed into the blood, leaving behind semi-solid waste. This collects in the rectum before being passed out of the body.

Review

Scrutiny of the children's work will give an indication of their understanding of the first part of how nutrients are transported around the body.

Objectives
● To know how the blood system transports nutrients around the body.

Resources
Stethoscopes or plastic tubing and funnels; data-logger with pulse rate monitor (optional); timers; wooden train sets; small balls; digital cameras/video cameras; secondary sources about the blood system such as books, CD-ROMs and internet access

Speaking scientifically
heart, heart beat, heart rate, nutrients, pulse, stethoscope

Lesson 3: The blood system

Introduction
Revisit the previous lesson and elicit the children's understanding of the role of the blood system as the main way of transporting nutrients from the food we eat around the body. The children will know that blood is pumped around the body by the heart. If you have some stethoscopes, give the children the opportunity to listen to one another's heart beats. If none are available, make some simple stethoscopes using plastic tubing with a funnel on either end.

Whole-class work
1. Ask the children to see if they can find their own pulse. Tell them to turn their arms so that they can see the two tendons running down the middle of their wrist. Now ask them to place their index and middle fingers together on the thumb side of the tendons and to feel for a pulse. Some children may need assistance to do this.

2. If you have access to a data-logger with a pulse rate monitor that clips onto the index finger, try using this with different volunteers.

Paired work
3. When the children have found their own pulse, ask them to work in pairs to find their partner's pulse.

4. The children should use timers or stopwatches to find each other's heart rate. They need to count the number of beats in 30 seconds, and then double this to get the number of beats per minute.

5. Now ask the children to try some simple exercise, such as running on the spot for one minute, before repeating the measurement. At this stage, ask the children to simply note the differences. Ask: *After exercise, what happens to your heart rate? Does it speed up? Does it slow down?*

6. Talk about the heart and its job as a simple pump. Ask the children why they think their heart rate changed (increased) after exercise.

Group work
7. Ask the children to work in groups of three or four. They should use secondary sources of information and the wooden toy train set to simply model the blood system. They should use the train set to show the journey that blood takes as it transports nutrients around the body.

8. The children could also use drama to role play the blood system. Some children can be the heart; others will represent blood vessels. Use small balls such as those from a child's ball pool to represent the blood and its journey around the blood system.

9. The children can record their modelling of the blood system using digital cameras to share their work and explain their understanding.

> ### Differentiation
> ● Some children may find it difficult to measure the heart rate and will need extra support from the teacher. Finding the pulse can also be a challenge and some children may need help with this.

Science in the wider world
Blood is the fluid that carries oxygen to all living cells in the body. It also transports food substances, water, hormones and waste matter. The human body has 10,000km of blood vessels and about 4 litres of blood.

Review
Through observation, assess the children's understanding (in simple terms) of the blood system and the way in which blood is pumped around the body.

Objectives
● To know that different people need different amounts of food to stay healthy.

Resources
Examples of food packaging with nutritional information panels; pictures of different people engaging in various activities

Speaking scientifically
calories, energy

Lesson 1: Food information

Introduction
Show the children pictures of different people engaging in various activities. Include a range of ages, physical sizes, genders and activities (strenuous to passive). Ask the children to talk about what each of these people needs in order to be healthy and carry out their activities. The children should be able to explain that all of the people shown need food.

Ask: *What do we get from the food we eat?* Talk about the energy we get from food and recap how that energy is transported around our bodies. Looking at the pictures, ask the children to think about which person would need the most energy. Lead the discussion to a point where the children are aware that a highly active, large person will need more energy and that males generally have higher energy requirements than females.

Whole-class work
1. Look at an example of a nutritional information panel from a food package with the children. At this stage we are not concerned with the Recommended Daily Allowance (RDA) or Guideline Daily Amount (GDA), although you may wish to make the children aware that these exist.

2. Focus on the section of the panel that refers to energy. Ask the children to talk about how energy helps us. Ask: *Do we all need the same amount of energy for the things we do? If an athlete is running a marathon, will they need a lot of energy or not?* Help the children to understand that what we eat and drink is 'energy in' and what we use through physical activity is 'energy out'. The more active we are, the greater the energy levels we need.

Paired work
3. Using a range of different food packaging, let the children examine how much energy (measured in kilocalories, (kcal)) there are in some different foods. They should do this by comparing the levels per 100g of food, which is generally shown in the nutritional information panel (together with that in the suggested portion size).

4. Ask the children to record their findings in tables and then to answer these questions:

- Which food had the highest number of kcal?
- Which food had the lowest number of kcal?
- What sorts of foods generally contain higher energy levels and which contain lower amounts?

> ### Differentiation
> ● Some learners may need help in identifying and understanding the correct nutritional information on the packaging. For some you may want to select some particularly straightforward examples.

Science in the wider world
Our bodies burn energy all the time, even when resting. If we take in more energy than we use in our daily lives and through physical activity then we will start to gain weight. An important part of staying healthy is maintaining a good balance between the energy we take in and the energy we expend. This will vary depending on individual levels of physical activity.

Review
Assess the children's understanding by scrutinising their answers. Do they demonstrate an understanding of the idea that high activity means high energy out, and therefore there needs to be a high level of energy in?

Objectives
• To know that food gives us energy.
• To know that there is a relationship between activity and the amount of food required.

Resources
Media resource 'Athlete' on the CD-ROM

Speaking scientifically
balanced diet, energy level, menu

Lesson 2: Exercise and diet

Introduction

Begin the lesson by recapping on previous work looking at nutritional tables on food packaging. Reinforce the children's understanding of the link between food and energy levels. Ask them to share with a talk partner what they feel like after they have taken part in physical exercise. Let them share some of their ideas with the rest of the class. These might include feeling tired, exhausted, hot, thirsty and hungry.

Whole class

1. Show the children the media resource 'Athlete' on the CD-ROM showing an athlete as they near the end of a race.

2. Ask: *What does the athlete have that has allowed them to race/take part in their physical activity?* (Energy); *Where did they get that energy from?* (Food); *Why do they seem tired and low in energy now?* (They have used a great deal of energy in their sport); *Do you feel the same? How do you recover your energy? Do you need to eat as much as this sportsperson?* (No, because the sportsperson takes part in more and harder physical activity.)

Paired work

3. Tell the children that they are going to be 'Young Apprentices' and that they have been asked to start an athletes' cafe. The cafe will serve food that is matched to the energy needs of the sportspeople who eat there.

4. Based on the findings from the previous lesson, children should design a meal for a sports personality of their own choice that can be served at the cafe. The meal should be part of a balanced diet and provide sufficient energy for the sports personality to compete successfully in their sport. Ask the children to think about the energy needs of a darts player compared to a marathon runner. Are they the same or different? Why? They should make sure they select foods that have a high enough calorie count but low fat and salt levels.

5. The children can write a letter inviting the sportsperson to the cafe, together with a copy of their menu. In the letter they should give an explanation of why they have chosen the foods they have on the menu.

Whole-class work

6. Come together as a class to share menus and display these for all to see. Ask the children to come up with an appropriate name for their cafe.

Science in the wider world

The diets of those who engage in sport are very important and can affect their performance. Athletes use the science behind food and nutrition to ensure that they tailor their food intake to help them perform at their best. There is no one food that can ensure a great performance; it is important to maintain a balanced diet that includes foods from various different groups.

Review

Assess the children's understanding of energy-giving foods and the relationship between activity and the amount of food required through scrutiny of their menus and letters. Have they selected appropriate foods and quantities?

Objectives
● To know that foods from different cultures contain healthy combinations of nutrients.

Resources
Pictures of foods from different places, for example, chilli from USA/Mexico, paella from Spain, fish and rice from Thailand, vegetable curry from India; recipes for meals from different countries (optional); menus from Indian, Chinese and Italian restaurants (optional); a collection of recipe books; paper plates; art materials; a visit from cooks in the local community

Speaking scientifically
cultures, diets, nutrients, nutrition

Lesson 3: Food from around the world

Introduction
Begin the lesson by asking the children to share details of their favourite meals with a talk partner. Ask: *What is your favourite main course? If you could choose any dessert, what would that be?* Ask the children to think about where these foods might typically be from as they share their ideas with each other. For example, pizza would typically come from Italy and chilli from the USA/Mexico.

Independent work
1. Give the children a paper plate and ask them to draw their favourite food from a different part of the world. Some of the children may have experienced food in other countries whilst on holiday – encourage them to draw on this experience.

Paired work
2. Show the children the pictures of foods from around the world. Ask them to identify the food items in each picture. Ask them to say whether they are energy-giving foods, body-building foods or maintenance foods.

3. The children could record their ideas in a simple table that they can devise themselves, using the headings 'Energy-giving foods', 'Body-building foods' and 'Maintenance foods'.

4. Ask the children to look at recipes for meals from different countries and assign the ingredients to food groups. Alternatively, they could look at menus from Indian, Chinese and Italian restaurants and do the same.

Whole-class work
5. Invite some cooks from your local community to bring samples of food from their culture and cuisine to share with the children. Ensuring that you are aware of any food allergies that the children might suffer from, let them sample a range of the foods.

6. Let the children ask the cooks about the ingredients, where they come from, and how they might fit into the groupings of energy-giving foods, body-building foods and maintenance foods. Ask: *Which is your favourite food? Can you identify some of the healthy components in each of the meals?*

Differentiation
● Some children will need support to identify ingredients in meals and in identifying the different cultures. It may be helpful for children to talk in more detail about the typical types of foods found in different restaurants they may have visited.

Science in the wider world
Different traditional foods from around the world have a long history, which may be associated with the local availability of particular foods. Within most cultures people have traditionally tended to eat a healthy and balanced diet, although there are some parts of the world where health is affected by the limitations of the diets available to people.

Review
Through discussion and observation throughout the lesson, assess the children's awareness of the nutritional value of meals from other cultures.

Objectives
● To recognise different types of teeth.
● To describe the functions of different types of teeth.

Resources
Secondary sources of information such as books and CD-ROMs; laptops with internet access; photocopiable page 76 'Teeth'

Working scientifically
● Using straightforward scientific evidence to answer questions or to support their findings.
● Recording findings using simple scientific language, drawings, labelled diagrams, bar charts and tables.

Amazing teeth

Revise

● Ability to identify and name the different types of teeth that we have.
● Knowing and understanding the purposes and functions of each of these different types of teeth.
● Understanding the role that each tooth type plays in the process of eating and food digestion.
● Using secondary sources of information as a means of answering a scientific question.

Assess

● Assess the children's understanding and knowledge of teeth, including the different types and their functions, by asking them to complete the photocopiable page 76 'Teeth'. The children should write inside the tooth everything they know and have learned about teeth. Remind them that there are different types of teeth and that each has a purpose, and encourage them to include this information on their sheets. They should also include how our teeth begin to break food down ready for it to be digested.
● When the children have completed their photocopiable sheets, ask them to use secondary sources of information to find out any amazing extra facts about teeth. This could be about our own teeth or those of other animals. Ensure that the children extract relevant information and do not simply copy sections of text from the secondary sources provided.

Further practice

● To take this topic further, you could explore with the children the importance of taking good care of their teeth by developing good dental health habits. Ask the children to design a simple poster to convey a message encouraging people to clean their teeth regularly and look after them well.

Objectives

- To consider what is meant by a balanced diet.
- To know that foods can be grouped into those needed for growth, activity and keeping healthy.
- To know what a healthy meal is like.
- To understand how knowledge of food groups can help build a healthy diet.
- To know that different people need different amounts of food to stay healthy.
- To know that food gives us energy.
- To know that there is a relationship between activity and the amount of food required.

Resources

Photocopiable page 'Healthy eating' on the CD-ROM

Working scientifically

- Gathering, recording, classifying and presenting data in a variety of ways to help in answering questions.
- Recording findings using simple scientific language, drawings, labelled diagrams, bar charts and tables.

Healthy eating

Revise

- Knowing the names of the three food groups: energy-giving foods, body-building foods and maintenance foods.
- Understanding which types of food fit into each group.
- Understanding the contribution each type of food makes to a balanced diet.
- Understanding that a balanced diet is needed in order to stay healthy.

Assess

- Assess the children's understanding of healthy eating by asking them to complete photocopiable page 'Healthy eating' on the CD-ROM. Their responses to this sheet will enable you to assess their ability to identify a range of foods that they regard as being healthy. Encourage the children to think about all the different foods they know and to include a variety of both sweet and savoury foods. You will also be able to assess the children's understanding of food groups and their ability to identify which of the three groups (energy-giving, body-building or maintenance) each of their chosen foods belongs to. This should help you to identify any children who have misconceptions about the constituents of a healthy diet. You will also be able to gauge the children's ability to express their ideas about whether or not they are eating a healthy, balanced diet.

Further practice

- Further understanding can be gained from a closer look at food groups and the importance of maintaining a balance across the different groups. Children need to be aware that some foods that seem to be 'healthy' may belong to only one of these groups and therefore cannot provide a balanced diet by themselves. You could provide some examples and consider these as a class. Children will have already looked at the way in which different levels of physical activity demand certain levels of energy-giving food, and you may want to explore this further with them.

Objectives
● To know that animals have different diets.
● To know the meaning of the terms carnivore, herbivore and omnivore.
● To be able to classify animals as carnivores, herbivores or omnivores.

Working scientifically
● Gathering, recording, classifying and presenting data in a variety of ways to help in answering questions.
● Recording findings using simple scientific language, drawings, labelled diagrams, bar charts and tables.

What's my diet?

Revise
● Awareness that animals (including humans) cannot make their own food but must get the nutrition they need from the food they eat.
● Knowing that different animals have different diets.
● Knowing that some animals eat only meat, some eat only plants and some eat both.
● Knowing the names we give to these three groups: carnivores, herbivores and omnivores.

Assess
● Ask the children to choose three different animals – a carnivore, a herbivore and an omnivore. They should draw pictures of each of these three animals showing the outlines only. They can then write on the inside of each of their pictures some examples of foods that this animal might eat. This will enable you to assess the children's understanding of the different diets eaten by animals, most importantly that they do not all eat the same kinds of foods. It will also give you an insight into the children's knowledge of the foods that typically make up the diets of carnivores, herbivores and omnivores.
● Finally, ask the children to identify on their diagrams which animal is the carnivore, which is the herbivore and which the omnivore, and to write a sentence or two explaining what each of these terms means.

Further practice
● Further understanding of these classifications can be gained by encouraging the children to think about the food chains involved and to trace the food relationships back further. So, for example, if a large animal eats a smaller animal, what in turn has that smaller animal eaten? The children will benefit from understanding that as we trace the food chains back, animals that are carnivores and never eat plants will have fed on animals that are plant-eaters.

SCHOLASTIC

Food (1)

■ Write down the foods you and your family like to eat in the "Foods eaten by humans" column.

■ Then think about the foods that animals eat. Write these down in the "Foods eaten by animals" column.

Foods eaten by humans	Foods eaten by animals

■ Now choose one animal and find out as much as you can about where it lives and what it likes to eat.

Animal diet factfile
Name of animal:
Habitat (where it lives):
Main foods eaten:

I can identify different foods eaten by humans and animals.

How did you do?

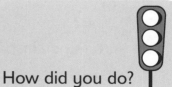

Animal I spy

■ Write an animal alphabet. Find out what each animal eats and tick the correct box. Finally, classify each animal as a herbivore, a carnivore or an omnivore.

Animal name	Eats plants	Eats animals	Eats both	Classification
A				
B				
C				
D				
E				
F				
G				
H				
I				
J				
K				
L				
M				
N				
O				
P				
Q/R				
S				
T/U				
V/W/X				
Y/Z				

I can name and classify animals.

How did you do?

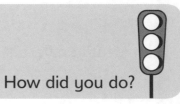

PHOTOCOPIABLE

■SCHOLASTIC
www.scholastic.co.uk

Food groups (1)

■ Look at the food in your packed lunch and draw it below.

■ Write the name of each item of your packed lunch under the correct heading.

Energy-giving foods	Maintenance foods	Body-building foods

■ Which foods in your packed lunch are you looking forward to eating the most and why?

_____

_____

I can identify different food groups.

How did you do?

Name: _____   Date: _____

Food groups (2)

■ Write in the table the foods you have eaten in the past 24 hours for breakfast, lunch, evening meal, supper and any other snacks.
■ ✓ Tick the correct food group.

Food groups	Body-building (for growth)	Energy-giving (for activity)
Breakfast		
Lunch		
Evening meal		
Supper		
Snacks		

I can identify different food groups.

How did you do?

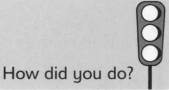

PHOTOCOPIABLE

■ SCHOLASTIC
www.scholastic.co.uk

Going shopping

■ Here are the shopping lists for two people. Look at them carefully. Think about the balance of the foods on each list.

LIST A
BANANAS
CARROTS
APPLES
CHICKEN
YOGHURT
SKIMMED MILK
LOW FAT SPREAD
RICE
PASTA
WHOLEMEAL BREAD
FISH

LIST B
CHIPS
CREAM
SAUSAGE
FULL FAT MILK
CHOCOLATE BISCUITS
BUTTER
FIZZY DRINKS
CHEESE
CHOCOLATE BARS

1. Write your thoughts about the balance of food on each list.

   List A _____

   List B _____

2. Which diet is healthy and balanced? _____

   Which diet is unhealthy and unbalanced? _____

■ Now write your own shopping list. Include a range of items to give you a healthy, balanced and tasty diet. A few "treats" are allowed!

My shopping list

I can identify healthy foods.

How did you do?

My teeth (1)

■ Look at the diagram below. Colour the teeth to show the position of each type.

Incisors – red   Canines – blue   Molars – green

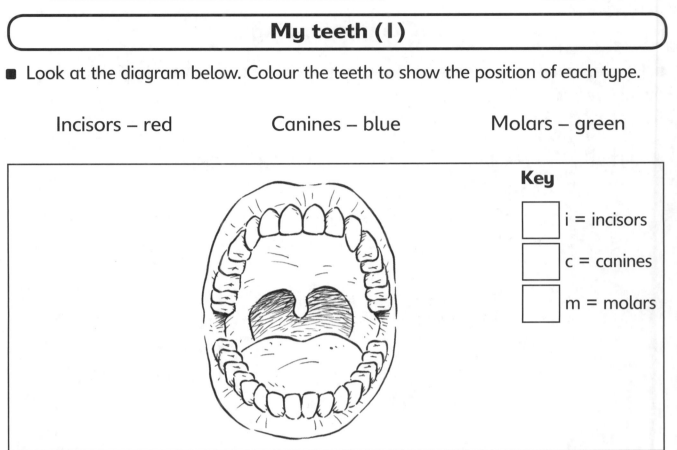

Key

☐ i = incisors

☐ c = canines

☐ m = molars

■ Use a mirror to look at your teeth.
■ Draw each different type of tooth and write about the job it does.

☐ Molar

_____

_____

☐ Canine

_____

_____

☐ Incisor

_____

I can identify and describe different types of teeth.

How did you do?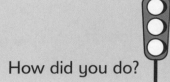

PHOTOCOPIABLE

SCHOLASTIC
www.scholastic.co.uk

The digestive system

■ Draw the different parts of the digestive system in the right places in the body. Add labels to show what each part is and what it does.

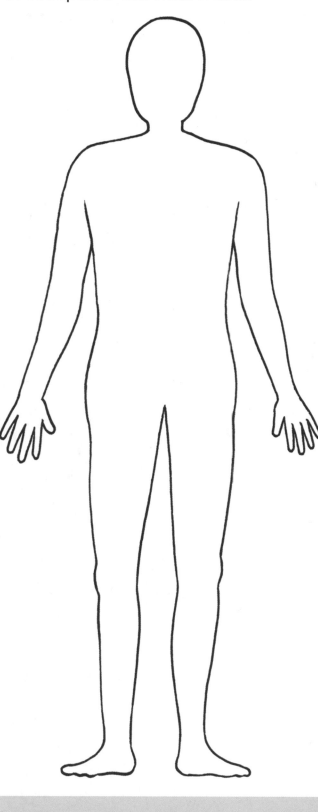

I can draw and label the digestive system.

How did you do?

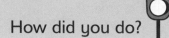

Name: _____   Date: _____

Teeth

■ What have you learned about teeth? Write in the tooth all you know about teeth.

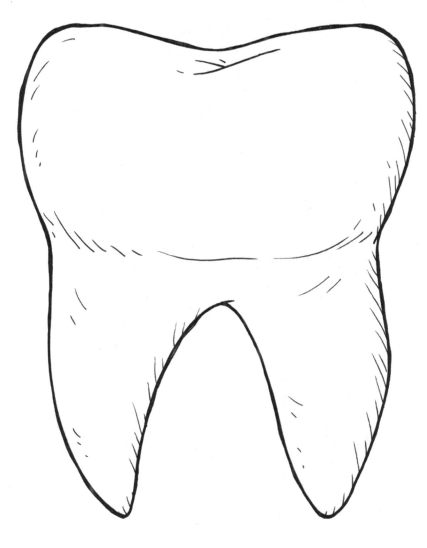

■ Why is it important to look after your teeth?

_____

_____

■ What should you do to make sure your teeth are healthy?

_____

_____

I can say why it is important to look after my teeth, and how I can do this.

How did you do?

PHOTOCOPIABLE

SCHOLASTIC
www.scholastic.co.uk

Light

Expected prior learning

● Know that the Sun is our main source of light but there are other light sources.

Overview of progression

In this chapter children will learn:

● about a variety of light sources
● that we can see because light travels to our eyes
● that light is needed to see and that 'dark' is the absence of light
● that light is reflected from surfaces
● that different materials let varying amounts of light pass through
● how shadows are formed when light is blocked by something.

Creative context

● This chapter provides opportunities for children to make shadow puppets and sundials.

Background knowledge

Light is a form of energy. It is transmitted by electromagnetic waves that (like other forms of energy) we cannot see. What we can see are the objects on which light falls. Light travels in straight lines at a speed of 300,000km per second. Nothing travels faster. When it meets the surface of a material, light can either be transmitted (travels through, such as with glass), absorbed (as in a black surface) or reflected (as with mirrors and all the objects we see).

Light sources can produce shadows, but their intensity will vary depending on the strength of the light source. A shadow is simply an area from which light is blocked. The intensity of a shadow can be varied by moving the object casting the shadow nearer to or further from its light source. The shadow also loses its definition, but gains in size, as the object is moved nearer to the light source.

Speaking scientifically

Children should be familiar with the terms: light source, shadow, reflect, opaque, transparent, translucent, arc and rotation.

Preparation

Many of the activities in this chapter need to be carried out on a sunny day and also require observations to be carried out over a whole day.

You will need to provide: Large circle of yellow paper; blackout materials/dark tent; mirrors; glowsticks; card tubes; various small objects; shiny and dull objects; image of the Moon; reflective armbands, signs or clothing; foil; art/craft materials; ray boxes (simple bulb and battery circuit in a short crisp tube with a slit at the bottom edge) torches; shoeboxes; lamps; 'Shadow' from *Star Poems* by Michael Rosen, table lamp; split pins; OHP; screen; garden canes; picture books; wooden posts; metre rules/measuring tapes; graph paper; road safety posters; decorating paint charts; pictures of emergency vehicles; pictures of camouflaged animals and bright flowers; example artworks using natural colours; eye-masks; curtain sample materials; opaque/translucent/transparent materials; coloured acetate; sheets of thin white cloth; data loggers or light meters; dowel; small pots of sand; sundial (or a picture of one); flat wooden boards with a central hole; wood glue; sundial templates; soundtrack of *Joseph and the Amazing Technicolor Dreamcoat*; balls

On the CD-ROM you will find: Photocopiable pages 'Fair test planning sheet', 'The Sun in the sky', 'Sundials'; media resource 'Graphing tool'; interactive activity 'Matching shadows'

Chapter at a glance

Week	Lesson	Curriculum objectives	Objectives	Main activity	Working scientifically
1	1	• (Y1) To observe and describe how day length varies.	• To review understanding of the apparent movement of the Sun during the day. • To introduce the idea that light travels from a light source. • To know that the Sun is a source of light.	Concept mapping ideas about the Sun. Tracking the Sun as it appears to travel across the sky.	• Asking relevant questions.
	2	• To recognise that they need light in order to see things and that dark is the absence of light.	• To identify sources of light. • To know a variety of light sources, both natural and artificial.	Identifying objects that are light sources and differentiating them from reflected light.	• Using straightforward scientific evidence to answer questions or to support their findings.
	3	• To recognise that they need light in order to see things and that dark is the absence of light.	• To understand the need for light to be able to see things. • To understand that light travels in straight lines.	How we see – using dark boxes to identify the need for a light source in order to see.	• Identifying differences, similarities or changes related to simple scientific ideas and processes.
2	1	• To notice that light is reflected from surfaces.	• To understand that light is reflected from objects. • To know that shiny objects reflect better than dull objects.	Finding out if shiny objects shine in the dark.	• Asking relevant questions.
	2	• To notice that light is reflected from surfaces.	• To know that light travels in straight lines. • To know that the sharp edge to a shadow is due to light travelling in straight lines.	Discussing how a mirror can be used to see behind you. Using mirrors, torches and ray boxes to explore how light travels in straight lines.	• Recording findings using simple scientific language, drawings, labelled diagrams, keys, bar charts, and tables.
	3	• To recognise that shadows are formed when the light from a light source is blocked by a solid object.	• To consider when shadows are formed outside.	Observing shadows in the playground. Creating annotated drawings to explain what a shadow is.	• Asking relevant questions. • Using straightforward scientific evidence to answer questions or to support their findings. • Using results to draw simple conclusions and raise further questions.
3	1	• To recognise that shadows are formed when the light from a light source is blocked by a solid object.	• To know that a shadow is formed when sunlight is blocked by an object.	Looking at how shadows are formed. Casting shadows and completing a worksheet.	• Identifying differences, similarities or changes related to simple scientific ideas and processes.
	2	• To recognise that shadows are formed when the light from a light source is blocked by a solid object. • To find patterns in the way that the size of shadows change.	• To know that light from a range of sources produces shadows. • To consider how the shape and size of a shadow varies with the position of the light source.	Using a variety of light sources to cast shadows. Completing a worksheet.	• Asking relevant questions. • Using straightforward scientific evidence to answer questions or to support their findings.
	3	• To recognise that shadows are formed when the light from a light source is blocked by a solid object. • To find patterns in the way that the size of shadows change.	• To know how the shape and size of a shadow varies with the position of the light source. • To consider the properties of an object needed to form a shadow.	Making shadow puppets using different materials, and using them to tell a story.	• Asking relevant questions. • Setting up simple practical enquiries, comparative and fair tests.

■SCHOLASTIC

Chapter at a glance

Week	Lesson	Curriculum objectives	Objectives	Main activity	Working scientifically
4	1	• To recognise that shadows are formed when the light from a light source is blocked by a solid object.	• To distinguish between opaque, translucent and transparent materials.	Demonstrating how to compare the amount of light that can pass through different materials.	• Making accurate measurements using standard units, using equipment including data loggers. • Gathering, recording, classifying and presenting data in a variety of ways to help in answering questions. • Using results to draw simple conclusions.
	2	• To recognise that shadows are formed when the light from a light source is blocked by a solid object. • To find patterns in the way that the size of shadows change.	• To understand that shadows change during the course of a day.	Observing and measuring shadows over a day. Drawing conclusions about how shadows change.	• Recording findings using simple scientific language, drawings and labelled diagrams. • Using results to draw simple conclusions.
	3	• To recognise that shadows are formed when the light from a light source is blocked by a solid object.	• To understand the properties needed in a fabric to block light completely.	Investigating the best fabric to use to make a blackout curtain or eye-mask.	• Gathering, recording, classifying and presenting data in a variety of ways to help in answering questions.
5	1	• To find patterns in the way that the size of shadows change.	• To know that the position of the Sun changes. • To consider the shape of the path of the Sun across the sky by looking at shadows.	Observing and recording the path of the Sun (children should be warned that it is not safe to look directly at the Sun).	• Recording findings using simple scientific language, drawings, labelled diagrams, keys, bar charts, and tables.
	2	• To ask relevant questions and use different types of scientific enquiries to answer them.	• To understand more about the Sun. • To identify a question that can be answered using secondary sources of information.	Research using secondary sources of information.	• Using straightforward scientific evidence to answer questions or to support their findings.
	3	• To find patterns in the way that the size of shadows change.	• To understand that a sundial can be used to tell the approximate time of day.	Looking at sundials and how they are used. Making and using a simple sundial.	• Making accurate measurements using standard units, using a range of equipment, including thermometers and data loggers.
6	1	• To recognise that they need light in order to see things.	• To know that there is a wide range of colours that can be seen.	Looking at colours in the spectrum.	• Using straightforward scientific evidence to answer questions or to support their findings.
	2	• To recognise that they need light in order to see things.	• To describe how plants and animals use colours.	Using secondary sources to investigate how plants and animals use colour.	• Using straightforward scientific evidence to answer questions or to support their findings.
	3	• To recognise that they need light in order to see things.	• To understand the use of light and colour in the local environment, for example, for road safety.	Looking at the messages different colours give us, including traffic light sequences.	• Using straightforward scientific evidence to answer questions or to support their findings.
Assess and review					

Objectives
● To review understanding of the apparent movement of the Sun during the day.
● To introduce the idea that light travels from a light source.
● To know that the Sun is a source of light.

Resources
A large circle of coloured paper to represent the Sun; copies of photocopiable page 102 'Tracking the Sun'; clipboards

Speaking scientifically
Earth, rotation, sky, Sun, sunrise, sunset

Lesson 1: The Sun

Note: This lesson needs a sunny day and must be started first thing in the morning and returned to throughout the day.

Previous knowledge

Children should already be familiar with the following:
● the apparent movement of the Sun during the day
● the changes that take place during the seasons of the year
● that the length of a day varies throughout the year, with the longest periods of daylight in summer and the shortest in winter.

Introduction

Ask the children to discuss with talk partners what they know about the Sun. Record their ideas and thoughts on the large paper Sun as a representation of their understanding. Encourage the children to think about the light and warmth we get from the Sun, and the enormity of its size and distance from us. There is no need at this stage for any awareness of the numerical size and distance, just a simple understanding of its vastness and tremendous distance. Some children may begin to talk about the Sun travelling across the sky and be able to articulate understanding of day and night.

Whole-class work

1. Ask the children to think about where the Sun was in the sky when they came to school this morning. Ask: *Did it shine on your face or on the back of your head? Was it high in the sky or low down near the horizon?* At this point it is worth discussing with the children the dangers of looking directly at the Sun, even if you are wearing sunglasses.

2. You might also talk about shadows at this point to see if any of the children have noticed that early in the morning the shadows are longer than they are towards the middle of the day.

Individual/Whole-class work

3. With appropriate adult support and supervision, take the children outside to observe where the Sun is now. Each child will need to take with them photocopiable page 102 'Tracking the Sun', a pencil and a clipboard. Again, reinforce to the children the danger of looking directly at the Sun.

4. Ask the children to choose an object such as a building, a tree or another nearby marker. They should then draw a sketch of that marker and the relative position of the Sun in the first box on the photocopiable sheet.

5. If you have time, make three more similar visits throughout the day to give a total of four (in the early morning, mid-morning, early afternoon and late afternoon, for example 9.00am, 11.00am, 1.00pm and 3.00pm). The children should record the position of the Sun and the time of day at each visit. If this is not possible, try to make at least three visits at times that are spaced so as to allow the children to observe the differences in the relative position of the Sun.

6. After the first observation, return to the classroom and refer back to the children's ideas about the Sun. Introduce further discussion about the Sun being a light source. Ask the children to share their ideas about how we see the things around us (because of the light that travels from the Sun, is reflected from an object, and then travels to our eyes).

7. At the end of the day, when all observations and drawings have been completed, encourage the children to describe what their pictures show. Ask them to complete the photocopiable sheet by describing what they have noticed in their own words.

8. Talk about their answers and elicit any misconceptions the children may have. Some may not understand that the Sun only appears to move and that it is actually the Earth that is moving and not the Sun.

Checkpoint
● What happens to the Sun during the day?
● What happens to the Sun at night-time?
● Does the Sun always take the same time to apparently travel across the sky?
● How does this journey differ during the different seasons of the year?
● What happens to the shadows of objects as the Sun travels across the sky?

Introducing the new area of study

As you begin to introduce this new area of study to the children, you may wish to consider some of the misconceptions they might have about light. Some will be aware of light sources but may also think that all bright or shiny objects are light sources rather than reflectors. The Moon is a typical example of this. We often refer to moonlight as though light was actually being emitted by the Moon. In fact, of course, it is light from the Sun that is being reflected from the Moon's surface towards the Earth.

Differentiation
● Some children will need support through additional discussion to help them to complete their sketches. Try modelling the process for them by completing an initial drawing of your own as an example.
● Challenge confident learners to give more detailed explanations of what is happening.

Science in the wider world

The Sun is at the centre of our Solar System and is orbited by planets including the Earth. The Earth takes 365.25 days to complete its journey around the Sun. At the same time as it is orbiting the Sun, the Earth is rotating on its own axis in an anti-clockwise direction. For the Earth to rotate once on its own axis takes 24 hours – or one Earth day. At any one time only half of the Earth is lit by the Sun and is in daylight; the other half is in darkness, so it is night-time.

An analogy for the ideas explored in this lesson is seen when you are sitting on one of two trains standing side by side in a railway station. If you watch the other train as your train departs, you will experience an illusion that makes it appear that the other train is moving, when, in fact, it is still. This happens because you have no fixed point of reference. Similarly with the Earth and Sun, it is the Earth's rotational movement that causes us to experience the illusion that the Sun is travelling across the sky.

Review

Through observation and discussion with the children throughout the day, assess their understanding of the path the Sun seems to take across the sky. Ask the children to explain the path that they have drawn.

Objectives
● To identify sources of light.
● To know a variety of light sources, both natural and artificial.

Resources
Photocopiable page 103 'Light sources'; blackout materials; torches; mirrors; glowstick

Speaking scientifically
light source, reflection, Sun

Lesson 2: Light sources

Introduction
Remind the children that the Sun is a light source. Ask them to think about what the Sun enables us to do. Elicit the idea that the Sun enables us to see things around us. Ask the children to describe what it is like around them when it is light and when it is dark. Ask them to share their ideas and record these on the board using the headings 'Light' and 'Dark'.

Whole-class work
1. If you have a room in school that can be blacked out, take the children along there to enable them to compare light and dark. As an alternative you could use a blackout cloth draped over a table and let the children explore the 'dark cave'.

2. Ask the children to share their ideas about what they need to enable them to see in the darkness of the 'cave' or darkened room. Ensure that the children understand that a source of light is needed.

3. Encourage the children to begin to think and talk about what other sources of light there are, apart from the Sun. Compile a list of these on the board. These could be grouped into those that are natural, such as lightning and fire, and those that are artificial, such as electrical devices. Children will be more likely to be able to identify light sources that are artificial rather than natural, and the 'Artificial' list is likely to be longer.

4. Discuss briefly the concept of needing light (whether it is light from the Sun or elsewhere) to be able to see anything. Explain to the children that we see because light bounces off (is reflected from) objects and enters our eyes. (This is covered in more detail in the next lesson.)

Paired work
5. To help the children differentiate between light sources and reflected light, let them use a torch to shine a light onto the ceiling, then use a mirror to reflect light onto the ceiling.

6. Ask the children to decide which of the two objects (torch and mirror) is the light source.

7. This activity enables the children to see that the effect may be the same, but whilst the light from the torch is being produced in the torch, the light from the mirror is being reflected from another light source (the classroom lights or the Sun).

Independent work
Ask the children to complete photocopiable page 103 'Light sources'. This will help them begin to understand the range of light sources they might come across.

Science in the wider world
There are some light sources that are chemical, producing light through a reaction between different chemicals. Examples seen in nature include the light produced by glow worms and fire flies. To illustrate this idea for the children, use a glowstick of the sort that can be bought for parties and outdoor events. These contain chemicals that produce a reaction when they are mixed, causing a release of energy that results in light.

Review
Assess the children's understanding of light sources through scrutiny of their work on the photocopiable sheet. Are they able to identify a range of light sources and differentiate light sources from reflected light?

Objectives
● To understand the need for light to be able to see things.
● To understand that light travels in straight lines.

Resources
Cardboard tubes (kitchen roll size), each with four small holes cut into its side down its length with flaps to cover the holes (these will be opened during the lesson); a selection of small objects that will fit at the bottom of the tube

Speaking scientifically
dark, light, reflect

Lesson 3: How we see

Introduction
Draw on the board an eye, an object and a light source, such as the Sun. Ask the children to work in pairs to decide where they might draw lines to show how we see the object. Ask the children to answer the very simple question: *How do we see?* Reinforce their conceptual understanding that light travels from a light source to an object and is reflected from that object to our eyes.

Independent work
1. Ask the children to each produce an annotated drawing showing the journey of light from the Sun to a different object, its reflection from that object, and its path to our eyes. This should include lines and directional arrows to show the path of the light.

Paired work
2. Give each pair of children a cardboard tube (with the four flaps closed) and a selection of small objects to be viewed.

3. Ask one of the children to close their eyes or turn away whilst the other places one of the small objects on their desk and puts the tube over the object.

4. When the object is hidden, the second child should look into the tube with one eye (in the same way as they might use a telescope) and close the other eye. Try to ensure they get close enough to make a tight fit around the end of the tube. They could use their hands to help with this.

5. Ask the second child to tell their partner what they can see.

6. The first child can then open the first flap at the top of the tube before again asking what the second child can see. This continues until the second child can clearly see and correctly identify the object.

7. The children can then change roles and a different object can be placed at the bottom of the tube. Make sure the flaps are all closed before they start again. This can be repeated as many times as required with different objects. The children can record what they see in the tube using a simple table like this:

Object seen in the tube when...				
0 flaps were open	1 flap was open	2 flaps were open	3 flaps were open	4 flaps were open

Whole-class work
8. Bring the children back together to talk about what they found out. Ensure that they are able to identify and understand that when the flaps were closed, the inside of the tube was dark and they were not able to see anything. As an increasing amount of light was let in when the flaps were opened, the children should have been able to see the object more clearly. Ensure that the children make the link and understand that in order to see they needed light.

Science in the wider world
Our ability to see an object clearly is dependent on the amount of light shining on it and the amount of light that the object reflects. This in turn is determined by the surface of the object. Smooth, light-coloured surfaces reflect more light than rough, dark-coloured ones.

Review
Consider the children's observations and their discussions in deciding if they know that light is needed for us to be able to see an object.

Lesson 1: Shiny objects

Introduction

Begin the lesson by showing the children an image of the Moon. Ask them why we can see the Moon. Is it because it shines and emits light? Or is it because it reflects light?

Show the children some shiny objects or images of shiny objects. (Christmas tree decorations such as baubles and tinsel can be shiny and will be familiar to the children.) Again, talk about the shiny objects and ask the children to explain what makes them shiny and glittery. The children might begin to think about the surface being smooth and reflecting light.

Group work

1. Set up a dark tent in the classroom and place a number of different objects (both shiny and dull) around the tent for the children to find.

2. Ask the children, working in groups of three or four, to find all of the objects that are in the tent. Ask them to do this in complete darkness initially and note whether they can easily see the objects, particularly the shiny ones, without using a light source. Ask: *Is it easier to find shiny or dull objects? Did the shiny objects shine when there was no light?*

3. After looking for the objects in complete darkness, the children can repeat the task using a torch. Again, they need to ask themselves whether it is easier to see the shiny or the dull objects. Ask: *Did the shiny objects shine when there was some light?*

4. Ask the children to record their findings using a simple Carroll diagram. This will enable them to record whether or not shiny or dull objects can be seen in the darkness, or whether a light source is required. (The Carroll diagram should end up without anything in the 'darkness' row.)

I could see...	Shiny objects	Dull objects
Darkness		
With a torch		

5. Ask: *Do shiny things shine in the dark?*

Paired work

6. Whilst a group of children are engaged in the above activity, the others can be looking at a range of objects ranging from bright and shiny to dull and matt.

7. Ask the children to put the objects in order of how effective they are at reflecting light. Encourage them to make predictions before using a torch to try each surface. You could include some highly reflective surfaces, such as cycle reflectors and road safety reflective armbands. You could also try a range of different coloured papers, including fluorescent paper, matt paper and shiny paper.

8. Using the simple motto 'At night wear something bright', ask the children to design a safety poster to encourage others to wear bright and reflective clothing on their way to and from school.

Science in the wider world

This lesson could be usefully linked to road safety and the children's understanding of the importance of being seen at night. Use your local road safety officers to support this, or link to the national 'Think!' campaign.

Review

Through discussion in the dark space, assess the children's understanding that a light source is required in order to see even shiny things, and that shiny objects reflect light more easily.

Objectives
● To know that light travels in straight lines.
● To know that the sharp edge to a shadow is due to light travelling in straight lines.

Resources
Flat mirrors; torches; cards with holes in the centre; a wall or other surface to shine the torch on to; ray boxes (home-made ones can be made using a simple bulb and battery circuit in a container such as a short crisp tube that has a slit cut into the bottom edge); cards with slits in them; card; scissors; an object to use to cast a shadow

Speaking scientifically
light, mirror, ray box, reflection

Lesson 2: How does light travel?

Introduction
Ask two children to come out to the front and stand one in front of the other. Give the child in front a mirror. Tell the child behind to pull a silly face and ask the child in front to see if they can copy the face by using the mirror. Ask: *How can Josh see what Alice is doing?* On a board or flipchart, model an annotated drawing that expresses the children's explanations of how Josh can see Alice.

Tell the children that they will need to record their ideas in this lesson by drawing and writing. Explain that there are three different activities and they will all get a chance to do each one in turn.

Paired work
1. Activity 1: as in the introduction, ask the children to stand or sit in pairs and take turns to use a mirror to copy the silly faces pulled by the child behind. The children should record their explanations of what is happening as an annotated drawing.

2. Activity 2: still in their pairs, the children shine a torch onto a card with a hole in it and look at the spot of light it makes on a wall. They then take another card with a hole in it and place it so that the light continues on its journey uninterrupted and there is still a spot of light. (The holes in the cards will be in a straight line, enabling the children to see that light travels in straight lines.) Can they do it with three cards? Children should record their ideas about what is happening as an annotated drawing.

3. Activity 3: the children look at the light coming out of a ray box. They explore putting different pieces of card with slits in front of the light and observe what happens. (These are often provided with commercially produced ray boxes.) They can cut their own design of slit in some card and see what happens.

Whole-class work
4. Ask the children to explain what they tried out in their explorations and to feed back any interesting observations they have made. Ask: *Can light go around things?* (No.) *How do you know that?* (There are examples from activities 2 and 3.)

5. Introduce the idea that light always travels in straight lines. Use a torch to cast a shadow on an object. Explain that because light travels in straight lines, when it is blocked it cannot get around the corner to fill up the gap, so there is a sharp edge to the shadow.

> ### Differentiation
> ● You may need to scribe or provide a key word bank for children with weaker literacy skills.

Science in the wider world
Although we know light travels in straight lines, it can be bent. When light travelling through the air meets another substance like glass or water, it changes direction slightly away from a straight-line path. This is known as refraction and is the basis for how lenses work. Although this is not part of this topic, you could demonstrate this idea for the children by simply standing a pencil in a clear tumbler, and then half-filling it with water. At the point where the pencil enters the water, it will appear to be slightly out of line with the rest of the pencil.

Review
Is light indicated by straight lines in the children's drawings? Do the children realise that light cannot go around corners unless a mirror is 'helping'?

Objectives
● To consider when shadows are formed outside.

Resources
'Shadow' from *Star Poems* by Michael Rosen (ASE Publications, 2000); drawing materials; a table lamp or torch

Speaking scientifically
light, shadow

Lesson 3: Shadow walk

Introduction

Read the poem 'Shadow' by Michael Rosen to the children and discuss it. Ask: *Have you ever noticed your shadow? Can you describe it to me? When do you notice that you have got a shadow?* (On a sunny day.) *What else can you tell me about shadows? Is your shadow always the same?* This will help to focus their observations during the 'shadow walk'.

Whole-class work

1. Go for a ten-minute 'shadow walk' in the playground or school field. Ask the children to look out for any shadows and to think about how they are made. (This could be replaced by five minutes of observation within the classroom if there are shadows cast by lights and windows.)

2. Ask the children to think about the shapes of the shadows they can see. What are the similarities and differences between the object and its shadow?

3. Back in the classroom, ask the children to briefly describe what they saw and explain that you are interested in finding out their ideas about light and shadows.

Independent work

4. Ask the children to work individually to complete an annotated drawing of themselves and their shadow on a sunny day. Explain that you want the picture and writing to show as much as possible of what they understand about light and shadows and how a shadow is made.

5. Circulate, asking questions to assess understanding, for example: *Do you ever get a coloured shadow? Why have you shown the shadow there – could it be on the other side? If I looked at your shadow would I see your eyes, nose and mouth?*

Whole-class work

6. Gather the children together to share their annotated drawings. Elicit some of their misconceptions – some will have included features on the pictures of their shadows that would not be there in reality.

7. Use a simple light source such as a table lamp or torch to create a simple sideways silhouette of one of the children. Ask the children to look at the shadow for any features that are on the lit side of the child.

> **Differentiation**
> ● You may need to scribe for children with limited writing skills. Your questions will depend on the children's responses.

Science in the wider world

During an eclipse of the Sun, the Moon passes between the Sun and the Earth. This casts a shadow of the Moon on the Earth's surface. Similarly, in an eclipse of the Moon, the Earth passes between the Sun and the Moon casting a shadow of the Earth on the Moon's surface.

Review

Analyse the children's annotated drawings – are shadows represented by solid blocks or are they like reflections? Are the shadows drawn starting at the children's feet? Are they in the correct place with respect to the light source? Is there evidence of understanding that the light has been blocked?

Objectives
● To know that a shadow is formed when sunlight is blocked by an object.

Resources
A light source such as a table lamp or torch; various opaque objects; a sunny day; photocopiable page 104 'Me and my shadow'; interactive activity 'Shadows: true or false?' on the CD-ROM

Speaking scientifically
block, light source, shadows, Sun

Lesson 1: Me and my shadow

Introduction

Read out the following clues to a mystery 'thing': *This thing can change shape. It can appear and disappear instantly. It can be anywhere, at any time. Its shape can change before your very eyes. It does not have any colour. One of these things can follow you around. Sometimes they can be scary. Sometimes they can be useful. They can move but they are not alive. Without light they simply do not exist.* When they think they know the answer (a shadow), the children should write it down secretly.

Whole-class work

1. Use the light from a light source such as a table lamp or torch to recap how shadows are formed. Use an object to create the shadow and explain that the light is being blocked when it reaches the object, hence the darker area behind it.

2. Ask the children to think about where most of our light comes from, and therefore what gives us most of our shadows (the Sun).

Group work

3. In the playground the children should work in groups of three or four to make shadows while other members of the group observe and sketch their observations.

4. Ask the groups to observe and record their shadows at several different times during the school day (perhaps at each break time). What, if anything, do the children think will be different each time?

Independent work

5. Distribute photocopiable page 104 'Me and my shadow' and explain the task. (It may be useful to have your demonstration from the whole-class activity available for the children to refer to.)

6. The final section of the sheet asks the children to draw a picture of the Sun and a shadow that it may cast. At this point it is worth reinforcing the importance of never looking directly at the Sun.

Science in the wider world

A shadow from the Sun is never still, unlike those made by many other light sources. Since the Earth is constantly moving in relation to the Sun, shadows cast by objects lit by the Sun change shape continually from sunrise to sunset. Of course, the Sun does not actually move at all. Shadows first thing in the morning and late in the evening are longer because of the angle of the Sun's light to the Earth; the Sun appears to be much lower in the sky at these times. As the day progresses towards midday, the shadows become shorter as the Sun apparently 'climbs' higher in the sky to its peak. The same situation occurs on a seasonal basis, too: shadows at midday in summer are much shorter than those at midday in winter, again due to the apparent path of the Sun across the sky.

Review

Mark the children's work, checking for evidence of an understanding of how shadows are formed. Their answers and diagrams should reflect their knowledge that a shadow is formed when light from the Sun (or another light source) is blocked. You can also use the interactive activity 'Shadows: true or false?' on the CD-ROM to check the children's understanding of key points.

- To know that light from a range of sources produces shadows.
- To consider how the shape and size of a shadow varies with the position of the light source.

Resources
A bright light source such as a table lamp; torches; a computer screen; desk lamps; coloured acetate or plastic film; copies of photocopiable page 105 'Light sources and shadows'; clipboards; objects to use to cast shadows; digital cameras (optional); interactive activity 'Matching shadows' on the CD-ROM; laptops/PCs

Speaking scientifically
light source, shadow, Sun

Lesson 2: Light sources and shadows

Introduction
Using a bright light source such as a lamp or a projector, cast a shadow on the board. Ask the children to think about ways in which this shadow could be changed. Encourage them to think about what will happen as the light source is moved nearer to or further away from the object.

Demonstrate and talk about how moving the object nearer to or further away from the light source changes the size of the shadow. You could show how this can be used for dramatic effect to make a small object seem frighteningly large!

Ask the children to suggest some other ways of changing how a shadow appears.

Paired work
1. Provide a variety of light sources so the children can see that shadows will be cast by any light source. Ask: *How can we produce shadows of varying quality and intensity? What happens if we use coloured light sources; do we get coloured shadows?* Ask the children to predict how the shadows from different light sources will vary, before using light sources of differing intensity, colour and distance from the objects to test their predictions.

2. Let the children explore their ideas and make their own decisions about how to record their findings. You could encourage the use of digital cameras as a means of recording the different shadows produced. Encourage the children to think not just about the size of the shadow but also its intensity, colour, shape and edge.

Independent work
3. After the children have investigated shadow quality in pairs as described above, distribute photocopiable page 105 'Light sources and shadows'. Ask the children to complete it based on what they have just seen and explored.

4. You could end the lesson by letting the children complete the interactive activity 'Matching shadows' on the CD-ROM.

Differentiation
- To support learners use the photocopiable sheet, but ask the children just to draw rather than write about their findings.
- To challenge confident learners, suggest that their descriptions are more detailed, perhaps continuing on the back of the photocopiable sheet.

Science in the wider world
All light sources can produce shadows, but their intensity will vary depending on the strength and intensity of the light source. The intensity of a shadow can be varied by moving the object casting the shadow nearer to or further away from the light source. The shadow also loses its definition but gains in size as the object is moved nearer to the light source – this happens because more reflected light is able to fall in the shadow. Similarly, the intensity and sharpness of shadows is affected by the intensity of the light source. On a bright sunny day, shadows are very sharp and distinct, whereas on an overcast day when the light is diffused by clouds, shadows are far less distinct.

Review
Check that the children have been able to identify a number of other light sources. Make sure their diagrams show that when a light source is nearer to an object, the shadow becomes larger. Aim only for a general understanding here – the children will explore this more systematically in future years.

Objectives
● To know how the shape and size of a shadow varies with the position of the light source.
● To consider the properties of an object needed to form a shadow.

Resources
Craft materials with varying light-blocking qualities; small garden canes or dowels; glue or tape; split pins; a light source such as an OHP; a screen (for example a wooden frame covered with tracing paper or thin white cloth); a few short story ideas or picture books

Speaking scientifically
block, light source, shadow

Lesson 3: Shadow puppets

Introduction
Talk to the children about traditional shadow puppetry. For example, in certain Asian cultures shadow puppets are sometimes used to tell the traditional legends of the gods at festival times. If you have access to any examples of these, use them in this lesson to tell a short story.

Whole-class work
1. Demonstrate for the class how the shadows are made in shadow puppet shows, using a range of materials.

2. Show the children how to make their own shadow puppets. For example, you could cut out a simple body shape from card or fabric and use split pins to make joints for arms and legs. Fixing a garden cane onto these will allow you to manipulate your shadow puppet so that it can move in an animated way.

3. In addition to demonstrating how to make the puppets, talk about some of the dramatic effects that could be used, following on from the previous lesson. Show the children how to make scenery for their shadow puppet show, for example from paper, plastics or other craft materials. A large tree could be created from a small twig by moving it further away from the light source. Coloured plastic film could be used for water or the Sun.

Group work
4. Ask the children to work in groups of three or four to come up with a simple story that they can re-tell using shadow puppets. They could use a well-known story or devise their own. Encourage them to plan their story using a simple storyboard.

5. Next the children must make the characters and scenery they will need for their shadow puppet show.

6. Encourage the children to use a range of techniques in their shadow puppet shows that demonstrate their understanding of shadows, including moving the puppets nearer to and further away from the light source. (Although this is covered in another lesson, the range of different materials you provide will give the children an introduction to the concept of transparent, translucent and opaque materials and how they can be used to create different effects.)

7. Allow time for the children to present their shadow puppet stories to the class.

Differentiation
● Some children may need support in coming up with their story. Have ready some short story ideas or picture books to help them.
● Challenge confident learners to include a range of sound effects in their puppet shows.

Science in the wider world
Shadow puppetry is one of the oldest forms of puppetry in the world and was used to tell traditional folk tales and legends. Early puppets were generally quite intricate silhouettes, whereas today shadow puppets are made by combining a range of materials and very often everyday objects.

Review
Engage with the children whilst they are making their shadow puppets and question them about their understanding of the materials they are using and the effects they are trying to achieve. Do they understand how to manipulate the quality, shape and size of the shadows?

Objectives
● To distinguish between opaque, translucent and transparent materials.

Resources
A selection of opaque materials such as card, aluminium foil and wallpaper; a selection of transparent materials such as sticky tape and cling-film; a selection of translucent materials such as tracing paper; light meters (or data-logging equipment if available); torches; photocopiable page 106 'Letting light through'

Speaking scientifically
light meter, opaque, translucent, transparent

Lesson 1: Letting light through

Introduction

The children should work in groups of three or four. Give each group a collection of different materials. Ask the children to sort their materials into different groups. This might be against any of a number of different criteria. Then ask the children to move around the other groups' tables to look at how they have grouped their items. Bring the children back together and ask them to suggest how each of the other groups classified their items.

Whole-class work

1. As a class, model grouping items by their ability to let light through. You could use some of the shadow puppets made in the last lesson.

2. Introduce the concept that some materials let no light through, some let a little light through, and others let most of the light through. Use the correct scientific vocabulary: *opaque*, *translucent* and *transparent*.

Group work

3. Ask the children to pick some items from their own collection of materials that they think let no light through, and some that let lots of light through.

4. Ask: *How could we test how much light each material lets through?* Suggestions will probably include holding them up and shining a torch on them. Ask: *How will we know how much light is coming through?*

5. Explain that there are devices that can measure how much light there is. Demonstrate how to use the light meters or data loggers. It is important to point out that the normal daylight level will be measured too, so they are looking for a change in the reading on the meter.

6. Ask each group to plan and carry out a test to find out how much light comes through the materials in their collection. They should decide in their groups how many materials to test. Encourage them to explain their test design and record their results in a table.

Independent work

7. Ask each child to write down two or three sentences about what they found out in their experiment.

8. Give each child the photocopiable page 106 'Letting light through' to complete.

> **Differentiation**
> ● The children can work in mixed-attainment groups to support each other. Target questions about the test according to the child, for example: *Why did you choose those materials? Which one do you think will let most/least light through? Why? Are you doing anything to make the test fair? What have you found out so far?* Scaffold the data interpretation by providing phrases such as: 'We found that (x) let the most light through and (y) did not let any light through. This is a list of objects in order of how much light went through.'

Science in the wider world

Opaque materials do not let any light through and so make dense shadows. Transparent materials let most light through and so do not form shadows. Translucent materials, such as bathroom windows, let some light through but scatter it, so the shadows are not as dark.

Review

Can the children use the light meter effectively? Have they carried out a fair test? Can they give examples of materials in their collection that are opaque, transparent and translucent?

Objectives
● To understand that shadows change during the course of a day.

Resources
A sunny day; wooden posts (such as rounders posts and stands); metre rulers or measuring tapes; graph paper; media resource 'Graphing tool' from CD-ROM

Speaking scientifically
graph, length, measurement, observation, shadow

Lesson 2: Changing shadows

Introduction
Remind the children of what they already know about shadows: that shadows are made by objects blocking the light and that the shadow formed is in the shape of this object. Ask the children if they have ever noticed that sometimes their shadow makes them appear very tall and sometimes it makes them appear very short.

Paired work
1. Ask the children to work with a partner to see how their shadows change during the day. At regular intervals throughout the day they should go and stand in the same place in the playground. One child should cast a shadow while the other observes and draws the shadow. They should then swap roles.

2. Encourage the children to look at each other's records and try to draw conclusions about how the shadows have changed as the day progresses – not just their position, but also their length. Ask: *At what time of day were your shadows longest? At what time of day were your shadows shortest? What happened to your shadows when the Sun was high in the sky?*

3. Some of the children could be challenged to say whether there are any differences between the parts of the shadow. Does it look the same all over or is there a difference between the main part of the shadow and the edges?

Group work
4. Use pieces of wood fixed vertically (rounders posts in stands would be ideal) to cast shadows on the playground. Leave them in the same place all day, choosing a spot where they will not be disturbed.

5. The children should work in groups of three or four. At regular intervals throughout the day (hourly on the hour, or at some other convenient regular time), the children should observe the shadows of the posts.

6. They should measure the length of their post's shadow and record the results in a simple table or chart. They should then use this information to draw a bar graph that will show how the shadow length shortens towards midday.

7. The children could use the interactive graphing tool on the CD-ROM to convert their table of results into a graph.

> ### Differentiation
> ● Some children may prefer to use the graphing tool (from the CD-ROM) to draw a simple bar chart. Alternatively they could make a cut-out of the shadow each hour and stick these on the wall to make a 'living' graph by the hour.
> ● Challenge confident learners to use the graphing tool to produce a variety of different graphs.

Science in the wider world
Shadows cast by the Sun have two parts. The area of total shadow is called the *umbra*, where the object blocks all light from the Sun. Around the edge is an area of partial shade called the *penumbra*.

Review
Through discussion with the children and scrutiny of their work, ensure that they understand that the shadows changed in two ways: position and size. Assess their work for evidence of an ability to collect the relevant data and present information as a clear graph.

Objectives
● To understand the properties needed in a fabric to block light completely.

Resources
A range of opaque and translucent fabrics of varying degrees of opaqueness; torches; light meters; data loggers; eye-masks; curtain sample materials; photocopiable page 'Fair test planning sheet' from the CD-ROM

Speaking scientifically
block, data logger, exclude, light meter, opaque, translucent, transparent

Lesson 3: Blackout

Introduction
Recap the ideas from the earlier lesson, 'Letting light through' (see page 90). Ask the children to recall the words we use to describe materials that let most light through, some light through and that block all light. Consolidate their use of the correct scientific vocabulary: *transparent*, *translucent* and *opaque*.

Paired work
1. Set the children the challenge of finding the best fabrics for either an eye-mask or a pair of curtains to ensure a good (and dark) night's sleep. Show the children examples of eye-masks and curtains and ask them to think about circumstances where we might want to exclude light completely.

2. Ask the children to plan how they might achieve this aim. Encourage them to think about how they tested materials that were transparent, translucent and opaque.

3. Give the children access to the fabrics to be tested. Encourage them to consider how they will ensure that they carry out a fair test when finding which of the fabrics will be best for their purpose.

4. Remind them that in fair testing they should only change one thing at a time. You could use photocopiable page 'Fair test planning sheet' from the CD-ROM to help the children identify what they will keep the same, what they will change and what they will measure.

5. As the children plan their investigations, question them to ensure that they will only change the fabric, keep the light source and the test the same, and know what they are measuring. They might choose to collect their results either visually, and order the fabrics, or numerically, by using a light meter or data logger.

6. Ask the children to carry out their investigation and then create a poster to report their findings to others.

Independent work
7. Ask the children to design an advertisement for their curtains or eye-mask. This should communicate to the reader the virtues of their product and demonstrate some understanding of the opaqueness of the fabric.

> **Differentiation**
> ● Some learners could simply order the materials by visually determining the amount of light they let through.
> ● Challenge confident learners to gather more accurate quantitative data using data loggers.

Science in the wider world
Opaque fabrics are used as blackout materials in a variety of different ways, ranging from the personal uses seen in this lesson to the exclusion of light from rooms in theatres and studios. The ability to control light levels allows us to produce different creative environments. Some people need complete darkness in order to sleep and the eye-masks considered in this lesson can help with that.

Review
Through discussion, observation and scrutiny of their work, assess the children's understanding of how to carry out a fair test, their ability to identify variables, and their understanding of opaque materials.

Objectives
- To know that the position of the Sun changes.
- To consider the shape of the path of the Sun across the sky by looking at shadows.

Resources
Charts from the lesson on 'Changing shadows'; clipboards; dowels; pots of sand

Speaking scientifically
arc, curved, Earth, rotation, sky, Sun, sunrise, sunset

Lesson 1: The Sun's path

Introduction
Remind the children of the work they have done previously, particularly their observations of how shadows change throughout the day. Look at the shape of the charts they drew in the lesson on 'Changing shadows' (see page 91). Ask them to explain what these charts show and what they tell them about the Sun and shadows.

Whole-class/Individual work
1. Early in the day, take the children outside to the playground and ask them to roughly sketch the general outline of the scene from where they are standing. Without looking directly at the Sun, they should mark on the position of the Sun relative to the objects in their outline drawing. They should also record the time of the observation alongside the position of the Sun.

2. Back inside, tell the children that throughout the day they are going to carry out observations of the position of the Sun in the sky. Ask them to predict where they think the Sun will be in one hour.

3. After one hour, the children should return to exactly the same spot and draw the position of the Sun again on their original sketch. Was their prediction correct?

4. Continue this pattern of observation and prediction every hour (if possible) throughout the day. Remind the children to record each time alongside the Sun's positions on their outline drawing.

Safety: Continue to stress the importance of not looking directly at the Sun. The children should simply observe its general location relative to their drawings.

Paired work
5. Each pair should fix a small length of dowel into a pot of sand to make a small 'sunshine recorder'.

6. Stand the pots on sheets of paper and position them on a sunny windowsill.

7. At regular intervals throughout the day, the children should take it in turns to mark the position of the end of the shadow.

8. When seen together, this simple record will indicate the path taken by the Sun across the sky. The points could be joined in a curve to give a more accurate representation of the path. More frequent observations and points of reference will make the task easier.

Science in the wider world
In Britain, the Sun appears to rise in the eastern sky and set in the western sky, following a path through the southern sky. The path it takes is always the same general symmetrical arc. The Sun is at its highest in our southern sky around midday (but this varies depending on GMT or BST).

Review
Through observation and discussion with the children throughout the day, assess their understanding of the path the Sun takes across the sky. Ask them to explain what they are doing and to describe the shape of the path that they have plotted.

Objectives
• To understand more about the Sun.
• To identify a question that can be answered using secondary sources of information.

Resources
Secondary sources of information relating to the Sun; art materials

Speaking scientifically
light source, orbit, solar, Sun

Lesson 2: More about the Sun

Introduction

Recap with the children the work they have done on the apparent journey that the Sun takes across the sky and its role as a light source in helping us to see. Ask the children to work in groups of four or five to create a concept map showing all that they currently know about the Sun.

Whole-class work

1. Ask the children, How could we answer a question that we might have about the Sun? Make a list of their ideas.

2. Explain that whilst scientific investigations are often about carrying out practical work, scientists sometimes do research using other forms of information and knowledge. These are called secondary sources.

3. Ask the children to think about what some of these secondary sources might be. Ensure that they are aware of books, CD-ROMs and websites. They should also be aware that they could choose to ask an expert when trying to answer their question.

Group work

4. Ask the children, in their groups, to look at the concept maps they have created. They should use their concept map to identify an area of study that can provide questions for them to answer either in pairs or independently.

5. As a group, ask the children to check that they have a range of questions that they can begin to answer. These questions might relate, for example, to the size of the Sun, its distance away from Earth, its age, how we get day and night, and what causes eclipses.

6. The children should use secondary sources to carry out their research in order to answer their questions. This will strengthen their background knowledge of the Sun.

7. The findings of the group could be presented on a large Sun cut from coloured paper, or in any other creative way that the children might choose.

> **Differentiation**
> • Some of the children will find coming up with a question quite difficult. You will need to support these children by using questioning to help them shape a question that they can research.
> • Challenge confident learners to engage with more complex questions and concepts, such as eclipses.

Science in the wider world

The Sun is at the centre of our Solar System. The planets, of which Earth is just one, travel around the Sun, each in a different orbit. The Earth's orbit takes 365.25 days, which we call one year. Because of the effective loss of one quarter day every year, we add an extra day into our calendar every four years, in a leap year.

At the same time as the Earth is orbiting the Sun, it is rotating about its own axis. The time taken for this to occur is 24 hours or one day. At any time, only half of the Earth is being lit by the Sun – the other half is turned away and is therefore in darkness. As the Earth rotates, the half of the Earth that is in darkness shifts. This is the change from night to day. Daytime begins as the Sun appears to rise. Of course, it does not actually rise; the effect is due simply to our perspective of it as we rotate.

Review

Through scrutiny of the children's work, assess their knowledge and understanding of the Sun, their ability to ask an appropriate question, and their skill in identifying useful and relevant information from secondary sources.

Objectives
- To understand that a sundial can be used to tell the approximate time of day.

Resources
A sundial (or a picture of one); flat wooden boards with a central hole drilled to fit pieces of dowel (one per group but can be shared if necessary); paper templates (one per group); art materials; glue to fasten the dowel in place; reference materials such as guidebooks for stately homes showing old sundials (optional); photocopiable page 107 'Telling the time with shadows'

Speaking scientifically
approximate, cast, estimate, measure, shadow, sundial

Lesson 3: Telling the time with shadows

Introduction
Ask: *What time is it? How do you know?* Most children will be able to tell you about clocks and watches and many will have a sound understanding of time. Ask if they know how people used to tell the time before watches and clocks were invented. They may identify some ways to measure the passage of time, such as sand timers or ticker-tape timers.

Whole-class work
1. Lead the discussion by suggesting that one method of telling the time uses something that is always present, even though we may not always be able to see it. Give clues that will lead the children to think about the Sun as a way to tell the time.

2. Introduce the idea of a sundial and show the children an actual sundial (or a picture of one). Set the sundial up (if available) and see if the children can use it to tell the time.

Group work
3. Use a flat board with a vertical piece of dowel to make a simple sundial.

4. A face can be made from a circle of paper with a central hole that can be slotted on to the sundial. The children could research historic designs of sundials, reproducing them or using them as inspiration for their own designs. Guidebooks from stately homes and historic houses or gardens often contain pictures.

5. The children may observe that real sundials do not usually cover the full 24-hour period; ask them why this is. (There is no sunlight at night.)

6. The sundial will need to be set up and calibrated by marking the position of the shadow at specific times, preferably on the hour.

7. The children can then use their sundial to estimate the time. Set them a series of challenges where they estimate the time using the sundial and check it on a clock. With experience, can they improve the accuracy with which they use the sundial to estimate time? (There will still be an accuracy range of several minutes at least.) The children can record their estimates in a table.

8. Distribute photocopiable page 107 'Telling the time with shadows' for the children to complete. Some children may need support to help them complete this sheet.

Science in the wider world
Shadows have been used for many centuries to help us mark time. We know that the Earth rotates around the Sun, giving the illusion that the Sun is travelling across the sky. This can be used to mark the passage of time over a day. It is thought that the first sundials were used over 4000 years ago by the Chinese. Today they are generally only used for decorative purposes due to their unreliability.

Review
Using their photocopiable sheets and through observation and questioning, assess the children's ability to tell the approximate time using a sundial.

Objectives
● To know that there is a wide range of colours that can be seen.

Resources
Soundtrack recording of Andrew Lloyd Webber's musical *Joseph and the Amazing Technicolor Dreamcoat* (and a suitable device to play it on); children's story Bible (optional); photocopiable page 108 'Colour'; painting equipment; collage materials; glue; scissors; interactive activity 'Colour' on the CD-ROM

Speaking scientifically
blue, green, indigo, orange, rainbow, red, spectrum, violet, yellow

Lesson 1: Colour

Introduction
Ask: *How many colours can you see in the classroom? What is your favourite colour?* Carry out a quick survey of favourite colours. You could also play 'When I went to market', where each item has to be a different colour.

Whole-class work
1. Talk about how we may wear clothes in our favourite colours. Introduce and play the song 'Joseph's coat' from *Joseph and the Amazing Technicolor Dreamcoat*.

2. Tell the children that Joseph's story is in the Bible, as is Noah's. There is also something multicoloured in Noah's story – the rainbow. You may like to read the end of the Noah story to the children. Ask them to name the colours of the rainbow.

3. Teach the children to remember the colours of the rainbow in order using a mnemonic such as: Richard Of York Gave Battle In Vain.

4. You may wish to explain, very simply, how we see colour (see 'Science in the wider world' below).

Independent work
5. Give out photocopiable page 108 'Colour' or ask the children to complete the interactive activity 'Colour' on the CD-ROM.

6. The children could paint pictures or make collages of rainbows. They could also make up new versions of the 'ROYGBIV' mnemonic to use as the centrepiece for a display of work from the unit.

Differentiation
● To challenge children, ask them to find out how a rainbow is formed. They could write about it in their own words on the back of their photocopiable sheet.

Whole-class work
7. Ask some of the children to share their work with the class. Reinforce the concept of a range of colours and check the children's knowledge of the colours of the spectrum.

8. Listen to their new versions of the 'ROYGBIV' mnemonic.

Science in the wider world
The light all around us is 'white', but it is made up from seven colours. Together, these colours are called the 'spectrum'. They are: red, orange, yellow, green, blue, indigo and violet. We can see these colours split apart in a rainbow, where red is on the outside and the rest follow in order, with violet on the inner edge. In this spectrum of light there are three 'primary' colours: red, green and blue. It is important to remember that the primary colours of light and the primary colours of paint (red, blue and yellow) are different. Different rules apply to mixing light than to mixing paint.

When white light hits, for example, a blue object, the red and green elements of the white light are absorbed by the object. The blue light is reflected into our eyes by the pigments in the object, and so we see a blue object. The same applies to the other primary colours. If the object is a mixture of colours, then the coloured pigments in the object reflect some of the constituent colours and absorb the rest.

Review
Look for evidence in the children's completed photocopiable sheets that they are able to name the colours of the spectrum and correctly complete the sentences.

Objectives
● To describe how plants and animals use colours.

Resources
Secondary sources of information about animals and camouflage and the internet; pictures (or real examples) of brightly coloured flowers; examples of the work of artists who use colours from nature; art materials; media resource 'Colour in nature' on the CD-ROM

Speaking scientifically
blend, camouflage, colour, hidden

Lesson 2: Colour in nature

Introduction

Show the children the media resource 'Colour in nature', which shows some examples of animal camouflage, where the animal's colour or shape has enabled it to blend into its background. Ask the children to talk in pairs about why these animals are the colour they are. Gather their ideas, which should be largely about camouflage and not being seen.

Now show them some images (or real examples) of flowers. Ask the children to discuss in their pairs why the flowers have such bright colours. Again, gather together their ideas, which this time should be about the flowers needing to be seen in order to attract insects.

Whole-class work

1. With appropriate adult support, take the children on a walk around the school grounds to look at the colours they can see in nature. This should be an observational walk – avoid taking any recording devices or sheets and simply engage the children, asking them to really focus on observing the colours around them.

2. Back in the classroom, allow the children time to reflect on and share what they have seen. Ask them if any colours were predominant. *What was the impact of the colours they saw?*

3. Share with the children some examples of the work of artists who draw on the colours of nature in their work, such as Andy Goldsworthy.

Group work

4. The children should use secondary sources to investigate how colours are used in nature. For example, they could look at how animals and plants use colour as a warning, as camouflage, or as a means of attracting a mate. They should work in small groups of three or four and present their findings with artwork to add to a class display.

5. Let the children make 'blot' butterflies. Discuss what colours they should use to give warnings (for example, red = 'I'm not nice to eat'; yellow and black = 'I sting'), or to attract a mate (the peacock's greens and blues, for example). Emphasise the symmetry of the patterns too.

> ### Differentiation
> ● Some children might benefit from being given one specific item to research, perhaps camouflage or warnings.
> ● Other children could try more complex research that includes a range of animals, plants and uses of colour. They could also use a range of media to present their findings, such as images from the internet.

Science in the wider world

Animals and plants have the colours they do for a reason. Plants have flowers and fruit with bright colours in order to attract creatures that will take their pollen or seeds away as part of the reproductive process. Animals have colours that are used as camouflage (and therefore a defence mechanism), or bright colours that serve either as a warning to other animals or as a means of attracting a mate. For example, in birds the male of the species usually has brighter plumage than the female.

Review

Look for evidence of an understanding of how plants and animals use colour for camouflage, attraction or warning.

Objectives
● To understand the use of light and colour in the local environment, for example, for road safety.

Resources
Road safety posters; pictures of emergency vehicles; photocopiable page 109 'Colour on the roads'; large sheets of paper; decorating paint charts; painting equipment

Speaking scientifically
amber, danger, green, red, reflective, safe, traffic

Lesson 3: Colour on the roads

Introduction
Begin by asking the children how they travelled to school this morning. As you do, introduce some elements of road safety. Remind the children of the earlier lesson on 'Shiny objects' (see page 84) and recap the importance of road safety in the dark. Ask the children how they keep themselves safe on the roads, particularly when it is dark. Encourage them to consider street lighting, pelican crossings (the green man), and wearing reflective clothing or armbands.

Whole-class work
1. Discuss with the children how important colour and light are in road safety: red is often used as a warning colour to tell people that there is danger ahead or to stop; green is generally used as a sign that it is safe and you can proceed, amber is used as a warning that danger may lie ahead and you should be careful. You could also mention warning lights on vehicles, such as the blue flashing lights on emergency service vehicles or the orange flashing lights used during road repairs or vehicle breakdowns.

2. Make a list of examples on the board. One of these should be traffic lights. Ask the children if they know the colours that are used in traffic lights. Tell them the sequence of traffic light changes and explain what each one means.

Independent work
3. Distribute photocopiable page 109 'Colour on the roads' and allow the children time to complete it. The children will have to recall the sequence of traffic lights, which should be: red; red and amber together; green; amber; red.

4. Ask the children to think about colour use outside in the local environment. Ask them to draw a picture of a street scene and to mark on as many uses of colour and light as they can. In particular, they should indicate how light and colour are used in road safety, including for example: traffic lights, street lighting, emergency vehicles, reflective clothing, road signs, cat's eyes, roadside barriers and markers. Alternatively, this could be done as a collaborative display, with the children drawing and cutting out their individual contributions to stick on to a group or class scene.

5. Ask the children to think about colour use inside the home. Give out some decorating paint charts and ask the children to look at variations in colour among the colour groups. Ask them to choose one colour 'family' and to create their own paint chart. Each chart should have about six blocks of colour and the children should give each an appropriate name. Encourage systematic mixing, with the children adding white or black to a starting hue.

Science in the wider world
Certain colours send out certain signals. In Britain, red is for danger and green is for safety. Colours can also send messages in a less obvious way – for example, some colours tend to be perceived as being vibrant, such as bright red, orange and yellow, whilst others are more relaxing, such as green and pastel shades.

Review
Have the children been able to indicate appropriate uses for colour and light in road safety and/or other human situations?

■SCHOLASTIC

Objectives
● To identify sources of light.
● To know that the position of the Sun changes.
● To consider the shape of the path of the Sun across the sky.

Resources
Photocopiable page 'The Sun in the sky' from the CD-ROM; sports balls; torches or table lamps

Working scientifically
● Asking relevant questions.
● Using straightforward scientific evidence to answer questions or to support their findings.
● Recording findings using simple scientific language, drawings, labelled diagrams, bar charts and tables.

The Sun in the sky

Revise
● Understanding that the Sun appears to travel across the sky during the day.
● Understanding that the Sun appears to rise in the east and set in the west.
● Awareness that the Sun's apparent journey across the sky is not the same throughout the year.
● Understanding that the Sun is a light source.
● Understanding that as the Sun appears to cross the sky, the shadows cast vary – long shadows are cast in the morning and evening and short shadows at midday.

Assess
● Use photocopiable page 'The Sun in the sky' from the CD-ROM to assess the children's knowledge of the general path that the Sun appears to take as it crosses the sky. The children's pictures should show their understanding that the Sun seems to rise in the east, set in the west, travel in an arc, and reach its highest point at midday. Children holding misconceptions may not show this journey as an arc but as a straight line.
● You can also use the children's completed photocopiable sheets to assess their understanding of how the Earth orbits the Sun. One misconception held by some children is that the Sun travels around the Earth rather than the Earth travelling around the Sun. Consideration of the children's drawings will indicate whether this misconception needs to be corrected.

Further practice
● Further understanding of the way in which the Earth orbiting the Sun causes day and night can be gained by modelling the process using sports balls and lamps. Commercially produced model Solar Systems are also available. Modelling the Earth orbiting the Sun (using a lamp to represent the Sun) enables the children to see that half of the Earth is always in darkness (night) while half is in light (daytime). They can also begin to understand why we talk about the apparent journey of the Sun – because it is actually we on Earth who are moving and not the Sun.

Objectives

- To consider how the shape and size of a shadow varies with the position of the light source.
- To understand that shadows change during the course of a day.
- To understand that a sundial can be used to tell the approximate time of day.

Resources

Photocopiable page 'Sundials' from the CD-ROM; torches; opaque objects to use to cast shadows

Working scientifically

- Asking relevant questions.
- Using straightforward scientific evidence to answer questions or to support their findings.
- Recording findings using simple scientific language, drawings, labelled diagrams, bar charts, and tables.

Sundials

Revise

- Understanding that shadows are formed when a light source is blocked by an opaque object. This can be reinforced by allowing the children to 'play' at casting shadows using torches and suitable objects.
- Understanding that shadows will change depending on where the light source is.
- Knowing that shadows can be used to tell the (approximate) time using a sundial.
- Awareness that using sundials to tell the time is not very accurate.

Assess

- Ask the children to complete photocopiable page 'Sundials' from the CD-ROM. An analysis of their work will allow you to assess the children's understanding of sundials, including how they are used, their accuracy and their reliability. The first activity on the photocopiable sheet will allow you to identify any misconceptions that the children may have about sundials. You may wish to support those who are having difficulty with reading the sentences so that you can be sure you identify their level of understanding and not their reading ability. This could be done by reading the photocopiable sheet aloud first as a class.
- The second activity on the phtocopiable sheet will help to assess the children's understanding of how sundials use shadows and the direction in which a shadow is cast in comparison to the location of the light source.

Further practice

- To consolidate the children's understanding of shadows further, try getting them to write an acrostic poem using the word SHADOW. Each line of their poem should have some connection with light sources and shadows. You could also get the children to create a storyboard that relates the adventures of the children and their shadows.

Light sources

Revise
- Understanding what is meant by a light source – that they provide us with light by giving out energy.
- Understanding that light sources can be either natural (such as the Sun) or artificial (such as an electric light).
- Ability to identify light sources and distinguish these from surfaces that reflect light.
- Knowing that the Sun is a light source but that the Moon only reflects light.
- Understanding that we see objects because light travels from these objects to our eyes.
- Understanding that light is reflected from surfaces.

Assess
- Show the children an example of a themed scene from your chosen book. Ask the children to individually draw an imaginary scene of their own on a large sheet of paper. This scene should have the theme of 'Light sources and how we see'. The children should draw a scene that includes as many different natural and artificial light sources as they can think of. In addition they should include a picture of a person in their scene and show how the light sources are being used to help this person see the objects around them. The children should annotate their drawings with further relevant information.
- An analysis of the children's drawings will enable you to assess their knowledge and understanding of light sources. You will be able to gauge their ability to identify light sources and also their understanding of how reflected light entering our eyes enables us to see.

Further practice
- Further understanding can be gained by letting the children explore their own immediate environment in school to identify the range of different light sources around them. These could each be classified as natural or artificial.
- The children could also explore reflected light further. They could experiment with mirrors to try to find out how we can use mirrors to see around corners if light travels in straight lines. Further experience of working with light sources and exploring dark spaces will consolidate their understanding that light entering our eyes allows us to see.

Tracking the Sun

■ Choose an object such as a building or tree as a marker. Draw a sketch of your marker in the first box. Mark the position of the Sun on your picture. (Do not look directly at the Sun.) Write the time at the top of the box.

■ Repeat this using the same marker three more times throughout the day.

Time:	Time:
Time:	Time:

■ In your own words, describe what has happened to the position of the Sun during the day.

_____

_____

_____

_____

■ Tick the sentence that best describes what has happened.
■ The Sun has travelled across the sky during the day.
■ The Earth has turned round during the day.

I can make and record observations.

How did you do?

PHOTOCOPIABLE   ■ SCHOLASTIC
www.scholastic.co.uk

Light sources

■ Think about the different things that provide us with light in different places. Write down as many light sources as you can think of.

At home	During a power cut
On a camping holiday	In the street at night

■ Some bright objects are light sources, but some are just reflecting light. Fill in this table by ticking the correct column for each.

Object	Light source	Reflects light
A star		
Clothes		
The Sun		
A fire		
The moon		
A book		
The television		
A candle		

I can identify light sources.

How did you do?

Me and my shadow

■ What is a shadow?

_____

_____.

■ How are shadows formed?

_____

_____.

■ What do you need to make a shadow?

_____

_____.

Draw a picture to support your answers.	Draw a picture of the Sun and a shadow of yourself.

■ Describe your shadow.

_____

_____.

I can explain how shadows are formed.

How did you do?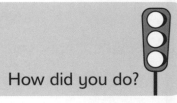

PHOTOCOPIABLE   **SCHOLASTIC**
www.scholastic.co.uk

Light sources and shadows

- All light sources can be used to produce shadows. Describe what happens when you use a torch to make shadows.
- Draw and describe what happens when you move the torch nearer to the object.

| Torch | Object | Shadow |

_____

_____

_____ .

- Draw and describe what happens when you move the torch further away from the object.

| Torch | Object | Shadow |

_____

_____

_____ .

I can explain how shadows are formed.

How did you do?

Letting light through

■ Some children did an investigation to find out how much light can get through different materials. They presented their results in a bar chart.

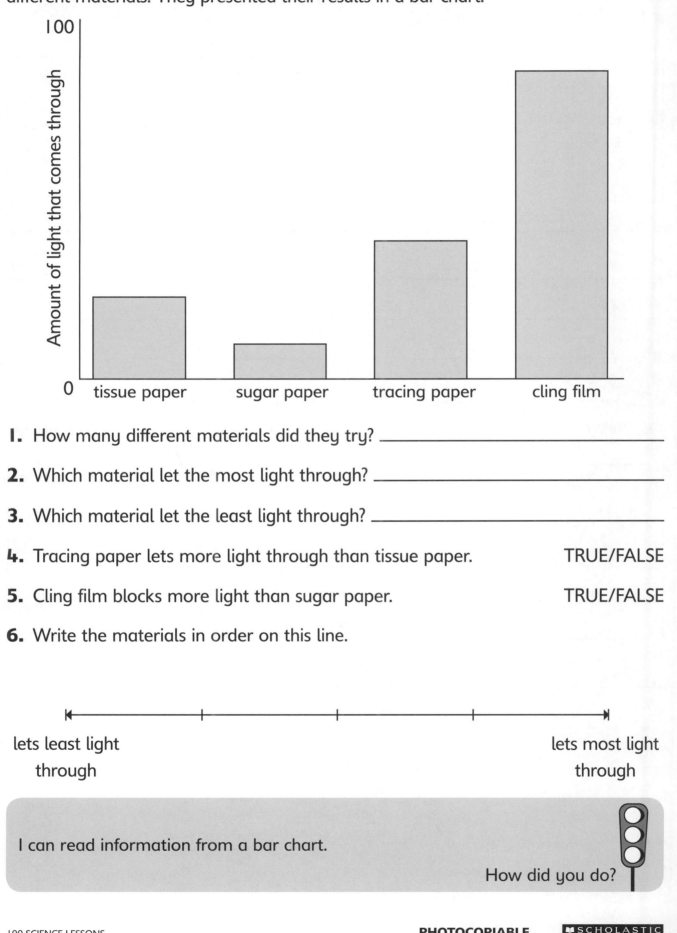

1. How many different materials did they try? _____

2. Which material let the most light through? _____

3. Which material let the least light through? _____

4. Tracing paper lets more light through than tissue paper.   TRUE/FALSE

5. Cling film blocks more light than sugar paper.   TRUE/FALSE

6. Write the materials in order on this line.

lets least light   lets most light
through   through

I can read information from a bar chart.

How did you do?

PHOTOCOPIABLE

SCHOLASTIC
www.scholastic.co.uk

Telling the time with shadows

- The first picture shows a stick's shadow at 9.00am. The other pictures show the stick's shadow later in the day.
- Label the other shadows with the correct time.

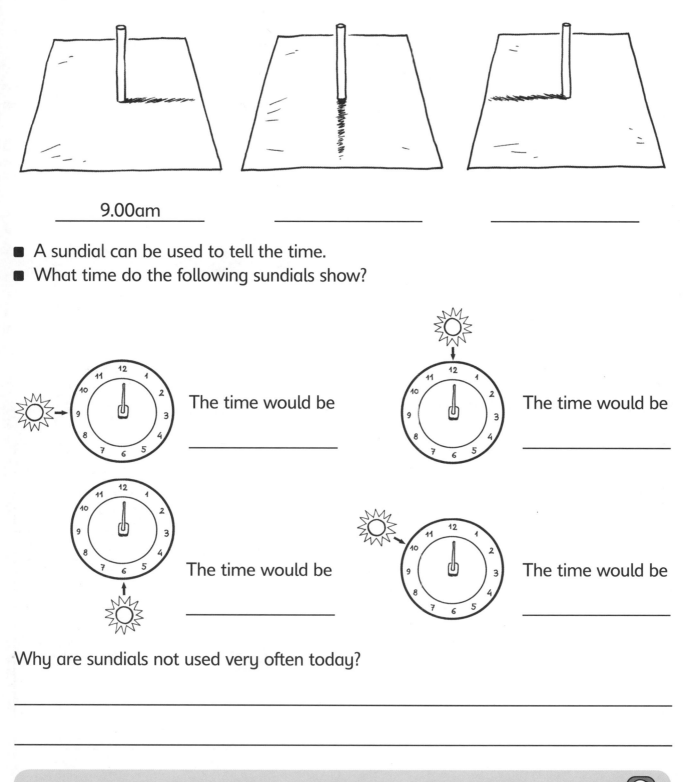

9.00am _____   _____   _____

- A sundial can be used to tell the time.
- What time do the following sundials show?

The time would be _____

The time would be _____

The time would be _____

The time would be _____

Why are sundials not used very often today?

_____

_____

I can explain how a sundial works.

How did you do?

Colour

■ Complete these sentences. Choose the correct words from the wordbank below.

orange	violet	rainbow	red	colour	light
indigo	seven	green	yellow	blue	

We are able to see things because of _____.

We can see the _____ of things because light is made up

from _____ colours.

The colours can be seen in a _____.

The colours are _____, _____,

_____, _____,

_____, _____,

_____.

■ Draw a rainbow and put the colours in the right order.

I can talk about the colours of the rainbow.

How did you do?

PHOTOCOPIABLE   ■SCHOLASTIC
www.scholastic.co.uk

Name: _____   Date: _____

Colour on the roads

- Colours are often used to give us a message or an instruction.
- Complete these sentences. Choose the correct words from the word bank.

a warning	dangerous	safe

Red is often used to indicate that something is _____.

Green is often used to indicate that something is _____.

Amber is often used to indicate _____.

- Now think about how traffic lights work. Can you remember the sequence in which the lights shine? Colour these traffic lights.

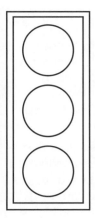 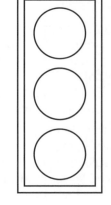 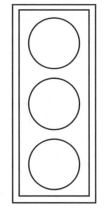 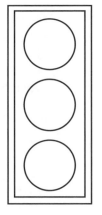 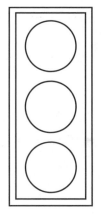

- Make a list of other uses of light and colour in road safety.

Light	Colour

I can explain how colour is used in road safety.

How did you do?

Plants

Expected prior learning

● Identify and name a variety of common plants including deciduous and evergreen trees.
● Identify and describe the basic structure of a variety of common flowering plants, including trees.
● Describe how seeds and bulbs grow and develop into mature plants.
● Describe how plants need water, light and a suitable temperature to grow and stay healthy.

Overview of progression

In this chapter children will learn about:

● the functions of different parts of plants, including the roots, stem/trunk, leaves and flowers
● the requirements of different plants for life and growth and how this varies from plant to plant
● how water is transported within plants
● the role of flowers in the life cycle of flowering plants.

Creative context

● This chapter provides opportunities for children to use different media to communicate their findings.

Background knowledge

Roots are vital to the well-being of a plant; they perform two very important functions in the plant. Roots supply water to the plant. If a plant becomes short of water it will eventually wilt and die. The roots of a plant draw up water and minerals from the ground. These are transported from the roots to the leaves, where photosynthesis happens. The plant also loses water as it evaporates into the air from the leaves and flowers. This water loss is called transpiration.

The root system also acts as an anchor to hold the plant in place. Without a well-established root system the plant would move about and become loose; it could even fall over and die. The root system often spreads out as far as the branches above ground. The roots of some larger plants and trees are very strong and can cause structural damage if allowed to develop near buildings.

Speaking scientifically

Children should be familiar with the terms: air, light, nutrient, water, starvation, anchor, root, evergreen, deciduous, leaf, soil, compost, fair test, plant, stem, trunk, flower, function, pollen, pollination, pollinator, transfer, nectar, stigma, petal, anther, seed dispersal, wind dispersal, animal dispersal, life cycle, compare, exploration, seedling, evaporation, investigation, observation and prediction.

Preparation

You will need to provide: art materials; flipchart; seeds; seedlings; various flowers, fruits, plants and plant parts; containers; shallow trays; beakers; cling film; plastic bags and ties; measuring cylinders; composts; soil samples; fruits; celery; food colouring; sticky labels; pictures of plants and overgrown gardens; art materials; secondary sources of information; clipboards; cardboard petals; woolly hats, socks and jumper; ping-pong balls; Velcro; bottles of juice; jar of honey; knives, bowls and spoons; sticky tape; pictures from the work of Maria Sibylla Merian; hoops; digital cameras and cameras; hand lenses; laptops; digital microscopes; wild flower identification charts; plan/map of the area around school; large diagram of parts of a plant

On the CD-ROM you will find: photocopiable pages 'Looking at climates' and 'Plant assessment'; interactive activities 'Plant parts'; 'Which parts do we eat?', 'Root, stem, and leaves' and 'Life cycles'

MSCHOLASTIC

Chapter at a glance

Week	Lesson	Curriculum objectives	Objectives	Main activity	Working scientifically
1	1	• (Y1) To identify and describe the basic structure of a variety of common flowering plants, including trees. • To identify and describe the functions of different parts of flowering plants: roots, stem/trunk, leaves and flowers.	• To revise the names of common plants. • To revise the names of parts of plants. • To know that we eat different parts of different plants. • To introduce the idea that different parts of plants have different functions.	Revising the names of plants and their parts and sorting them into groups. Identifying foods from plants and naming the parts we eat. Supermarket visit. Introducing the idea that each part of the plant has a specific function.	• Using straightforward scientific evidence to answer questions or to support their findings.
	2	• To identify and describe the functions of different parts of flowering plants: roots, stem/trunk, leaves and flowers. • To investigate the way in which water is transported within plants.	• To know that roots take up water and anchor the plant to the ground.	Looking at plant specimens. Drawing a labelled diagram of a plant. Investigating the function of roots.	• Recording findings using simple scientific language, drawings, labelled diagrams, bar charts, and tables.
	3	• To identify and describe the functions of different parts of flowering plants: roots, stem, leaves and flowers. • To investigate the way in which water is transported within plants.	• To know that the stem of a plant carries water and minerals from the roots and also gives the plant shape.	Looking at the root and stem structure as a transportation system.	• Setting up simple practical enquiries, comparative and fair tests.
2	1	• To identify and describe the functions of different parts of flowering plants: roots, stem/trunk, leaves and flowers.	• To recognise that leaves are needed for healthy plant growth. • To investigate the relationship of plant leaves to plant growth.	Investigating plants with and without leaves to determine the importance of leaves.	• Setting up simple practical enquiries, comparative and fair tests.
	2	• To explore the requirements of plants for life and growth (air, light, water, nutrients from soil, and room to grow) and how they vary from plant to plant.	• To understand the need for plants to have a supply of air to grow healthily.	Looking at how air is needed by plants. Finding out what happens when plants are starved of air.	• Asking relevant questions. • Setting up simple practical enquiries, comparative and fair tests. • Gathering, recording, classifying and presenting data in a variety of ways to help in answering questions.
	3	• To explore the requirements of plants for life and growth (air, light, water, nutrients from soil, and room to grow) and how they vary from plant to plant.	• To know that light is needed for healthy plant growth.	Investigating light as a variable factor in plant growth.	• Asking relevant questions. • Setting up simple practical enquiries, comparative and fair tests. • Gathering, recording, classifying and presenting data in a variety of ways to help in answering questions.
3	1	• To explore the requirements of plants for life and growth (air, light, water, nutrients from soil, and room to grow) and how they vary from plant to plant.	• To know that too little or too much water prevents healthy plant growth.	Considering the effects that under- and over-watering plants can have.	• Asking relevant questions. • Gathering, recording, classifying and presenting data in a variety of ways to help in answering questions.
	2	• To explore the requirements of plants for life and growth (air, light, water, nutrients from soil, and room to grow) and how they vary from plant to plant.	• To know that plants need a supply of nutrients for growth. • To understand that plants produce their own food.	Comparing plant growth in different soils.	• Setting up simple practical enquiries, comparative and fair tests.
	3	• To explore the requirements of plants for life and growth (air, light, water, nutrients from soil, and room to grow) and how they vary from plant to plant.	• To understand the ideal conditions for plant growth.	Writing a guide to the care of plants.	• Gathering, recording, classifying and presenting data in a variety of ways to help in answering questions.

SPRING 2

Plants

Week	Lesson	Curriculum objectives	Objectives	Main activity	Working scientifically
4	1	• To explore the requirements of plants for life and growth (air, light, water, nutrients from soil, and room to grow) and how they vary from plant to plant.	• To understand that different species of plant have different requirements for healthy growth.	Using secondary sources to identify some common wild plants. Exploring some of the similarities and differences in plants growing in different places.	• Identifying differences, similarities or changes related to simple scientific ideas and processes.
	2	• To explore the part that flowers play in the life cycle of flowering plants, including pollination, seed formation and seed dispersal.	• To understand the process of pollination in plants and the role of flowers in that process.	Playing the pollination game.	• Gathering, recording, classifying and presenting data in a variety of ways to help in answering questions.
	3	• To explore the part that flowers play in the life cycle of flowering plants, including pollination, seed formation and seed dispersal.	• To understand that seeds can be dispersed in a variety of ways.	Looking at the range of methods used to disperse seeds in nature, including by wind and by animals and birds.	• Identifying differences, similarities or changes related to simple scientific ideas and processes.
5	1	• To explore the part that flowers play in the life cycle of flowering plants, including pollination, seed formation and seed dispersal.	• To know the conditions that seeds need to germinate.	Planning an investigation into seed germination using different variables to determine ideal conditions.	• Setting up simple practical enquiries, comparative and fair tests. • Reporting on findings from enquiries, including oral and written explanations, displays or presentations of results and conclusions.
	2	• To explore the part that flowers play in the life cycle of flowering plants, including pollination, seed formation and seed dispersal.	• To understand the contribution of the work of Maria Sibylla Merian to our understanding of plant life cycles.	Introducing the scientist Maria Sibylla Merian. Looking at the life and work of Merian.	• Recording findings using simple scientific language, drawings, labelled diagrams, keys, bar charts and tables.
	3	• To explore the part that flowers play in the life cycle of flowering plants, including pollination, seed formation and seed dispersal.	• To know how to order the life cycles of common plants.	Investigating life cycles in plants.	• Recording findings using simple scientific language, drawings, labelled diagrams, keys, bar charts, and tables.
6	1	• To explore the part that flowers play in the life cycle of flowering plants, including pollination, seed formation and seed dispersal.	• To know that after pollination takes place, a fruit is produced that contains seeds.	Recording/presenting findings about fruits in the style of Merian through the use of detailed illustrations.	• Recording findings using simple scientific language, drawings, labelled diagrams, keys, bar charts, and tables.
	2	• To explore the requirements of plants for life and growth (air, light, water, nutrients from soil, and room to grow) and how they vary from plant to plant.	• To know that different plants are found in different habitats. • To know that there are reasons why different plants grow in different habitats.	Predicting how plants might vary in different habitats. Carrying out a plant survey.	• Gathering, recording, classifying and presenting data in a variety of ways to help in answering questions.
	3	• To explore the requirements of plants for life and growth (air, light, water, nutrients from soil, and room to grow) and how they vary from plant to plant.	• To understand the relationship between the physical aspects of a habitat and the plants living there.	Researching and communicating their findings about different plant habitats.	• Using straightforward scientific evidence to answer questions or to support their findings.
Assess and review					

Objectives
● To revise the names of common plants.
● To revise the names of parts of plants.
● To know that we eat different parts of different plants.
● To introduce the idea that different parts of plants have different functions.

Resources

A flipchart; pictures of common plants including trees (such as oak, sycamore, holly and horse chestnut), wild plants (such as dandelion, daisy, buttercup and nettle), and garden plants (such as daffodil, crocus, snowdrop and rose); computer and online shopping service (optional); extra adult supervision (if visiting a shop or supermarket); photocopiable page 135 'Food sources' If arranging to visit a local shop or supermarket, contact the manager first to arrange permission. Ensure that you have extra adult supervision for each group. If this is not a practical option, you could access supermarket websites and use the online shopping service.

Speaking scientifically

animal, deciduous, evergreen, flower, function, leaf, plant, root, stem, trunk

Lesson 1: What do we know about plants?

Previous knowledge

Children should already be able to:

● identify and name a variety of common plants, including some garden plants, wild plants and trees
● identify trees as evergreen or deciduous
● identify and describe the basic structure of a variety of plants, including knowledge of roots, stem/trunk, leaves and flowers
● observe and describe how seeds and bulbs grow into mature plants
● find out and describe how plants need water, light and a suitable temperature to grow and stay healthy.

Introduction

Ask the children to tell you some of the foods they have eaten recently. Write them down on the board. Encourage the children to consider where each food came from originally, before it arrived in the shops. Ask them to see if they can put the foods into groups, not according to the type of food or its benefits to us, as in Chapter 2, but in some other way. Guide their thinking towards the idea of food from plants and food from animals.

Whole-class work

1. As a class, re-write the earlier food list as two lists on the flipchart, one headed 'Plants' and the other headed 'Animals'. Before recording their ideas, encourage the children to predict which they think will give the longest list, plants or animals.

2. When the table is complete, discuss it as a class. Reinforce the idea that whilst we might eat some foods that are animal-based, much more of our food comes from plants.

3. Put the children into mixed-ability teams of three or four. Give them a simple picture identification quiz using the pictures of common plants, including trees. Ask the children to identify each of the plants in turn and to record their answers.

4. Review the answers together as a class. Ask the children to explain how they identified each of the plants in the pictures. Encourage them towards an understanding that they need to look at observable features such as the flowers, leaves and stem/trunk, in addition to size and shape. Make sure each part is named and discussed.

5. Having identified the parts of a plant, ask the children to think about the functions of each of these parts. They could discuss their ideas with a talk partner first, before sharing them as a class. Elicit ideas about the function of the roots, stem, leaves and flowers. Gather the children's ideas together and record them on the board. Explain to the children that you will be looking at these parts in more detail in later lessons.

Independent work

6. Ask the children to complete the interactive activity 'Which parts do we eat?' on the CD-ROM.

7. Give the children photocopiable page 135 'Food sources'. Ask them to list some plant-based foods and the parts of the plants that we eat. Ask: *With some plants, do we eat more than just one of these parts?*

Whole-class/Group work

8. Arrange a visit to a local shop or supermarket. If that is not possible, you could look at an online shopping service on a supermarket website via the interactive whiteboard instead. These are often organised into aisles, just like the real thing.

9. Divide the children into groups of four or five. Either using the computer or in the real supermarket, allocate an aisle to each group.

10. Ask the children to consider and record the different types of food in their aisle and to decide whether each comes from plants or animals. The results will reinforce the principle that most of our diet comes from plants.

Introducing the new area of study

As you begin to introduce this new area of study you may wish to consider some of the misconceptions children often hold about plants. Some will think that all plants have flowers, green leaves and a stem and that they grow in pots. This is based on their experience of house plants. A distinction between plants and trees is often made – some children think that a tree is a plant when small but that as it grows it becomes a tree and not a plant. Some children will not identify parts of plants that they eat as being plants, so for them carrots are not plants but vegetables. Children (and indeed some adults) also tend to get confused about the difference between seed germination and plant growth and do not appreciate the different requirements for each.

Science in the wider world

A characteristic of all living things is their need to obtain nutrition. Almost all plants and animals depend either directly or indirectly on the Sun for their food. Unlike animals, plants are able to make their own food. The plant then becomes food for animals, which in turn may be food for other animals, including humans. Thus all of the food we eat can be traced back along a food chain to plants, and ultimately to the Sun. These links in the food chain are often difficult to trace when faced with some of the processed foods we eat today and the many additives and preservatives they contain. Nonetheless, the vast majority of foods that children will come across will be linked in some way with plants.

Review

Marking the children's work will give an indication of whether or not they have understood the concepts covered in this lesson. All of the children should have been able to sort the foods into groups, so will have understood that foods come ultimately from one of these two sources (plants or animals). Most children should be able to identify the parts of a plant and many will have a basic understanding of the functions of these parts.

Objectives
● To know that roots take up water and anchor the plant to the ground.

Resources
A wilting plant; washed weeds with intact roots in shallow trays; photocopiable page 136 'Plant parts (1)'; photocopiable page 137 'Plant parts (2)'; beakers; water; cling film

Speaking scientifically
anchor, roots, water

Lesson 2: The roots

Introduction
Ask the children to think about what they feel like on a hot and sunny day, particularly if they have just been for a long walk or played games. Elicit the idea of being hot and in need of refreshment. Ask them to think about what being thirsty does to you. Show them a wilting plant and ask them to think about what this plant may need and why it is wilting. They should suggest that the plant needs a 'drink' of water. Draw on the analogy between the children themselves needing water and the plant needing water.

Whole-class work
1. Discuss with the children how we drink to take in water and how the plant takes in water through its roots.

2. Distribute the weeds that you have prepared and photocopiable page 136 'Plant parts (1)'. Ask the children to take great care with their plants as they will be using them again in an investigation.

3. Ask the children to look carefully at their plant – its roots, stem and leaves. Talk about how water moves up the roots and stem to the leaves and about the functions of the roots, stem and leaves.

Independent work
4. Ask the children to draw a labelled diagram of their plant on the photocopiable sheet. They should then pair up the names of the parts with the descriptions of their functions.

5. Suggest to the children that, while we *think* water is taken up through the roots of the plant, we want to find out for sure. Therefore they are going to carry out an investigation to show that water does travel through the roots of the plant.

6. The children will need photocopiable page 137 'Plant parts (2)', the weeds, plastic beakers, water and cling film. During the investigation, which could last a week, the children will need to observe the water levels every day and record their observations on the photocopiable sheet.

Differentiation
● Some children will need support during the setting up of the investigation and may benefit from using a simplified scale on the beaker (or writing on the beaker with a waterproof pen to mark the falling water level).
● Challenge other children to give reasoned answers to questions and use a beaker marked in smaller units, such as millilitres, that can be read off and recorded.

Science in the wider world
Roots are vital to the well-being of a plant. Without a strong root system the plant would become unhealthy and die. This is because the roots perform two very important functions. Firstly, they supply water and trace minerals to the plant. The water in the roots and stem moves due to a combination of pushing and pulling. The roots often push the water a little way up the stem, while evaporation from the leaves draws up more water to replace that which is lost. Secondly, the root system acts as an anchor to hold the plant firmly in place.

Review
Mark the children's photocopiable sheets to gauge their understanding of the functions of the roots. Have they been able to identify the two main functions? During the investigation, assess the children's ability to take simple measurements.

Objectives
● To know that the stem of a plant carries water and minerals from the roots and also gives the plant shape.

Resources
A vase of flowers such as tulips; celery (both full stems with leaves and stems cut into 2cm slices); containers; water; food colouring; hand lenses; digital microscope(s); laptop(s)

Speaking scientifically
bud, petal, stem, transport

Lesson 3: The stem

Introduction
Take a bunch of cut flowers and put them in a vase of water. Ask the children to use descriptive words to talk with a talk partner about the flowers. Encourage them to think about why we put cut flowers into water. Ask: *What would happen if we left the flowers without water for too long? Why does the plant have a stem when we are really only interested in the flower? When we buy a bunch of flowers, what are the flowers often like at first?* (The buds are closed.) *What happens over the next few days after buying the flowers?* (The buds open.)

Whole-class work
1. Gather together the children's thoughts and ideas about the flowers. Ensure that they understand that the stem has two purposes. Check that they understand that the stem transports water and gives support to the plant.

2. Point out to the children that we can see the function of the stem in supporting the plant just by looking. Ask them how we might be able to see that the stem carries water.

Paired work
3. Talk about the tiny pipes through which a plant carries water. The water carries minerals, which are nutrients from the soil. Look at the ends of the cut flowers. The children will find it difficult to see any of these 'pipes' clearly. Pass around some sliced-up pieces of celery and encourage the children to look at the small pipes that can be seen using hand lenses.

4. If you have access to digital microscopes, set these up for the children to use to see the pipes in more detail. Alternatively, you can use just one microscope and display the image on the board.

5. Suggest to the children that even though they can see the pipes, they can't yet be sure that water travels in them. Then give out beakers containing water and a few drops of food colouring. Ask the children to place a celery stem in their container and put it near a window. They should keep a diary record of what the celery stem and leaves look like over the next hour or two. This could be in the form of annotated diagrams or annotated digital images. Keep repeating the observations over the next 24 hours (after which time the leaves should be saturated with the dye).

6. When there is a noticeable difference let the children look at the leaves and stem closely and examine the end of the celery. The children can write about and draw their observations of how water travels in tiny pipes through plants. Again, if you have access to digital microscopes or hand lenses, use these to let the children get a close-up view of the channels and leaves.

Differentiation
● Some children may prefer to present their results using annotated drawings alone.
● Challenge confident children to present their findings in written narrative with accompanying illustrations and to provide clear explanations and evidence of understanding.

Science in the wider world
The movement of water through a plant is known as the transpiration stream. The water in the stem (as with the roots) moves upwards due to a combination of pushing and pulling. The roots can 'push' the water (and so, also the minerals) a little way up the stem, and evaporation from the leaves draws up more water to replace that which is lost.

Review
Examine the children's observation diaries to assess whether they understand the concept of water travelling through the 'pipes'.

Lesson 1: The leaves

Objectives
● To recognise that leaves are needed for healthy plant growth.
● To investigate the relationship of plant leaves to plant growth.

Resources
Potted plants; twigs from evergreen and deciduous trees/bushes (obtainable during pruning; do not use yew or holly for safety reasons); leaves from different species of plant/tree (obtainable during pruning or natural falling; avoid damaging trees to gather these); hand lenses/digital microscopes; laptops; art materials; interactive activity 'Root, stem and leaves' on the CD-ROM

Speaking scientifically
deciduous, evergreen, leaves

Introduction

Talk to the children about their prior knowledge and understanding of the different parts of plants. Recall the parts they know about and talk briefly and in simple terms about the functions of those parts: roots take up water and minerals and anchor the plant; stems/trunks carry water to the leaves and keep the plant upright; flowers allow the plant to reproduce; leaves absorb sunlight and make food.

Whole-class work

1. Discuss what might happen if the plant was deprived of one of these parts. Ask: *What would happen if a plant had no roots? How would a plant survive without a stem? What happens when the flowers of a plant are cut off?*

2. Ask the children to think about the leaves of trees. What happens to the leaves of trees in the autumn and winter? Elicit the children's understanding of evergreen and deciduous trees/bushes.

3. Have either some twigs from evergreen and deciduous trees for the children to examine, or pictures on the board to show the differences. Make the point that whilst conditions are too cold and dark for growth to continue, deciduous trees lose their leaves and are therefore unable to make food and grow during the winter.

Paired work

4. Give each pair of children a selection of four different leaves to look at. Let them have the opportunity to use hand lenses or digital microscopes to make close and careful observations of the leaves. Ask them to consider the shape, size, toughness, colour and feel of the leaves. Let them make observational drawings of their leaves.

5. The children should plan and carry out an investigation into the importance of leaves to plants. They should use two plants (preferably of the same species) – one that has leaves and one that has had its leaves removed. You could do this either with some potted wild plants/weeds or with some (relatively cheap) small plants bought from a garden centre. The children can keep them in the same conditions, observe what happens and measure their growth over a period of time.

6. The children can discuss their observations and draw conclusions about what happened to the plants without leaves. Reinforce their knowledge that leaves are important in order for plants to grow well.

Science in the wider world

The leaves of plants are vital to their health and survival. Plants may suffer damage to their leaves either through disease (such as Dutch elm disease, which starts in the leaves and spreads) or by being eaten by other creatures (for example caterpillars on brassicas such as cabbage and cauliflower). Plants that suffer in this way may die, or at best their growth rate during that particular growing season is impacted.

Review

Discussion with the children during their investigation and scrutiny of their written work will help to indicate their understanding. You can also use the interactive activity 'Root, stem and leaves' on the CD-ROM to revise some of the key learning from the last three lesssons. Look for evidence that they know that without leaves a plant is unable to grow. Some children may be able to explain that without leaves the plant cannot produce food and therefore cannot grow.

Objectives
● To understand the need for plants to have a supply of air to grow healthily.

Resources
Small potted plants (bedding plants would be ideal); plastic bags and ties

Speaking scientifically
air, light, need, nutrient, starvation, want, water

Lesson 2: Air and growth

Introduction
Introduce the lesson by asking the children to think about the difference between the things they *need* and the things they *want* in life. A general discussion might raise several things that children think are needs rather than wants. Ask them to share their needs and wants, and as they do so, compile two lists on the board. Explain to the children that a need is something that is essential in order to live, while a want is something that may well be non-essential and does not affect our ability to stay alive.

Whole-class work
1. Ask the children to think about the needs of plants. Together add a third column to your lists that shows the needs of plants.

2. Write down the children's ideas of what a plant might need in order to stay alive. As the discussion develops, guide the children to ensure that the list contains air, light, water, nutrients (minerals) from the soil and room to grow.

3. Explain that they will be looking at each of these things in the coming lessons.

Paired work
4. Ask the children to talk with a partner about what they think will happen to plants if they do not have the things they need to stay alive. Ask: *What would a plant be like if it was kept in the dark? What would a plant be like if it was too close to other plants? How would a plant survive if it did not have any water?*

5. Encourage the children to think about how they might investigate what would happen if a plant was starved of air. The children should share their ideas with the class.

6. Give each pair of children a small plant and a small plastic bag with a tie, or a ziplock bag. They should place the plant inside the bag and seal it inside. The children could very carefully exclude as much air as they can without damaging the plant.

7. Place the plants somewhere suitable in the classroom and ask the children to observe what happens to them over the coming days. The children could devise and keep a simple daily record of their observations.

Independent work
8. Ask the children to draw and annotate two pictures of their plant. The first should show the plant at the start of the experiment. The second should show what they think it will look like when it does not get the air it needs.

9. After carrying out the investigation, the children can record their result by drawing a third picture of what actually happens to the plant.

Differentiation
● Most children should be able to engage with the observations in this lesson. Allow some learners to record the changes to their plant in picture format only.
● Challenge confident learners to give something of an explanation, in addition to a descriptive observation.

Science in the wider world
To grow well, plants need air. They use carbon dioxide from the air to make their food, and release oxygen as a by-product. Plants also need to use oxygen for respiration in order to release energy from their food, just as animals do.

Review
Through scrutiny of the children's work and by engaging them in discussion, assess their understanding of the differences between wants and needs and the need that plants have for air.

Objectives
● To know that light is needed for healthy plant growth.

Resources
Small plants or seedlings (cress can be germinated quickly) – use small containers to germinate some seeds and grow the seedlings

Speaking scientifically
dark, growth, light

Lesson 3: Light and growth

Introduction

Ask the children to image what life would be like without light. If appropriate you might make reference to other topics where the children have looked at different light sources (see Chapter 3) and encourage them to identify the Sun as one of several different light sources. Ask the children to recall the purpose of the leaves on plants. Talk about plants not gathering food but making their own. There is no need to talk about the process of photosynthesis, but simply introduce the idea that plants use sunlight and air to make their own food.

Whole-class work

1. Give the children small containers of growing cress seedlings for them to look at. Can they see the leaves?

2. Ask them to notice what the small cress plants are like, thinking about the colour and orientation. Ask: *Are the stems leaning or straight? Are the leaves green or another colour?*

Paired work

3. Using the seedlings, set up an investigation in which light is a variable factor. Ask the children to decide how they might investigate the effects of light on how the seedlings grow.

4. Together, place some of the pots of seedlings in a dark place, some in partial light and some in bright light. Ask the children to predict what might happen to the seedlings kept in each of the different light levels.

5. The children should then observe the growth of the seedlings over the course of several days. They can record their observations in a 'Seedling diary'.

6. After several days, encourage the children to comment on the differences and similarities between the seedlings in the different conditions. Ask: *What differences can you see in the size of the seedlings? What differences can you see in the colour of the leaves of the seedlings? Are all the seedlings growing in the same direction?* (Those near the bright light of a window will have bent in order to grow towards the light. Why have these seedlings grown so that they lean towards the light?)

Science in the wider world

Plants need light for the process of making food (called photosynthesis). Lack or low levels of light will affect this and therefore affect the growth of the plant (though in the early stages, a seedling deprived of light may grow taller in order to try to reach the light). Plants will also grow *towards* the light. Where many plants are found very close together, they will grow straight upwards towards the light. This can be seen in pine forests where the trees grow very straight to keep their leaves (needles) in the sunlight. The lower branches, which are in the dark, tend not to have many needles.

Review

Through discussion and analysis of their seedling diaries, assess the children's understanding of the role that light plays in healthy growth and the impact it can have on the direction that a plant grows in.

Resources
A bunch of flowers that has been left in coloured water overnight (and one flower that has not been kept in water and has dried out); food colouring (for the coloured water); seedlings; small pots or containers; compost; measuring cylinders; water; digital cameras or video cameras (if available); rulers

Speaking scientifically
evaporation, investigation, observation, prediction, seedling, travel, water

Lesson 1: Water and growth

Introduction
Take a bunch of cut flowers into the classroom that has been in coloured water overnight. Ask: *Why do we put cut flowers into water? What happens if we don't? How do we know that the flowers actually need water in order to open and bloom?* Look carefully at the petals of the flowers together. (The children should notice that the food colouring has coloured the edges of the petals.) Have an example of a flower that has not been in water to show them. Talk about the need that plants have for water in order to stay healthy.

Paired work
1. Using seedlings that you have grown previously, give each pair three seedlings, some small containers and a quantity of compost. Ask the children to very carefully pot up the seedlings, one into each pot.

2. Tell the children that they are going to investigate the effect that water has on the growth of these seedlings. One will be over-watered, one under-watered and one will get about the right amount of water.

3. Let the children discuss and agree what these definitions might mean in terms of the frequency and amount of water given to the seedlings. Suggest something like: one of the pots will be watered three times a day, one will never be watered and the third will be watered when the soil feels dry.

4. Encourage the children to make predictions about what they think will happen to each of their three seedlings.

5. The children should observe and measure the growth and general health of their plants over a period of a week or two. They can usefully make their own decisions about how to do this. Suggestions might include using digital still or video cameras to produce some time-lapse images, drawings, measurement of the height of the seedlings, and general observations described in words in a diary.

6. At the end of the experiment, encourage the children to draw conclusions about their observations and the data they have collected and to produce a written account of their investigation.

> **Differentiation**
> ● Some children will need assistance in formulating their ideas into a written account of the investigation. You could provide a wordbank or writing frame for these children to use.
> ● Challenge confident learners to use secondary sources to find out more about the importance of water to plants.

Science in the wider world
Getting the right amount of water is essential for healthy growth in plants. Too much water and the roots will not get sufficient oxygen and may begin to rot, as we often see when there are prolonged periods of rain. Conversely, when there is a prolonged period of dry weather the plant does not get the water it needs for photosynthesis and other reactions, and to allow nutrients to travel through it. The resulting lack of water in the plant cells causes the plant to droop rather than standing upright.

Different plants require different amounts of water. Some can only survive with a regular supply of water but others (such as succulents and cacti) can go for much longer periods of time without water.

Review
Through scrutiny of the children's work, assess their understanding of the importance water has for the health of a plant. Can they identify what happens when a plant receives too little or too much water?

Objectives
● To know that plants need a supply of nutrients for growth.
● To understand that plants produce their own food.

Resources
Pots; different soil samples (some sandy, some stony, some with a good humus level such as compost); cress seeds; photocopiable page 138 'Growing seeds in different soils'

Speaking scientifically
compost, fair test, nutrient, sandy soil, stony soil

Lesson 2: Nutrients in plant growth

Introduction
Recap on the work done in previous lessons and the factors that lead to healthy growth in plants. Check that the children are able to identify that air, light and water are needed for plants to stay healthy, before introducing the idea that plants also need a supply of nutrients.

Whole-class work
1. Ask the children to think about themselves and what keeps them fit and healthy. Encourage them to talk about shelter, safety, warmth and food.

2. Talk again about the fact that as animals we are not able to produce our own food in the way that plants use air, water and sunlight to produce theirs. Introduce the idea that plants also need certain other nutrients in order to grow well.

3. Tell the children that a nutrient is a substance that can be used by animals for energy while plants use it to make their own food. Ask: *What would happen if a plant did not have access to a supply of nutrients?* (It would not make sufficient food and would become unhealthy.)

Paired work
4. Ask the children to work in pairs to plan a fair test investigation to see what the effect is of germinating seeds in different soil samples. This will affect the levels of nutrients supplied to the seedlings as they grow.

5. Make available a range of soil samples. Ask the children to set up their investigation so that the only thing they change is the soil sample. The amount of water, the light and the temperature should be kept the same for each sample.

6. Distribute photocopiable page 138 'Growing seeds in different soils' and ask the children to follow the instructions carefully. They should plant cress seeds in two different types of soil and care for them both equally well. A record of their work can be kept in the form of a simple storyboard.

Science in the wider world
Different soils and sub-soils have different properties. Some are fine, some are gritty and open and some are more solid with finer particles that stick together. These different soil types allow the water that falls on them to drain away at different rates. When it rains, you will notice how the water lies for longer in some areas than in others. The levels of humus in the soil also impact on the nutrients that are retained in it, and therefore available to plants.

Review
Scrutiny of the children's work and your questioning will help you to assess their ability to identify an investigation that is and is not a fair test. Ask: *Did you use the same amount of water for each plant? Why? Did you use the same amount of soil? Why? How was this fair or unfair?*

Objectives
● To understand the ideal conditions for plant growth.

Resources
Copies of the letter from Vera Wild (see below); pictures of overgrown gardens

Speaking scientifically
healthy, overgrown, space

Lesson 3: Space in plant growth

Introduction
Recap with the children that so far they have considered the needs of plants for air, light, water and nutrients, but that there is one more thing to consider. Tell the story of an imaginary garden that has been left for a long time without anyone looking after it so that it has become overgrown. Show the children pictures of overgrown gardens. Ask the children to imagine what it might be like. Ask: *What do you think might have happened to some of the plants? Will some have grown more than others? Which ones?* Try to encourage the children to create a picture in their minds of a garden where the plants are 'fighting each other' for space.

Whole-class work
1. Explain that all plants need space in which to grow. Plants that are too close together will compete for the available light and soil-based nutrients. This competition can lead to unhealthy plants and can affect the way they grow.

2. Read out the letter below, from someone who has an overgrown garden.

Dear children,

I have just moved into a house that has a garden full of overgrown plants all trying to survive. Some have grown so big that they are really squashed and some are completely covering others. I understand that you have been learning about how plants stay healthy and I wondered if you could help me by suggesting what the plants in my garden need in order to make them healthy again.

I look forward to hearing from you,

Vera Wild

Independent work
3. Give the children copies of the letter and ask them to suggest what Vera Wild could do to solve the problems with her garden. The children should write a short guide or leaflet to send to Vera, which will explain how to keep the plants in the garden healthy. They should include illustrations and written text to help Vera Wild solve her problem, and should use these headings: light, soil, water and space.

4. Encourage the children to recall the work they have already done in previous lessons and to use some of what they have learned in relation to this practical situation.

Science in the wider world
Generally, if the space available for a plant is small then the plant will be small and its growth may be stunted. Big plants need big spaces so that their leaves and branches can grow freely.

Review
Assess the children's understanding of the needs of plants, especially the need that plants have for sufficient space.

Objectives
● To understand that different species of plant have different requirements for healthy growth.

Resources
Secondary sources of information to help with plant identification; large hoops; clipboards; art materials
Ensure that you have extra adult supervision for children carrying out their surveys outside the school grounds, if necessary.

Speaking scientifically
field, hedge, plant, survey, waste ground, wild

Lesson 1: Variation between different plants

Introduction
Begin the lesson by telling the children that they are going to be explorers and explore local plant life. Ask them if they can name any wild plants that they think they may be able to see and identify locally. Most of the children should be able to identify some common wild plants such as the dandelion, daisy and buttercup. It may be worth discussing here the definition of a weed. (Weeds are plants that are not wanted in the location where they are growing.)

Whole-class work
1. Together, plan a plant survey. Tell the children that they are going to look at the plant life that is growing in a certain area. They will be considering the similarities and differences between the plants in that area.

2. Ask the children to suggest ways that they might do this. Lead them to the idea that they look at one small area and use a large hoop to define that area.

3. Have available a range of secondary sources of information that the children can use before carrying out the survey to familiarise themselves with some of the wild plants they may see.

4. Discuss with the children exactly what it is they are going to be observing and how they might compare similarities and differences between the plants they find. For example, it would be a good idea to record the characteristics of the patch of ground (damp, dry, dark, light and so on), as well as comparing the plants growing there (tall, short, few, many, in view, hidden).

Paired work
5. Let the children carry out their surveys in pairs. They should choose an appropriate way in which to record their observations. They could devise a simple record sheet that includes details such as the identification of the plants growing in the area (if known), or draw a sketch of the plants.

6. The children should then try to identify any unknown plants they have seen using secondary sources as an aid.

7. Ask the children to investigate some of the plants that they have found in more detail. Ask: *What are the similarities and differences between them? How many different plants did they find within this one area? How does this compare with others in the class?*

Differentiation
● Some children may prefer to present their findings in simple picture form.
● Challenge others to present their observations with additional research notes and background information.

Science in the wider world
Most gardeners will tell you that different plants like to grow in particular types of soil and in certain conditions. Many garden centres will set out their stocks of plants according to whether those plants prefer, for example, clay soil or sandy soil, shady sites or sunny sites, and so on. As we look around our environment, we see a real variety of wild plants that also prefer certain conditions. Some, such as the dandelion, grow well in dry, open, sunny sites, whilst others, such as mosses, prefer the shady dampness offered by a sheltered north-facing position.

Review
All of the children should be able to identify a few of the more common wild plants. Most should be able to identify some of the differences and similarities between the plants that they have found.

Lesson 2: Flowers and pollination

Introduction
Show the children a flower and a jar of honey. Ask them to discuss with a talk partner the link there might be between them. Gather together the ideas. Direct the discussion towards bees gathering nectar from flowers in order to make honey. Ask the children further questions to elicit their understanding, such as: *What attracts the bees to the flowers?* (Smell and colour); *What else may be happening when the bees are flying from flower to flower?* (Pollen is being transferred); *Do other insects move pollen about in the same way?*

Whole-class work
1. Introduce the role play of the process of pollination. This needs to be carried out in a large space, either outside or in the school hall or gym. Decide how many flowers you will make and the number of petals needed depending on the number of children in your class.

2. You will need to make at least two flowers. Nine children are needed for each flower and one child is needed to be the bee:
● The 'bee' wears the woolly jumper.
● One child, wearing a woolly hat, can be the stigma.
● Four children wearing woolly socks on their hands will be the anthers.
● Four children will need to hold the petals in an open flower shape around the anthers. They should also each hold a bottle of juice.
● Stick the ping-pong balls of one colour to the anthers of one flower, and the ping-pong balls of the other colour to the anthers of the second flower.

3. The 'bee' can start buzzing around and should travel to a flower seeking the nectar, which they can drink. As they do so, the children who are the anthers should put some of their ping-pong balls onto the back of the bee (these should stick onto the woolly jumper).

4. The bee can then 'fly' to the other flower for another drink. The 'anthers' again stick some of their pollen onto the bee, while the stigma takes off some of the pollen from the previous flower and sticks it to their hat.

5. To complete the process, the bee could return to the first flower for a final drink. Again, the anthers transfer some more of their own pollen to the bee and the stigma removes some of the second flower's pollen.

6. At the end of the game, ask the children to discuss what happened and to explain how pollination takes place.

Independent work
7. Back in the classroom, ask the children to draw an annotated drawing to show the process of pollination, using pictures of real flowers.

> **Differentiation**
> ● Some children may need support to complete their annotated drawings; you could provide a wordbank to help them.
> ● Challenge confident learners to annotate their drawings with more detailed, complex comments.

Science in the wider world
The flower produces seeds through sexual reproduction. Pollination is the first part of this process. Bats and birds can act as pollinators as well as bees. In some cases this process can happen in the same flower (self-pollination). When two flowers are involved the process is called cross-pollination.

Review
Through observation and discussion with the children, assess their awareness and understanding of the process of pollination.

Objectives
● To understand that seeds can be dispersed in a variety of ways.

Resources
A variety of seeds and fruits such as beech nuts, acorns, sycamore spinners, burrs; plants such as the cleavers (sometimes known as 'sticky willy'); dandelion flowers at the 'feathery' stage; hand lenses and/or digital microscope(s); photocopiable page 139 'Seed dispersal'

Speaking scientifically
animal dispersal, seed dispersal, wind dispersal

Lesson 3: Seed dispersal

Introduction
Begin the lesson by giving the children a variety of fruits and seeds to handle and look at.

Paired work
1. Give the children a tray containing a selection of the fruits and seeds, together with hand lenses. Encourage the children to think of different ways of grouping the seeds and fruits according to chosen criteria (for example, colour, shape, fruit or seed).

2. Ask the children to group their own seeds and fruits, and then to work with another pair to see if they can decide what criteria were used. (The actual criteria chosen are not overly important here; it is more about the process.)

Whole-class work
3. Bring the children back together and show them a grouping that you have used. This should be based on how the seeds are dispersed.

4. Play a 'yes/no' question game where the children have to ask you questions to find out your sorting criterion. You may want to give some subtle clues before revealing that the criterion is how the seeds are spread.

5. Introduce the idea of seed dispersal. Use your seeds and fruits to show examples of those that disperse in the air (by wind) and those that disperse using animals.

6. Together produce a mind-map of ideas about why seeds might disperse. Ask: *Why is it important that seeds are moved away from the parent plants? What would happen if they were not?*

Paired/Whole-class work
7. Ask the children to return to their own collections and to re-classify them according to how they think the seeds and fruits are dispersed. Let the children handle and re-examine the seeds and fruits as they consider this.

8. Discuss their answers as a class. Where practical, show the children how the dispersal occurs. For example, the sycamore seeds can be dropped so that they spin away, the dandelion 'feathery' seed carriers can be blown, and the burrs can be placed on clothing to show how the seeds are moved.

Independent work
9. Ask the children to complete photocopiable page 139 'Seed dispersal' independently using some of the seeds and fruits they have been examining.

Science in the wider world
Plants need to disperse their seeds away from themselves in order to prevent the young plants growing nearby. This avoids overcrowding and the plants competing for light, water and other resources. Some plants have seeds that are adapted to be carried away on the wind or in water, whilst others are moved by animals. Animal dispersal can be through seeds that fasten themselves onto the coats of certain animals, or through being eaten as part of a fruit and passed through the animal's digestive system.

Review
Assess the children's understanding of seed dispersal through scrutiny of the photocopiable sheets. Identify whether the children have demonstrated an awareness of the two different means of seed dispersal. Can they explain how the seeds are actually transported, and why?

Objectives
• To know the conditions that seeds need to germinate.

Resources
Cress or mung beans (or other fast-germinating seeds); compost; eight small containers per group; sticky labels; photocopiable page 140 'Growing seeds'

Speaking scientifically
conclusion, fair test, observation, prediction, results

Lesson 1: Germination

Introduction
Remind the children of the investigations they have carried out in recent lessons, particularly looking at plants and light, and plants and water. Ask: *What do plants need to grow? Can anybody tell me what effect light has on plants? Why is water important to plants?* Address any misunderstandings that may become apparent as a result of your questions and ask other children to share and discuss their ideas.

Whole-class work
1. Tell the children that they are going to carry out an investigation to find the ideal conditions for germinating seeds. At this stage you may wish to clarify the difference between germination and growth. (Germination is the first stage, where the seed swells, splits and roots and shoots begin to emerge. Growth is the later stage, where leaves have formed and the plant begins to produce food for further development and growth.)

2. Ask the children what they think might be required for seeds to germinate. Encourage discussion of all the possible conditions and list these on the board. Ensure that at the very least your list contains light, water and a suitable temperature (heat).

3. As a class, begin to plan a fair test to investigate the germination of seeds with different amounts of light, heat and water.

4. Ask the children to work out how many different combinations there are and therefore how many samples they will need to grow. They will also need to consider the following: how much water they will give the plants and how often (for example daily, every three days, weekly); where to keep the plants needing light and those needing dark (for example in a store room, on a window sill); where to keep those that need heat or cold (for example in a cold store room, outside, in a fridge).

Group work
5. Provide the resources the children need, and distribute and talk through photocopiable page 140 'Growing seeds'.

6. The children can work in groups of three or four to set up their investigation. Remind them to put sticky labels with their own names, the plant number and the conditions (whether given water, light or warmth) on the pots.

7. The children can use the photocopiable sheets to help them observe and keep a record of what happens in their investigation over the next two weeks. The questions at the end should help them to reach a conclusion.

Science in the wider world
The success of plants is vitally important to humans, since we harvest and use a large range of fruits, vegetables, cereals and grains as food. Many different food crops are grown throughout the world and are a major part of the diets of most of the world's population. It is humankind's general success in growing crops that has allowed us to thrive throughout the world, despite problems in some countries.

Review
During the investigation, try to find time to talk to each child about it individually. Aim to gauge their level of understanding about what they are doing and why. The children's written work should also help to indicate their understanding. They should have been able to keep accurate records of their work, presenting their results and drawing some conclusions that show they understand that seeds that have water, light and heat will grow better. Some may also be able to suggest why.

SCHOLASTIC

Objectives
● To understand the contribution of the work of Maria Sibylla Merian to our understanding of plant life cycles.

Resources
Encyclopaedia or other large reference book; pictures by Maria Sibylla Merian; examples of flowers and plants; hand lenses; digital microscopes and laptops (if available); art materials

Speaking scientifically
illustration, life cycle, observational drawing

Lesson 2: The scientist Maria Sibylla Merian

Introduction
As a visual stimulus, have available an encyclopaedia or other large reference book to show the children. Ask the children to think about how we know so much. Ask: *Where do we get all the information we have from? How do we find out about the world around us? How do we answer the many questions we have?* Encourage the children to think about the ways in which we explore and observe. You might relate this to some of the many programmes they may have seen on television that feature explorers of various kinds.

Whole-class/Independent work
1. Introduce the work of Maria Sibylla Merian by sharing with the children some examples of her work, particularly those featuring plants. Talk about the work she carried out, emphasising that her observations have contributed to our knowledge and understanding of plant life cycles.

2. Encourage the children to look at the examples carefully and to consider how the artist might have been able to make such detailed and careful observations and paintings.

3. Explain to the children that they are going to carry out some observations and attempt to record these in the style of Merian. Ask the children to suggest what media Merian might have used. Why didn't she use photographs to record her observations instead of artwork?

4. Have available a range of wild flowers and plants for the children to look at. They can initially just use the naked eye to look at the flowers and plants, before examining them in more detail using hand lenses or digital microscopes. Remind the children that the purpose of their observation is not to look for something specific, but to make very general observations and learn what they can about the shape, colour and structure of the flower or plant.

5. Encourage the children to make sketches of what they see.

6. Let the children select one of the plants or flowers to draw and paint in detail. You can also provide them with a copy of a Merian illustration so they are able to follow the Merian style. Ask the children to first sketch and then carefully paint their chosen flower or plant. Reinforce the need to be observant. Remind them that they should not paint what they might like to see, but what they actually do see.

Differentiation
● Some of the children will find this activity a challenge, as they will need to exhibit a good level of fine motor skills when making a detailed painting. You may need to support and encourage these children and model the process with them.

Science in the wider world
Maria Sibylla Merian was a naturalist and illustrator who developed her skill as a botanical artist in the 17th century. She was born in Frankfurt in 1647 and spent several years travelling around, carefully and scientifically observing and sketching both plants and animals. She published three collections of her work between 1675 and 1680. Because her work was not published in Latin (the official language of science at the time) it was largely ignored by scientists.

Review
Assess the children's ability to record accurate observations, rather than their artistic style or merit.

Objectives
● To know how to order the life cycles of common plants.

Resources
Children's paintings from the previous lesson; pictures of seeds, seedlings, plants, fruits and dead plants of various species (one species for each group of three or four children); real examples of each of these stages from a particular plant species; photocopiable page 141 'Plant life cycles'; interactive activity 'Life cycles' on the CD-ROM

Speaking scientifically
death, fertilisation, flower, fruit, germination, growth, life cycle, plant, pollination, seed, seed dispersal

Lesson 3: Maria Sibylla Merian investigation (1)

Introduction
Remind the children of the work of Maria Sibylla Merian. Look together at some of the paintings the children completed in the last lesson. Talk about Merian's work on the life cycles of animals and plants. Introduce the idea of plant life cycles. Ask if anyone knows what we mean by a plant life cycle. Encourage the children to discuss their thoughts, ideas and suggestions with talk partners before sharing them with the whole class.

Group work
1. The children should work in groups of three or four. Give each group a set of pictures of the different stages in the life of a plant to study.
2. Ask the children to sort these pictures into the correct order to show the plant's life cycle. Given that this is a life cycle, the children can decide the starting point for themselves.

Whole-class work
3. Bring the class together to talk about the various stages in the plant life cycle. Ask: *What might the correct order be? What happens at each stage?*
4. Ensure that the children have a clear understanding of the stages of seed germination, plant growth, pollination/fertilisation, seed dispersal and plant death. You could demonstrate this by showing the children real examples of each of these stages. You might use seeds, a young plant, a flower (perhaps still on the plant), some fruit and a dead plant. Ask some of the children to hold these to physically create a cycle for the others to see.

Independent work
5. Give out photocopiable page 141 'Plant life cycles'. Ask the children to complete this by drawing and describing the stages in the pictures you gave them for the group work. Reinforce this work further, by using the interactive activity 'Life cycles' on the CD-ROM.

Differentiation
● Allow some learners to concentrate on just drawing the pictures.
● Encourage confident learners to write more complex explanations on their life cycle worksheets.

Science in the wider world
A life cycle progresses through the different stages of development that living things go through from the beginning to the end of their lives. The typical life cycle of a plant would be:
● Seed germination: the point at which the roots and shoots emerge from the seed.
● Growth: the plant begins to produce food and grows and develops into a mature plant.
● Pollination and fertilisation: the process of producing fruit and seeds resulting from the joining together of pollen (the male sex cells) and ovules (the female sex cells).
● Seed dispersal: the seeds are distributed away from the parent plant.
● Death: some plants die after one year of growth (annuals). Others die after two years (biennials), whilst some live for many years (perennials).

Review
Assess the children's work for evidence of their understanding and ability to order the stages in the life cycle of a plant.

Objectives
● To know that after pollination takes place, a fruit is produced that contains seeds.

Resources
A range of fruits (some common and others more unfamiliar and exotic, some whole and others cut in half); hand lenses; access to the internet; books about fruit; knives; bowls; spoons; photocopiable page 142 'Finding fruits'

Speaking scientifically
fruit, life cycle, observation, seed

Lesson 1: Maria Sibylla Merian investigation (2)

Introduction
Ask: *What is a fruit? Where does it come from? What is the fruit for?* The children may talk about fruit being a food, so you might need to focus their attention onto the purpose fruit serves in the life cycle of a plant.

Paired work
1. Give each pair a selection of whole fruits. Tell the children to take it in turns to close their eyes while their partner gives them one of the fruits. Using just their senses of touch and smell, they need to identify the fruit.

2. With their eyes open again, ask: *What shape is the fruit? What colour is it? Does it have a hard shell or a soft skin? Where on the plant do you think it would have grown? If we had not picked the fruit to eat, what do you think might have happened to it?*

3. When both children in each pair have tried this activity, give out some cut fruits so the children can look inside the fruit. Ask: *Is it soft or hard? Is it juicy? What is there inside the fruit other than the flesh?* (Make sure you have chosen fruits that contain seeds.)

4. Ask the children to use hand lenses to make a more careful observation of the inside of the fruit and the seeds. Ask: *Where are the seeds? Are they in the centre or on the outside of the fruit? What shape are the seeds? Are they small or large compared to the size of the fruit?*

Independent work
5. The children should draw and paint a selection of the fruits in the style of Merian. They should paint both the outside and the inside of the fruits, including the seeds.

6. Give children photocopiable page 142 'Finding fruits' to complete. The children should try to name at least one fruit for each letter of the alphabet, before using secondary sources of information such as books and the internet to find out an interesting fact about each one. They may not be able to find a fruit for every letter of the alphabet but for some letters there are several. The most popular is the letter P.

Differentiation
● Some children will need support to locate the seeds on fruits such as raspberries and strawberries.
● Challenge confident learners to name a greater number of fruits independently.

Science in the wider world
Fruits are the seed-bearing parts of a plant. In this lesson you will probably have only used what might be regarded as culinary fruits. Some plant parts that are botanically fruits are regarded in culinary terms as being vegetables – tomatoes, cucumbers and peppers are all actually fruits because they contain seeds. In botanical terms, vegetables are the plants where we eat the leaf, stem or root.

Review
Assess the children's understanding of the role of the fruit in the life cycle of a plant through discussion and observation. Are they able to identify that the fruit contains the seeds of the plant?

Objectives
● To know that different plants are found in different habitats.
● To know that there are reasons why different plants grow in different habitats.

Resources
Hoops; clipboards; adhesive tape; digital cameras (optional); wild plant identification charts; reference books or keys on wild plants; a plan of the area you are surveying

Speaking scientifically
compare, explore, habitat, hoop

Lesson 2: Plant habitats

Introduction

Explain to the children that in this lesson they will be learning about some different plant habitats near school and about the plants that live in them.

Whole-class/Paired work

1. Write descriptions of some local habitats on the board, such as 'Under a large tree', 'In the middle of a field' or 'Under a hedge'. Ask the children to discuss with talk partners the plants that they expect to find in one of these. Ask: *What plants might we expect to find under the tree or in the field? What differences might there be in the plants growing in each place? Why?*

2. Their discussions might raise points such as fewer plants under the tree because it is dark, fewer plants in the school playing field because it is mown and trampled, and so on.

3. Write some of these predictions on the board. Ask: *How could we find out if our predictions are correct?* (We can look.) *How can we ensure we look at the same shape and size of area when comparing the two different locations, to make sure it is fair?* After some discussion, suggest that the children could put a hoop down and look at the plants that are growing inside the hoop.

Paired work

4. Each pair should decide which two habitats to explore. Model for the children a way of recording their observations in a table. Ask them to write down predictions of what they will find and whether they expect any differences between the plants in the two habitats.

5. The children can go outside to investigate the plants in each habitat and record their findings. They could take photos of the location of their habitat and their hoop in place on the ground. Encourage them to identify the plants they find and record them in their table. If they cannot name the plants, they should use identification charts, books or keys to help them.

6. Discuss questions that arise as the children are working, such as: *Do you count the number of flowers, or try to work out if they all belong to one plant? How do you record the number of grass plants?* (You estimate.) *Did you choose where you put your hoop or did you drop it randomly? Which would be fairer?* (Random dropping, so there is no pre-selection of 'interesting bits'.)

Whole-class work

7. Gather together the data on the board to show the number of different species of plants, the number of each of these species, and their locations.

8. Encourage the children to look at the data and draw conclusions. Ask them to write at least a sentence comparing what they found in their two different habitats. You may want to provide a structure for this, for example:

- 'We found _____ in both habitats, but we only found _____ in the _____.
- We think this is because _____.'

9. Encourage the children to compare the different habitats by asking: *Did you find different plants in each habitat? Can you suggest why that might be?*

Science in the wider world

A habitat is a place where a community of organisms lives. It can only support plants (and animals) that are adapted to its conditions.

Review

Can the children record the different plants that they find accurately? Can they make comparisons between the two habitats and suggest reasons for the differences?

■SCHOLASTIC

Objectives
● To understand the relationship between the physical aspects of a habitat and the plants living there.

Resources
Photocopiable page 'Looking at climates' from the CD-ROM; secondary sources of information on plants that grow in different climates

Speaking scientifically
climate, habitat, weather

Lesson 3: Our findings

Introduction
Discuss the weather briefly. Ask the children to sum up what the weather has been like over the past week. *Has it been warm and dry, sunny, wet and windy, or cold?* Ask the children to think about how our weather changes and what happens to plants when it does. Some children will be able to tell you about how in cold weather plants stop growing or die altogether. Ask them why this happens.

Whole-class work
1. Talk about why some plants prefer certain habitats and climates. Introduce the idea that certain climates are not suitable for some plants to grow in at all times of the year and that different plants prefer different climatic conditions.
2. Give examples of climatic conditions with different combinations of heat and moisture levels: hot and dry; hot and wet; cold and dry; cold and wet.

Individual work
3. Give out photocopiable page 'Looking at climates' from the CD-ROM. It provides a simple Carroll diagram on which the children can see the different possible combinations of temperature and moisture. This will help them to identify four examples of environments with these climates.

Paired work
4. In pairs, the children can use secondary sources of information to find out about some of the plants that live in a chosen habitat and climate.
5. Their findings could be presented in a novel way. For example, information about rainforests on paper in the shape of a large tree, research about the poles on paper in the shape of an iceberg, or findings about deserts on paper in the shape of a sand dune.
6. Ask the children to write an estate agent style description of three or four habitats of living things, for example, 'Lots of room here. Bigger than it looks. A bit damp and dark. Would ideally suit a plant that does not like the sun...'

> ### Differentiation
> ● Some children may need support in using secondary sources to help with their ideas.
> ● Challenge confident learners to make greater use of estate agent jargon in their descriptive writing.

Science in the wider world
The climate of a region affects the plants that live there. Different plants are able to thrive in different climates. A number of climatic factors affect living things and their environment. These include temperature, light intensity, rainfall and wind speed. The most influential of all these climatic factors is probably temperature. Generally speaking, living things prefer to inhabit an environment with warm temperatures and a good supply of the resources they need. This is why as you travel from temperate climates to those that are more extreme, like the poles or deserts, there is a marked reduction in the number of different species of living things to be found.

Review
Most children should be able to complete the photocopiable sheet. Discuss their ideas with them in order to gauge the depth of their understanding.

Objectives

● To know that we eat different parts of different plants.
● To introduce the idea that different parts of plants have different functions.
● To understand the ideal conditions for plant growth.

Resources

Photocopiable page 'Plant assessment' from the CD-ROM; interactive activity 'Plant parts' on the CD-ROM; large unlabelled diagram of the different parts of a plant; examples of plants that the children have grown during this topic

Working scientifically

● Asking relevant questions.
● Recording findings using simple scientific language, drawings, labelled diagrams, keys, bar charts, and tables.
● Using results to draw simple conclusions.

Plants

Revise

● On the board, display a large unlabelled diagram showing the different parts of a plant. Ask the children to identify these plant parts and to explain the function of each one. Talk about the important role that each part plays in keeping the plant healthy.
● Ask the children to talk about how they could identify a plant that was unhealthy. What would be some of the signs? Possible answers might include: leaves in poor condition; the plant not growing; or the stem wilting and not holding the plant upright.
● Ask the children to talk about some of the foods they have eaten recently and whether each food was plant-based or animal-based. Encourage the children to recall that most of our food is derived from plants.

Assess

● Show the children some of the plants that they have grown during this topic. Ask them to think about the different factors that have led to these plants germinating and growing as they have. Can they see and identify the different parts of the plant on these plants as they did for the plant on the board?
● Give the children photocopiable page 'Plant assessment' from the CD-ROM and ask them to complete it. This will allow you to assess their overall knowledge of the topic, including the functions of the different parts of a plant, what plants need to stay healthy, and the role of plants in providing us with food.
● Let the children engage with the interactive activity 'Plant parts' from the CD-ROM.

Further practice

● Engage the children in discussions and ensure that they are able to verbally explain their understanding of the different parts of plants and their functions.

Objectives

- To understand the process of pollination in plants and the role of flowers in that process.
- To understand that seeds can be dispersed in a variety of ways.
- To know the conditions that seeds need to germinate.
- To know how to order the life cycles of common plants.
- To know that after pollination takes place, a fruit is produced that contains seeds.

Resources

Pictures of seeds, seedlings, plants, flowers, pollination (such as bees), fruit and seed dispersal

Working scientifically

- Gathering, recording, classifying and presenting data in a variety of ways to help in answering questions.
- Recording findings using simple scientific language, drawings, labelled diagrams, keys, bar charts, and tables.

The life cycle of a plant

Revise

- Use a variety of pictures that show seeds, germination, seedlings, plant growth, pollination, fruit and seed dispersal to encourage the children to revisit many of the stages in the plant life cycle that they have considered in this topic.
- Let the children work in groups of three or four. Give each group one of the stages in a plant life cycle and ask the children to create a short role play or dramatised scene that illustrates their particular stage. The children can also prepare a narration for their scene with one of the children acting as the narrator.
- Ask the class to share their role plays in the order of the plant life cycle.
- Ensure that the children have a clear understanding of: seed germination (including the factors that can affect whether it takes place); plant growth (including some of the factors that can affect this); pollination (for example how bees move from flower to flower and transfer pollen as they collect nectar); the production of fruit and seeds; and seed dispersal (this is covered in more detail in the next assessment activity).

Assess

- Show the children the pictures that you used earlier. They should work together to put these in the correct order to show a plant life cycle.
- Ask the children to draw their own series of annotated drawings in the form of a cartoon strip or storyboard to illustrate the life cycle of a plant from germination to dying. If you wish, you could make reference to the work of Maria Sibylla Merian here and encourage some children to adopt her style.
- Ensure that the children have ordered their drawings correctly based on a starting point of the seed.

Further practice

- Engage the children in further work on plant life cycles. Although the focus so far has been on plant reproduction through pollination and seed production, you could begin to develop the children's understanding of some other ways in which plant life cycles progress. For example, some plants (such as strawberries) reproduce by sending out 'runners', which root themselves and then become detached from the parent plant. Others can be reproduced by taking cuttings of stems or leaves, which then root and grow independently as a new plant. The children could explore and investigate some of these through practical activities.

Objectives
• To know that after pollination takes place, a fruit is produced that contains seeds.
• To understand that seeds can be dispersed in a variety of ways.

Resources
Examples of seeds that are dispersed in different ways (real or photographs); 'junk' modelling materials

Working scientifically
• Gathering, recording, classifying and presenting data in a variety of ways to help in answering questions.
• Recording findings using simple scientific language, drawings, labelled diagrams, keys, bar charts, and tables.

Seed dispersal

Revise

• Use the seeds or photographs of seeds to revisit the idea of seed dispersal. Ask the children to recall the different ways in which seeds can be dispersed.
• Ask the children to share their understanding with a talk partner.
• Share the children's ideas as a class in order to consolidate their understanding that seeds are usually dispersed by animals or the wind.

Assess

• Ask the children to work individually and imagine that they have been exploring a previously unknown island and have discovered a new species of plant.
• Ask them to use their understanding of plants to draw and colour a picture of their new plant. They need to think particularly about the leaves, flowers and seeds of their plant, in addition to its overall size and shape.
• The children should then name their plant. This name might be based on the features of the plant, where it was found, its similarity to other plants, the conditions it lives in or their own names.
• Next ask the children to design and make a model of the seed that their plant produces. They need to think about how the seed would be dispersed away from the parent plant. Does it have features that would allow it to roll away, to be carried on the wind, or to float? Is the fruit attractive to animals so they might eat it and so consume the seed? Might it have some sort of hook mechanism to attach itself to the coat of an animal? They should use 'junk' modelling materials and paints to build a model (not to scale) of their seed. The junk materials you need to make available should be chosen to give the children an opportunity to develop their ideas.
• Gather the children together and ask each child to share their new species and the model of the seed. Ask them to explain the seed design and how it links to the method of seed dispersal.

Further practice

• You could look at a wild area of land to see if it is possible to identify patterns in the plants growing there that indicate how their seeds are dispersed. For example, a species that has berries (such as hawthorn) might grow some distance from the next-nearest example of this same species. A collection of wind-borne seeds might have settled against a wall and germinated in a corner, or a water-borne seed might have germinated alongside the water following a rise and fall in water levels.

Food sources

■ List some plant-based foods in the first column of the table below. For each one, say which part(s) of the plant we eat. There is an example shown below.

Name of food	Part of the plant that we eat
Carrots	Roots

I can identify which parts of plants we eat.

Name: _____   Date: _____

Plant parts (1)

- Look carefully at the plant in front of you.
- Draw it in the box on the right.
- Label these parts of the plant:

roots

stem

leaves

- Each part of the plant has a special job to do.
- Match the part of the plant with its job.

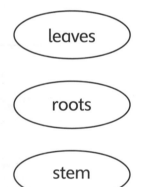

leaves

roots

stem

| These take water into the plant from the soil. |

| These are where the plant makes its food. |

| This keeps the plant upright. |

- One of these plant parts has another job. Which one is it and what does it do?

_____

_____

_____

I can explain the functions of different parts of a plant.

PHOTOCOPIABLE   ■ SCHOLASTIC
www.scholastic.co.uk

Name: _____   Date: _____

Plant parts (2)

■ You are going to carry out an investigation to show that water is carried up the roots of a plant. Use your weed, beaker, cling film and water to set up your investigation as shown in this diagram.

■ Why is it important to put a seal around the top of your beaker?

_____

_____

_____

Now put your plant in a safe place and record the water level every day, starting with today.

Date	Days after start	Water level
Difference between first and last water levels		

■ What has happened to the water level?

_____

■ Why do you think this has happened?

_____

I can carry out and record an investigation.

Name: _____   Date: _____

Growing seeds in different soils

- You are going to grow some cress seeds in two different soils.
- Put different types of soil into each of the two pots. Label them A and B.
- Sprinkle the seeds onto the soil and gently press them in.
- Water the seeds carefully before putting the pots on a window sill.
Make sure you give each the same amount of water.
- Draw a storyboard to show what you have done so far.

- Keep an eye on the seeds, water them regularly and equally.
- Predict in which soil the seeds will grow the best and why.

_____

_____

- Draw a storyboard of the pots as the cress grows.

A	A	A
B	B	B

I can carry out and record an investigation.

PHOTOCOPIABLE   **SCHOLASTIC**
www.scholastic.co.uk

Seed dispersal

■ Choose three seeds or fruits that are dispersed either by wind or by animals. Answer these questions for each one.

1. Draw pictures of your three chosen fruits/seeds in the boxes below and write their names underneath.

2. How is each seed dispersed? Draw a more detailed picture to show how each seed is dispersed. Write underneath either "wind dispersal" or "animal dispersal".

3. Write a sentence to explain how this helps each seed to be dispersed.

_____

4. Explain why it is important that seeds are dispersed away from the parent plant. What would happen if all the young plants tried to grow in the same place?

_____

_____

I can explain how some seeds are dispersed.

Name: _____   Date: _____

Growing seeds

■ Use this table to record the conditions that your plant will be kept in.

Plant number	Water?	Light?	Heat?
1			
2			
3			
4			

■ Use the table below to keep record of how well your plants are growing.
■ You may want to draw or write your observations down. You may be able to measure the growth of your plants.

Plant	Day 1	Day 2	Day 3	Day 4	Day 5
1					
2					
3					
4					
Plant	Day 6	Day 7	Day 8	Day 9	Day 10
1					
2					
3					
4					

■ As you observe plants what do you begin to notice?
■ Remember to write down everything that is happening in your diary.
■ At the end of two weeks what has happened?
■ Write down which of your plants has grown the best. What do you think this tells us about the conditions that this plant was kept in?

I can make scientific observations and record them.

How did you do?

Plant life cycles

■ In the spaces draw pictures of each stage of the life cycle of a plant. Write a sentence to explain what happens at each stage.

I can describe the life cycle of a plant.

How did you do?

Finding fruits

■ Are there fruits that begin with each letter of the alphabet? See if you can find one fruit for each letter, then use books or the internet to find one interesting fact about each fruit.

	Fruit	Interesting fact
A		
B		
C		
D		
E		
F		
G		
H		
I		
J		
K		
L		
M		
N		
O		
P		
Q		
R		
S		
T		
U		
V		
W		
X		
Y		
Z		

I can name a variety of fruits.

How did you do?

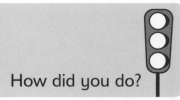

Rocks

Expected prior learning
- Distinguish between an object and the material from which it is made.
- Identify and name a variety of everyday materials, including wood, plastic, glass, metal, water and rock; and to compare and group them together.
- Compare and group together a variety of everyday materials.
- Identify and compare the uses of a variety of everyday materials, including wood, plastic, glass, metal, brick/rock and paper/cardboard.

Overview of progression
In this chapter children will learn:
- to compare and group together different types of rocks on the basis of their simple physical properties
- to relate the simple physical properties of some rocks to their formation
- to describe in simple terms how fossils are formed when things that have lived are trapped within sedimentary rock
- to know that there are different types of soil
- to understand the scientific reasoning behind decisions to use particular materials in particular ways.

Creative context
- This chapter provides opportunities to write creatively and make models.

Background knowledge
Rock is classified according to how it was formed, millions of years ago:
- Igneous rocks (granite) formed from molten material during volcanic eruptions and make up nearly 95% of the Earth's crust.
- Sedimentary rocks (sandstone, limestone) make up about 5% of the Earth's crust and formed when sediment settled and became compressed.
- Metamorphic rocks are made from igneous and sedimentary rocks that underwent changes due to heat or pressure.
Soil is a mixture of tiny pieces of rock and decaying plants. This decaying vegetation becomes a substance called 'humus'. The humus sticks all the particles together and absorbs water. Different types of soil are produced depending on the rock types under an area.

Speaking scientifically
Children should be familiar with the terms: material, property, hard, soft, transparent, translucent, smooth, rough, chalk, granite, limestone, sandstone, slate, igneous, metamorphic, sedimentary, permeable, impermeable, archaeology, fossil, sediment, layer, pressure, renewable, non-renewable, core, mantle, crust, humus, particle, clay, sandy, chalky, peaty, germinate.

Preparation
You will need to provide: rock samples; soil samples; hand lenses; digital microscopes; digital cameras; clipboards; laptops; various pots, beakers and trays; art materials; an unusual/old object; a roofing slate; selection of everyday objects/materials; pipettes; gloves; sandpaper; nails; secondary information sources; plastic cups; tank; modelling material; old artefacts/documents/pictures; pictures of rock uses, archaeological digs, the Earth from space, rock formations and volcanoes; sand; pasta shells; rice paper; leaves; shells; twigs; fossils; plastic cubes; plaster of Paris; papier-mâché; plastic bugs/dinosaurs; coal; plastic bottles; newspaper; muslin; elastic bands; sieves; worms; compost; saucers; bin liners; ping-pong balls; sticky notes; food colouring; bottle of sparkling water; vinegar; bicarbonate of soda; crushed rock; trowels; flour; gravel; stones; books; construction materials; wafer biscuits; honeycomb candy

On the CD-ROM you will find: interactive activities 'Materials', 'Rocks and soils', 'Types of rock'; media resource 'Volcano'

Chapter at a glance

Week	Lesson	Curriculum objectives	Objectives	Main activity	Working scientifically
1	1	• (Y2) To identify and compare the suitability of a variety of everyday materials including wood, metal, plastic, glass, brick, rock, paper and cardboard for particular uses. • To compare and group together different kinds of rock.	• To review a range of everyday materials. • To revise how materials are used. • To understand a range of simple properties of materials. • To introduce the concept that there are different types of rock.	Reviewing Year 2 work on the uses of everyday materials. Identify a variety of everyday materials such as wood, metal, plastic, glass, brick/ rock and paper/ cardboard.	• Reporting on findings from enquiries, including oral and written explanations, displays or presentations of results and conclusions. • Asking relevant questions.
	2	• To compare and group together different kinds of rocks on the basis of their appearance and simple physical properties.	• To consider a range of different rocks.	Observing, examining, naming and sorting rock samples.	• Identifying differences, similarities or changes related to simple scientific ideas and processes.
	3	• To compare and group together different kinds of rocks on the basis of their appearance and simple physical properties.	• To learn about the ways in which humans use rocks.	Identifying ways in which rocks are used, for example as a construction material on buildings, walls and roads. Concept mapping and drawing uses of rocks.	• Identifying differences, similarities or changes related to simple scientific ideas and processes.
2	1	• To compare and group together different kinds of rocks on the basis of their appearance and simple physical properties.	• To know that rocks can be tested to see how hard-wearing they are.	Comparing rock samples for wear by rubbing. Ranking rocks by how hard-wearing they are.	• Identifying differences, similarities or changes related to simple scientific ideas and processes.
	2	• To compare and group together different kinds of rocks on the basis of their appearance and simple physical properties.	• To know that rocks can be tested for their permeability.	Comparing rock samples for permeability by dripping water.	• Setting up simple practical enquiries, comparative and fair tests. • Gathering, recording, classifying and presenting data in a variety of ways to help in answering questions.
	3	• To compare and group together different kinds of rocks on the basis of their appearance and simple physical properties.	• To know that rocks are used for particular purposes because of their properties.	Going on a 'rock trail' around the school or the neighbourhood to identify the ways in which rocks have been used because of their characteristics.	• Identifying differences, similarities or changes related to simple scientific ideas and processes.
3	1	• To describe in simple terms how fossils are formed when things that have lived are trapped within rock.	• To know what fossils are. • To understand how fossils can be used to help us learn about the past.	Looking at different types of fossils and examining the patterns and shapes created.	• Gathering, recording, classifying and presenting data in a variety of ways to help in answering questions.
	2	• To describe in simple terms how fossils are formed when things that have lived are trapped within rock.	• To know how fossils are formed.	Looking at how fossils are formed from animal and plant remains. Making reproduction fossils using modelling materials.	• Gathering, recording, classifying and presenting data in a variety of ways to help in answering questions.
	3	• To describe in simple terms how fossils are formed when things that have lived are trapped within rock.	• To know what is meant by a fossil fuel. • To understand that fossil fuels are non-renewable.	Looking at how we use fossil fuels (such as oil, coal and gas) and showing that they are non-renewable and will run out one day.	• Gathering, recording, classifying and presenting data in a variety of ways to help in answering questions.

Chapter at a glance

Week	Lesson	Curriculum objectives	Objectives	Main activity	Working scientifically
4	1	• To compare and group together different kinds of rocks on the basis of their appearance and simple physical properties.	• To understand, in simple terms, some of James Hutton's ideas about geology.	Introducing the work of James Hutton, the 'father of geology'.	• Gathering, recording, classifying and presenting data in a variety of ways to help in answering questions.
	2	• To compare and group together different kinds of rocks on the basis of their appearance and simple physical properties.	• To understand the structure of the Earth's crust.	Creating a model of the Earth's structure.	• Reporting on findings from enquiries, including oral and written explanations, displays or presentations of results and conclusions.
	3	• To compare and group together different kinds of rocks on the basis of their appearance and simple physical properties.	• To understand what volcanoes are and how they are formed. • To know that igneous rocks are formed from volcanic lava.	Looking at and modelling volcanoes.	• Gathering, recording, classifying and presenting data in a variety of ways to help in answering questions.
5	1	• To recognise that soils are made from rocks and organic matter.	• To know that soil lies on top of rock. • To know that there are different kinds of soil.	Learning how soil is formed. Describing soil samples using secondary sources.	• Gathering, recording, classifying and presenting data in a variety of ways to help in answering questions.
	2	• To recognise that soils are made from rocks and organic matter.	• To know that different soils have different sized particles and colours.	Mixing soil with water and observing settlement. Discussing the layers of different soil samples.	• Asking relevant questions. • Setting up simple practical enquiries, comparative and fair tests. • Gathering, recording, classifying and presenting data in a variety of ways to help in answering questions.
	3	• To recognise that soils are made from rocks and organic matter.	• To know that rocks of different sizes can be separated by sieving.	Devising ways of separating and grading particles of different sizes.	• Setting up simple practical enquiries, comparative and fair tests.
6	1	• To compare and group together different kinds of rocks on the basis of their appearance and simple physical properties.	• To understand the scientific reasoning behind decisions to use particular materials in particular ways.	Explore a range of stories in which the properties of materials are drawn upon, such as Three Little Pigs.	• Asking relevant questions.
	2	• To compare and group together different kinds of rocks on the basis of their appearance and simple physical properties.	• To understand the reasoning behind decisions to use particular materials in particular ways.	Use some of the stories from the previous lesson to create physical models to demonstrate the use of appropriate materials.	• Recording findings using simple scientific language, drawings, labelled diagrams, keys, bar charts, and tables.
	3	• To compare and group together different kinds of rocks on the basis of their appearance and simple physical properties.	• To understand how igneous and sedimentary rocks are formed. • To be able to relate the simple properties of rocks to their formation.	Looking at rock formation and properties using confectionary as a model.	• Recording findings using simple scientific language, drawings, labelled diagrams, keys, bar charts, and tables.
Assess and review					

Objectives
● To review a range of everyday materials.
● To revise how materials are used.
● To understand a range of simple properties of materials.
● To introduce the concept that there are different types of rock.

Resources
An unusual or old object (see Introduction for suitable examples); a selection of small, everyday objects or samples of materials made from wood, metal, plastic, glass, rock and paper; photocopiable page 168 'Materials'; interactive activity 'Materials' on the CD-ROM

Speaking scientifically
hard, material, opaque, property, rough, smooth, soft, translucent, transparent

Lesson 1: Everyday materials

Introduction
Bring into the classroom an unusual or old object that the children are unlikely to recognise, or something that has changed over recent years. Suitable objects could be a vinyl record, a flat iron or a chamber pot! Ask the children to look at the object and then tell you what they think the item is/was used for. Discuss how they identified the object – which senses did they use?

Paired work
1. Present the children with a selection of samples of materials. Ask them to tell you how they would identify each material. Talk about how they find out anything about the world around them. Encourage the children to recall the senses they would use in identifying an unknown material – sight and touch mainly.

2. Distribute photocopiable page 168 'Materials' and tell the children that they are going to use their senses to identify a range of materials around the school that have been used to make particular objects. They should then go out and survey the chosen area to complete the photocopiable sheet. When they have completed their survey, ask the children to think about how they knew, or what helped them to decide, what an object was made from.

3. Ask the children to work in pairs to complete the interactive activity 'Materials' on the CD-ROM.

Whole-class work
4. Recap on how the children identified the various materials, then ask: *How would you tell the difference between two different people?* Begin to introduce the children to the idea that just as humans have certain characteristics that make them who they are, so too materials have certain 'properties'.

5. Explore this further by asking: *How would you tell the difference between two different materials? We use our senses to help us identify materials, but how do we sort one material from another? How do we know that what we are touching is glass or plastic?*

6. Let the children again observe and handle the selection of materials you have provided. Talk about the properties of those materials, asking the children to describe them as: hard or soft; opaque, transparent or translucent; and smooth or rough. You may like to keep the number of properties limited at this stage (depending on the ability of your class), as too many could lead to confusion. Compile a list of properties that the children could use in describing materials.

7. Look at a variety of the objects the children identified in their survey. Ask the children to suggest sensible reasons why each object was made from that material. Ask them to suggest alternative materials that could have been used and explain their choices. Then ask them to suggest materials that would be unsuitable, again explaining why they are unsuitable. Does the place where the object is used affect the choice of materials it is made from? For example, you could ask: *Why are our chairs made from metal or plastic and not finely carved wood?*

8. Play a sorting game with the materials you have provided. You sort the materials by an unknown criterion and let the children ask questions to determine the criterion. Some of the children could have a turn at choosing the criterion and playing this with the rest of the class, before you present a set where the criterion is rock.

Introducing the new area of study

Ask the children to talk with a talk partner about all the things they know about rocks. They should start to discuss some of the different types of rocks they know. These can be recorded as a simple list.

As you begin to introduce this new area of study, you may wish to consider some of the misconceptions children may hold in relation to the topic of rocks. Some children may think that all hard materials that are similar to rocks, such as bricks and concrete, are actually rocks. They may also have some misunderstandings linked to size, assuming that rocks are large and that because stones are small they are not rocks. Some children may also think that all rocks are the same.

Science in the wider world

No matter how we choose to classify different materials, it is important to remember that all materials ultimately come from the natural resources of the Earth. This may be either in a form that makes them useful immediately, like wood, or as a raw material used in the production of other materials, such as oil for plastics.

Review

All the children should know that they use their senses to help them identify materials, and which senses are most often used. Most should be able to complete the activities and identify the uses of these materials.

Objectives
● To consider a range of different rocks.

Resources
A selection of rock samples, including small and large pieces of similar rocks, with their names written on cards (rock kits containing samples of sandstone, limestone, marble, granite, chalk and slate are available from Hardy Aggregates, www.hardy-aggregates. co.uk); secondary sources of information about rocks; internet access

Speaking scientifically
chalk, granite, igneous, limestone, marble, metamorphic, sandstone, sedimentary, slate

Lesson 2: Types of rock

Introduction

Show the children a selection of different rock samples and ask them if they know where rocks come from. Discuss whether rocks are artificial or natural. Ask for suggestions of some ways in which rocks are used. Introduce to the children the idea that rocks are part of the structure of the Earth and that they are a natural material.

Group work

1. Divide the children into groups of about four and give each group a selection of rock samples to look at and touch. Ask the children to describe the rock samples using characteristics such as: size of particles (or grains) – none, tiny, small or large; shape of particles – angular or smooth and round; colour – black, white, grey, pink, green or yellow; appearance – shiny or dull; texture – rough or smooth. Create a class table of their observations.

2. Now put the name labels with the correct larger rock samples, and associate the characteristics from the children's descriptions with the different rock types.

3. Using the labelled rocks to reinforce the variety of distinguishing characteristics, ask the children to identify some similar small rock samples. Ask them to group the rocks by considering their characteristics. The children can record their work by drawing carefully coloured observational sketches of their rock samples, naming them, and (depending on their ability) writing a brief description of one or more of the rock samples.

Whole-class work

4. Bring the children back together to share the results of the sorting and sketching activities they have done.

5. Introduce the idea that there are three main rock types: igneous, sedimentary and metamorphic. Sort the rock samples you have been using into these three types.

Independent work

6. Ask the children to use secondary sources to find out more about the three rock types: igneous, sedimentary and metamorphic. They can present their findings as a 'rock factfile', or mounted on to coloured rocks that are either painted stones or papier-mâché rocks. These can be used to form a 'mountain' as a display.

> **Differentiation**
> ● Some children may need to restrict their research to a few basic facts about one or two rock types.
> ● Challenge confident learners to research in more detail and find different examples of each rock type.

Science in the wider world

Rocks are widely used for building and a walk around any town will provide plenty of examples. Towns are often characterised by the colour of the local stone used for their buildings: pink or grey mottled granite, red-brown sandstone, or white or yellow limestone, for example. There are many different types of rock that can be identified by looking at factors such as colour, texture and hardness.

Review

Assess the children's work for evidence of their ability to recognise the different samples of rock. Most should be able to recognise the majority of the samples having studied the bigger pieces; the most confident learners should be able to recognise them all.

Objectives
● To learn about the ways in which humans use rocks.

Resources
A3 paper for concept maps; samples of rocks (from the previous lesson, with the addition of some 'shaped' examples if possible – see Introduction); secondary sources of information on how rocks are used; pictures showing how rocks are used in building or for artistic/decorative purposes; interactive activity 'Rocks and soils' on the CD-ROM

Speaking scientifically
property, rock type

Lesson 3: Uses of rocks

Introduction
Begin by letting the children look at and handle the rock samples from the previous lesson. Try to supplement these with some samples that have been shaped in some way, such as a roof slate. Alternatively, give the children some pictures as a comparison. Encourage the children to look carefully at the materials both in their raw state and after they have been altered so we can make use of them.

Whole-class work
1. Ask the children to think about some of the ways in which rock is used – for example, as a construction material in buildings, walls and roads. The children may also be able to identify other uses for rocks, such as for decorative or artistic purposes and in garden features.

2. You may want to explain how some rocks are modified, worked or changed before they are used. Concrete, for example, is a mixture of sand, cement and gravel. It is not itself a rock but is clearly made using rocks. This is a good starting point for discussion.

Paired work
3. The children can work in pairs to complete the interactive activity 'Rocks and soils' on the CD-ROM.

Group work
4. In groups of three or four, the children should discuss what they know about rocks and draw a concept map based on their initial thoughts. Encourage them to share all they know about rocks and soils with each other, including the uses of rocks. They should write down some of the key words and phrases they use in their concept maps.

5. Avoid correcting any misconceptions at this stage, since it is important that the children feel free to air all their ideas. Try to ensure that they make links between some of their words and phrases to establish concepts and ideas. This could also be done using one of the many concept-mapping software packages that are available.

6. When the concept maps are complete, the children should work in their groups to make an annotated drawing showing some uses of rocks. Some children may be able to find out more about different types of rock and how they are used by carrying out research.

Differentiation
● Most children should be able to record their ideas using a simple concept map. When drawing their concept maps, some children could use pre-prepared words, cards or pictures to simplify the process.
● Challenge others to develop more complex links between words and phrases.

Science in the wider world
Depending on their composition, rocks are used for a variety of purposes such as building and landscaping. Many rocks used in the construction of buildings are extremely hard-wearing. There are numerous examples of historic buildings that are many hundreds of years old and that were often built using locally quarried rock.

Review
Share and discuss the concept maps, encouraging children to ask questions and make suggestions in order to gauge their understanding. Begin to group the ways in which rocks are used and discuss criteria for these categories.

Objectives
● To know that rocks can be tested to see how hard-wearing they are.

Resources
A rock selection with samples ranging from soft to hard; sandpaper; nails; hand lenses; photocopiable pages 169 and 170 'Rock investigation'

Speaking scientifically
hard, rough, scratch, smooth, soft

Lesson 1: Rock rubbing test

Introduction
Talk with the children about some of the reasons they gave for using particular materials for particular purposes when carrying out their materials survey (see page 146). Establish an understanding that we choose certain rocks for certain uses because of their properties. Ask the children to talk with a partner about the properties of rocks. Get them to share their ideas and list these on the board. Ensure that the list includes: weather-proof, hard-wearing, rigid, hard, can be shaped, and so on. Rock is used because it is hard-wearing.

Whole-class work
1. Tell the children that they are going to carry out an investigation to find out how hard-wearing some different rocks are. Explain that they will need to compare different rock samples to see how easily they are worn away.

2. Ask the children to decide how they might carry out their investigation. Encourage them towards an understanding that to test for wear some repeated action such as rubbing or scratching needs to be used.

Paired work
3. Before the children begin, ask them to examine the rock samples and predict which will be the most and most hard-wearing. Ask the children to place the samples in order based on the look and feel of the samples.

4. Try to ensure that all pairs carry out a 'scratch test' or 'rubbing test' to compare how easily the samples can be marked or ground down. They could rub each rock sample the same number of times with a piece of sandpaper, or use a nail to scratch each rock the same number of times. They must try to do this in the same place each time and with the same force. They should use the hand lenses to carry out observations before the test and again after.

5. Ask the children to record their investigation on photocopiable pages 169 and 170 'Rock investigation' using annotated observational drawings.

Whole-class work
6. Bring the children back together to share their findings. Ask: *Which of the rock samples was most easily worn or scratched? Which would be the most hard-wearing? How does this compare to your predictions?*

7. Ask the children to draw some conclusions from what they have found out. Encourage discussion about how this information could be used to decide on suitable uses for each rock. (For example, a cobbled road would need a very hard-wearing rock.)

Differentiation
● Some children may need extra support in developing a suitable plan.

Science in the wider world
Rock is made from chemicals called minerals. It is the hardness of these minerals that determines how easily the rock is worn away. The Mohs Scale is used for the hardness of minerals. These range from the softest (talc), which can be scratched with a fingernail, to the hardest (diamond). This explains why diamonds are used in the tips of drills to bore through other rocks in mining and tunnelling.

Review
All children should be able to identify properties such as hard, soft, and so on. Most should be able to look at examples of materials and list some of their properties. Some will be able to use that information to group materials by property in increasingly sophisticated ways.

Objectives
- To know that rocks can be tested for their permeability.

Resources
A selection of rock samples, some permeable (such as pumice, chalk, sandstone) and some impermeable (such as flint, granite, slate); a roofing slate; pipettes; water; plastic cups; a range of papers, such as blotting paper, kitchen paper, writing paper, glossy paper (optional)

Speaking scientifically
chalk, flint, granite, impermeable, permeable, pipettes, pumice, sandstone, slate

Lesson 2: Rock permeability

Introduction
Begin the lesson by re-capping the properties of the rock samples that the children have already looked at. The idea of permeability is likely to be new to the children and is not a property they would identify through observation. Ask the children to think about some of the uses of rocks they have looked at. Show them the roofing slate and ask them what they think it might be used for and why. Encourage them to identify that slate is a rock that will not let water pass through it. Introduce the words *permeable* and *impermeable*. Explain that permeable rocks let water through and that impermeable ones do not.

Paired work
1. Tell the children that they are going to test a variety of rock samples for permeability – that is, whether they let water through or not. They will do this by dropping small amounts of water onto the samples and observing how quickly the water is absorbed, if at all.

2. If you think it would be useful for your class, they could try this using different types of paper first to help develop their understanding of permeability.

3. Let the children handle the rock samples before sorting them into two groups, permeable and impermeable, as a way of making a simple prediction.

4. Working in pairs, the children should drop five drops of water onto each rock sample using a pipette. They should observe and record the results in a table they devise for themselves. This should enable them to identify permeable and impermeable rocks.

5. As a second test for permeability, give each pair two plastic cups. Ask them to take one of the rocks that they think is permeable and one that they think is impermeable and to place them in a plastic cup each. They should then cover the rocks with water and observe what happens.

6. Tell the children to watch for any bubbles that might be coming from the rock samples. (They must observe very carefully, as some bubbles may actually be coming from the surface of the rock and not from the inside.) The rocks that release bubbles are permeable (let water through) and the ones that don't are impermeable (don't let water through). The children can then repeat this test with the other rock samples.

Whole-class work
7. Bring the class back together again and ask the children to share their findings and explain which rocks were permeable and which were impermeable.

8. Ask if anyone can explain why some rocks released bubbles. Explain that the rocks that released bubbles have spaces between the grains that make up the rock. These spaces hold air. When the rock is placed in water, the air is forced out of the spaces and rises to the surface. These are the rocks that will let water through (because of the spaces) and so they are permeable. In the other rocks there are no spaces, so bubbles are not released and they are not permeable.

Science in the wider world
Rocks are used in a variety of ways depending on their permeability. Clay (which is used to line reservoirs and in the making of pottery) and slate (which is used in roofing) are impermeable, whereas chalk allows water to pass through it and is a permeable rock. In the natural world, underground reservoirs of water are often found in areas of sandstone because it too is a permeable rock.

Review
Look for evidence in the children's investigation work that they have understood the two types of rock and that the property of permeability can be tested.

Objectives
● To know that rocks are used for particular purposes because of their properties.

Resources
Clipboards; a pre-determined route for a 'Rock Trail'; digital cameras; appropriate numbers of adult helpers; examples of small rock samples from previous lessons

Speaking scientifically
identification, property, rock type, survey

Lesson 3: Rock trail

Introduction
Remind the children about previous lessons. Ask them to recall the three main types of rock. Use the rock samples from previous lessons to reinforce the children's ability to identify them. Ask the children to remember some of the ways we use rocks and compile a list. Ask if all rock types can be used in all these different ways. Establish that this is not so and that we select specific rocks for particular uses. Explain to the children that they are going to go on a 'Rock Trail' to see if they can find out how different rocks are used depending on their properties.

Whole-class work
1. With adequate support and preparation, take the children on a 'Rock Trail'. Walk around the school or local area to identify how rocks are used and the characteristics these rocks have that determine their use. For example, particular types of rock are used in building walls, or on roads. Others are used for decorative purposes.

2. Use the rock samples to help the children identify which rocks have been used. Some of the uses are quite obvious, since the rock has only been shaped and is used in its pure form. Other uses are less obvious, as the rock may have been turned into a different material.

3. Talk with the children initially about uses of rock that are clearly seen. Ask them to write down examples of uses of rock in buildings, roads and pavements, and decoration. They should try to give reasons why the rocks were chosen for these purposes.

4. If you have access to digital cameras, ask some children to record their observations by taking photographs.

Group work
5. Back in the classroom, ask the children to work in groups of four to prepare their findings ready to share with the class. Suggest some different methods they could use, for example: pictures on a map; drawings of a street scene; an ICT presentation using digital photos taken.

6. Whichever method is used, ensure that the children consider why each of the rock types was used for each purpose.

Differentiation
● Ask children who need support to find just one example of rock use in a building, a road or pavement, and a decorative item, and suggest reasons for its use.
● Challenge confident learners to find three or four examples of each and also to try to identify the rock type.

Science in the wider world
Rocks are used for a variety of purposes, largely in the construction of buildings and roads. Many rocks have distinctive characteristics that make them appropriate for use in very specific ways. For example, sandstone and flint are often used in buildings and walls, and marble for statues, monuments and fireplaces. However, there are a number of other building materials that are manufactured from different kinds of rock. Brick, concrete and plaster are all derived from rocks, as are glass and ceramics.

Review
Through scrutiny of their work and via questioning and discussion, assess the children's understanding that rocks are used for specific purposes due to their characteristics. Ask: *Can you tell me which rock is good for building walls? Why is that rock used? Why not other rocks?*

Objectives
● To know what fossils are.
● To understand how fossils can be used to help us learn about the past.

Resources
A selection of different fossils (search online for one of the many stockists); hand lenses or digital microscopes; art materials; a collection of old artefacts, documents or photographs (see Introduction); pictures of an archaeological dig

Speaking scientifically
archaeology, fossil, preserve

Lesson 1: Fossils

Introduction
Ask the children to think about how we know about the past. Try to ensure that you make this relevant to the children by asking them how they know what their town or city was like 10, 20 or more years ago. Encourage them to identify some of the different types of evidence that we have, for example, photographs, films and videos, documents, word of mouth and artefacts.

Whole-class work
1. Ask the children how we know about life further back in time. Introduce the idea of archaeology and how digging in the ground can unearth evidence of how we lived many hundreds of years ago. Share some pictures with the children that show how the remains of ancient villages and settlements have been revealed.

2. Take the children even further back in time by asking them how we know about the creatures that lived many thousands and millions of years ago. Introduce the idea of fossils to the children.

Paired work
3. Let the children work in pairs to look at some of the fossils that you have provided using hand lenses or digital microscopes. At this stage, the children do not need to be able to identify the fossils (there are many different types) but simply understand what they are.

4. Ask the children what they think the fossils are made from and to share their ideas in their pairs.

5. Tell the children to work with another pair to group their fossils according to some observable features. For example, they might choose the shape, colour or texture of the fossil, or whether it looks like a fossil of a plant or animal.

Independent work
6. Give the children some art materials and let them make some observational sketches of a selection of the fossils. Encourage them to look carefully at the patterns in the fossils and to replicate these on their sketches.

Whole-class work
7. Bring the children back together again to share their sketches.

8. Ask them what they know about the fossils after studying them carefully for their sketches. What do they think the fossils are made from? What do the patterns on the fossils look like? Can they see the shapes of any plants or animals in the fossils? If these fossils are millions of years old, what does that tell us about the past?

Differentiation
● Some children may need additional support and encouragement when making careful observational drawings, as this requires concentration. You may want to check that individual children have suitably simple or complex fossils to look at.

Science in the wider world
The discovery of fossils helps us to trace back this ancestry and identify the relationships between different living things. In the eighteenth century, Mary Anning from Dorset became one of the most famous fossil collector when she discovered the first complete fossilised skeleton of a reptile – an Ichthyosaurus.

Review
Through discussion, assess the children's understanding that fossils help us to understand the past.

Resources
Fossil examples from the previous lesson; small plastic tank; soft modelling material; sand; water; pasta shells; rice paper; leaves; small plastic dinosaurs or bugs; shells; twigs; plastic cups; plaster of Paris; paints

Speaking scientifically
fossil, layer, pressure, sediment

Lesson 2: Fossil formation

Introduction
Begin by looking again at the fossil examples you have. Ask the children if they can recall what fossils are and what they tell us. Ask if they have any idea about how these fossils might have formed.

Whole-class work
1. Model how fossils are formed for the children. Place a layer of soft modelling material in the small plastic tank. What might this represent? (The sea bed.)

2. Next take a pasta shell that has been wrapped in rice paper so that it looks like a creature. Tell the children that this creature has died and fallen to the sea bed. Place the shell in the modelling material and press it down a little before covering it with sand.

3. Explain (adding sand as you do) that over many millions of years more and more sand layers are added on top of the creature.

4. Ask: *If this is the sea, is there anything in our model that is missing?* (Water.) Carefully pour water onto the sand without disturbing it. Push down on the sand over the pasta shell to represent the pressure of sand and sediment piling up. Ask: *What do you think might happen to this creature over time?* (It will decay and become fossilised, or a hole in the rock will be left in the shape of the creature.)

5. Now remove the water and ask the children to imagine how, over many years, the Earth's surface has changed and the fossil has been exposed. Remove the sand and expose the pasta. Without the rice paper (which should have dissolved in the water) it can represent a fossilised skeleton. Removing the pasta should also expose an imprint, representing a fossil where a hole is left in rock.

Independent work
6. Tell the children that they are going to make fossils of their own. Give them each a plastic cup and some soft modelling material. Ask them to push this into the bottom of the cup.

7. They should then select an object (leaf, dinosaur, bug, shell or twig) to push into the modelling material. They should carefully remove the item, mix a small quantity of plaster of Paris with water, and pour it into the mould until level with the top.

8. When the plaster of Paris has set, they can remove the modelling material from the cup and carefully peel it from the reproduction fossil. This can now be painted and a class fossil collection created.

Whole-class work
9. Bring the children back together to share their fossil models.

Science in the wider world
Fossils are found in sedimentary rocks, which form through the compression of layers of sediment and water. Most fossils are found in areas that were once under the sea and have since been revealed due to changes to the landscape over many years. Fossils of creatures that appear to be land-based were probably fossilised in the same way but covered in water from lakes, rivers and estuaries.

Review
Assess the children's understanding of fossil formation through discussion.

Lesson 3: Fossil fuels

Introduction

Begin the lesson by asking the children to think about how we keep our homes and school warm and lit. Ask: *What do we use to heat the classroom?* (Gas, coal or electricity.) *How do we run vehicles?* (Diesel or petrol.) *Can anyone tell me what we call gas, coal, petrol and diesel?* (They are all sources of energy.) Show the children a piece of coal and ask what it is and where it came from. This will not be as familiar to children as it once was. Tell them that coal is what we call a fossil fuel. Explain that it was formed many millions of years ago in the same way as fossils, but from large trees and plants that once covered huge areas of the country.

Paired work

1. Tell the children that they are going to go looking for 'coal'. Give each child a plastic cup and allow them just one minute to look around the classroom and locate the cubes representing coal. They should collect as much 'coal' as they can in their plastic cups.

2. After the minute is up, ask the children to count and record how much coal (number of cubes) they were able to find. Give them another minute to find more supplies of 'coal' before again counting and recording their collection.

3. Repeat this until the children can find no more.

4. Ask the children to look at their results and to talk about what they found. Ask: *Did you find the same amount of coal each time you looked?* (To start with, probably yes.) *What happened as you looked later?* (It was harder to find the 'coal' as most of it had already been collected.) *How many cubes are there still to find?* (None, they have all been found.)

Whole-class work

5. Talk about how this activity models the real situation with fossil fuels. We have collected and used so much of the fossil fuels that in years to come there will be none left.

6. Ask the children to think about alternatives. Introduce the idea that fossil fuels are non-renewable (once used they are gone forever) but that there are also renewable fuels that will never run out.

7. Make a list of renewable and non-renewable energy sources based on suggestions from the children.

Independent work

8. Ask the children to design a poster to encourage people to use more renewable energy sources, rather than fossil fuels. This should show the advantages of renewable fuels and the disadvantages of non-renewable fuels and include examples of both types.

Science in the wider world

Coal, oil and natural gas are called fossil fuels because they are made from the fossilised remains of plants and animals. Millions of years ago the Earth was covered in huge forests and the oceans were full of living creatures. As these living things died and decayed, they were covered by sediment, which compressed the decaying matter. Over millions of years, oil and gas were formed from the sea creatures and coal from the plant life. In recent years we have used fossil fuels at such a rate that it is expected they will run out completely in less than 250 years.

Review

Through scrutiny of the children's posters, assess their understanding that fossil fuels are in limited supply and what some of the alternatives are.

Objectives
● To know what is meant by a fossil fuel.
● To understand that fossil fuels are non-renewable.

Resources
A lump of coal; plastic cups; 150 plastic cubes or similar to represent coal reserves (before the lesson you should hide these around the classroom in a variety of increasingly less obvious places)

Speaking scientifically
energy, fossil fuel, fuel, non-renewable, renewable

Objectives
• To understand, in simple terms, some of James Hutton's ideas about geology.

Resources
Images of the Earth taken from space; plastic drinks bottle with the top cut off and holes in the base for each pair of children; worms; sand; newspaper; compost; water; squares of muslin; elastic bands; saucers; black plastic (cut from bin liners) Note: Please ensure that you follow your school's health and safety policy with regards to washing hands after this activity. You might also want to refer to the Association for Science Education publication *Be Safe*, http://www.ase.org.uk/resources/health-and-safety-resources/health-and-safety-primary-science/

Speaking scientifically
geologist, geology, layer, sediment

Lesson 1: James Hutton

Introduction

Begin the lesson by showing the children some images of the Earth taken from space. Ask them how we might have found out about what the Earth was like before we were able to see that view from space. Talk about how scientists have asked questions and explored the Earth for many years. Tell them that for a long time the study of geology was the main source of information about the structure of the Earth.

Tell the children about James Hutton, who was a Scottish geologist. Over 300 years ago he suggested the idea of 'rock cycles', in which old rocks are destroyed by weathering and new ones are formed from their sediments. The children can explore this idea by observing a wormery, which can be used as a model to represent the movement of layers and the effect they have on each other.

Paired work

1. Give each pair of children a plastic bottle with the top cut off and three or four drainage holes in the bottom.

2. Ask them to put a 3cm layer of sand in the bottom of the bottle, followed by a 2cm layer of newspaper torn into fine shreds and moistened.

3. Next they should add a 10cm layer of compost, and then another layer of damp shredded newspaper.

4. Tell them to add five or six of the worms and then to cover the bottle with a square of muslin secured with an elastic band.

5. They should then cover the bottle with black plastic, and stand it on a saucer in a cool, shady place.

6. Ask the children to keep a diary to record what happens over the following week. This could include a series of drawing or digital photographs taken by the children. They may need to occasionally provide some food for the worms – small pieces of vegetables or fruit are fine but nothing acidic.

Whole-class work

7. After the worms have had a chance to settle in and start to move about, look at the layers of sand, newspaper and compost. The movement of the different layers in the wormery can be likened to the way in which the layers of rock in the Earth move, as identified by Hutton. He suggested that there was a continuous cycle of rocks and soil being compacted into bedrock, forced to the surface by volcanic processes, and eventually worn away into sediment again.

Science in the wider world

Geologists study the layers of rock under the Earth's surface. They can use what they discover to work out a lot about the environment at the time these layers were laid down. Generally (if left undisturbed) the lower layers are older, since in sedimentary rock the sediment is laid down layer upon layer. The layers of rock effectively represent periods of time in the history of the Earth.

Review

Through discussion assess the children's understanding that there are different layers of rock. See if they can explain how the ideas of James Hutton can be represented by the movement between the layers in the wormery.

Objectives
● To understand the structure of the Earth's crust.

Resources
A4 labels ('igneous rock', 'metamorphic rock' and 'sedimentary rock'); pictures of rocky outcrops, cliff faces and quarries; yellow or orange ping-pong balls; soft modelling materials in different colours (yellow, orange, blue and green if possible); photocopiable page 171 'The structure of the Earth'; secondary sources of information about the structure of the Earth; interactive activity 'Types of rock' on the CD-ROM

Speaking scientifically
core, crust, igneous, layer, mantle, metamorphic, sedimentary, structure

Lesson 2: Under our feet

Introduction
Take the children to the school hall or another large space. Around it place the three large labels with the rock types on them. Tell the children that you are going to read some descriptions that will lead to the identity of each of the three rock types. The children must stand by the label for the correct rock as soon as they recognise it from your description.

● Igneous:
  ● I was formed from molten rock.
  ● Granite is an example of me.
  ● I come out of the ground in a volcano.
● Sedimentary:
  ● Sandstone is an example of me.
  ● I sometimes contain fossils.
  ● I was formed from bits of other rocks squashed together in layers.
● Metamorphic:
  ● I didn't come out of a volcano and I never contain fossils.
  ● Slate is an example of me.
  ● Another example of me is marble.

Whole-class work
1. Ask the children to think about what might be below the surface of the Earth. What is the Earth like under their feet? Give them time to think, discuss and share their ideas. Gather these together, then ask: *How do we know what the Earth is like under our feet?*

2. Show the children pictures of rocky outcrops, cliff faces and quarries. Ask the children to consider why they can see the rocks. Talk about the way in which rocks move and become exposed so that we can see what they are like.

Paired work
3. Tell the children that they are going to make their own model of the Earth to show the different layers.

4. Ask them to mould the yellow modelling material around the ping-pong ball, then the orange, and finally the blue. They can then flatten some small pieces of green into the surface of the 'Earth' they have shaped. Ask the children in their pairs to explain what each part of the model represents:
  ● ping-pong ball – the solid inner core
  ● yellow layer – the Earth's liquid layer
  ● orange layer – the mantle of the Earth
  ● blue layer – the Earth's crust
  ● green – the land masses on the surface.
When it is completed they can cut away a segment to show all the layers.

5. Give the children photocopiable page 171 'The structure of the Earth' to complete. They should identify the layers and use secondary sources of information to write sentences about each.

6. You can revise the three different types of rock, by asking the children to complete interactive activity 'Types of rock' on the CD-ROM.

Science in the wider world
Due to the size of the Earth and the very limited way in which we are able to drill into it, geologists have found out most of what is known about its structure by studying earthquake vibrations.

Review
Through scrutiny of their photocopiable sheets and discussion during the lesson, assess the children's understanding of the layered structure of the Earth.

Objectives
● To understand what volcanoes are and how they are formed.
● To know that igneous rocks are formed from volcanic lava.

Resources
Sticky notes; rock samples of granite and basalt; small bottle of sparkling water; small plastic drinks bottle; papier-mâché or plaster bandages; paint; food colouring; vinegar; bicarbonate of soda; media resource 'Volcano' on the CD-ROM

Speaking scientifically
erupt, eruption, pressure, volcano

Lesson 3: Prehistoric plants

Introduction

Begin the lesson by showing the children the media resource 'Volcano' on the CD-ROM. Ask them to imagine what it must be like when a volcano erupts. Give the children a sticky note each and ask them to write down some words, phrases and ideas about volcanoes. Give each child a second sticky note and ask them to write a question they have about volcanoes (this could be done in pairs).

Whole-class work

I. Tell the children that a volcano occurs when rocks within the Earth's structure move and molten rock bursts up from deep inside the Earth. This rock cools as it reaches the surface and becomes igneous rock such as granite and basalt (you might have some samples to show the children).

2. The temperatures are immensely high and the pressure can throw rocks high into the air. You can demonstrate the pressure that forces the molten rock out of a volcano by opening a small bottle of sparkling water that has been slightly shaken. (This is best done outside.) The pressure forces the water to spray in many directions.

Paired work

3. Tell the children that they are going to build a model of a volcano. (Depending on time this could be a very simple or a more complex model.)

4. Give each pair a small plastic drinks bottle. Using either papier-mâché or plaster bandages, they can create a volcano shape around the bottle, leaving the top of the bottle clear. If time allows, let this dry and then allow the children to paint it to look like a volcanic mountain.

5. To make the volcano erupt, give each pair a small quantity of bicarbonate of soda and a small quantity of vinegar. For a colourful effect you can add food colouring to the vinegar or some powder paint into the bicarbonate of soda.

6. To make the volcano erupt the children should add a teaspoon of bicarbonate of soda to their bottle and then a small amount of vinegar.

7. If you wish, you could ask the children to record the exact quantities of bicarbonate of soda and vinegar they used. They could then try some different (but appropriately small) quantities until they are able to create an ideal model. (Be sure to limit the children's access to vinegar and bicarbonate of soda to safe levels.) Ensure the children take care, that they avoid spills and that they wash their hands after the activity.

Independent work

8. Ask the children to use the word bank created earlier to write a science poem about volcanoes. The poem does not need to rhyme but should use scientific vocabulary and ideas, therefore demonstrating what the children know about volcanoes.

Science in the wider world

Volcanoes tend to occur in bands across the world, with some regions having a much greater concentration than others. Many lie dormant for years whilst others are active more frequently. The impact of volcanoes upon the Earth can be tremendous. Large areas of vegetation can be destroyed by an eruption, along with everything else that lived there. The area can remain a very barren and inhospitable place where little can survive for long periods afterwards.

Review

Through scrutiny of the children's poems and the vocabulary used, assess their understanding of what volcanoes are and how they form.

Objectives
- To know that soil lies on top of rock.
- To know that there are different kinds of soil.

Resources
A piece of rock; some crushed rock; a container of soil; a container of water; a dead plant (a weed); soil samples; hand lenses; dishes or shallow trays; plastic gloves; trowels; small plastic containers; secondary sources of information

Speaking scientifically
bedrock, humus, soil, subsoil, topsoil

Lesson 1: Types of soil

Introduction
Take into the classroom a piece of rock, some crushed rock, a container of soil, a container of water and a dead plant (a weed). Ask the children if they can think how these things are all linked. Talk about the possible links that the children suggest. Record these on the board.

Whole-class work
1. Introduce the idea of how the soil was created. Tell the children that soil is a mixture of tiny pieces of rock that have become mixed with decaying plants. This decaying vegetation becomes a substance called 'humus'. The humus sticks all the particles together and absorbs water. This mixture slowly changes and becomes a habitat for plants and minibeasts that we call *soil*.

2. Ask the children to help you put the items in order to show how soil is made. This should be: rocks become the crushed rocks, to which the decaying plant material and water is added, resulting in the soil.

3. Ask the children to draw a series of illustrations to explain how soil is formed. Remind them of the importance of washing their hands after handling any soil samples.

Independent work
4. Ask the children to carefully collect some soil samples from the school grounds using the trowels and plastic containers. The children could also bring in samples from their own gardens. (In an urban area you may need to provide trays of local soils for the children to use.) Ask the children to describe each type of soil and how they differ from those found in the school grounds.

5. Ask the children to use secondary sources of information to investigate the different recognised soil types. Can they find sufficient information to draw an illustration showing the different layers of soil to be found under the ground? This could become a group collage picture.

Science in the wider world
As you dig down into the ground you go through different layers of soil, each slightly different in composition. In Britain you are likely to find three layers: topsoil, which is the decomposed remains of living things mixed with tiny rock particles; subsoil, which is larger pieces of rock with less decaying plant life; and bedrock, which is the rock from which the soil is made. Each different layer then has different amounts of rock and water in it, thus giving them different colours and textures.

Review
Through scrutiny of the children's work, assess their level of understanding. All of the children should be able to describe how soil lies on top of rock and most should recognise that there are different types of soil.

Objectives
● To know that different soils have different sized particles and colours.

Resources
Soil samples; plastic beakers; water; plastic gloves; photocopiable page 172 'Looking at soil'

Speaking scientifically
chalky, clay, peat, sandy

Introduction
Using the soil samples collected for the previous lesson, discuss with the children their findings about how soils vary. Try to begin to identify these soils by their look and texture:
- Sandy soil is crumbly, light and contains only a little organic matter.
- Chalky soil is stony.
- Clay soil is a heavy, sticky and wet soil.
- Peat soil is a dark-coloured mixture of sand and clay and has a large amount of organic matter.

Independent work
1. Give the children photocopiable page 172 'Looking at soil' and samples of each of the four types of soil. Ask them to complete the photocopiable sheet by looking carefully at the soil samples.

Paired work
2. Using the different soil samples collected from different locations, ask the children to put approximately 5cm of one sample into a clear plastic container. Different pairs of children can look at different soil samples.

3. They should fill the container with water, stir the mixture and leave the solution to settle (this may take some time). Ask the children to draw a series of containers on a time line so that they are able to record their observations at intervals as the mixture settles out. It does not really matter about the regularity of this; what is more important is that they notice what happens over time. Encourage the children to make careful observations and to try and record the colours or shades they notice.

4. As the water clears and the materials settle, the children should begin to see different layers of particles, with the heaviest ones generally settled at the very bottom. Ask them to explain what they notice and why they think this is happening.

5. The children may be able to describe how darker soils usually contain more humus; pale, gritty soils may be very sandy; and reddish soils with fine particles tend to be clay-based.

6. Discuss the different layers with the children and compare the contents of the different soil samples.

Science in the wider world
The type of soil in an area is extremely important for gardeners and farmers, as different soil compositions are favoured by different plants. Loam soils are usually the best type for gardens and farms due to their clay and sand content mixed with a high level of organic matter.

Review
Through discussion and observation, assess the children's ability to compare the particles in soil. Most should be able to explain the observable differences.

Objectives
● To know that rocks of different sizes can be separated by sieving.

Resources
Wholemeal seeded flour; a range of sieves with different sized holes (these may range from a garden sieve to a cook's sieve – sieves can also be made using plastic pots or containers with holes punctured into the base using different sized tools or nails); a pre-prepared mixture of sand, gravel and stones

Speaking scientifically
sieve, sieving

Lesson 3: Separating soil particles

Introduction
Talk to the children about a problem you have been presented with. Somehow the local DIY store had a mix-up in its deliveries and has unfortunately now got lots of different sizes of sand, gravel and stone mixed together. The store manager has asked if the class can suggest some method of sorting out the mixture. Ask the children to share their ideas about how the large and small particles could be separated. You may like to demonstrate the time-consuming task of separating these by hand as an encouragement to the children. Gather together some of their ideas and, if needed, give some helpful hints to lead the children towards the idea of using sieves.

Whole-class work
1. Talk about different types of sieve and how the sieving and grading process works.
2. Demonstrate sieving something like wholemeal seeded flour using sieves with different-sized holes. The sieved flour products can then be clearly presented, sorted into groups of different sizes.

Group work
3. The children should work in groups of three or four. Give them the prepared sand and gravel mixture and have available a selection of sieves with different-sized holes. The children should then sieve and classify the materials by their size.
4. Ask the children to prepare a poster in a collage style to illustrate and record the activity. The poster should indicate the initial problem and explain in simple illustrated steps how the process was carried out.

Differentiation
● Children could be given simpler or more complex mixtures of materials that require fewer or more sieves.

Science in the wider world
Rock and stone excavated from a quarry is brought out in a huge range of shapes and sizes. In order to be useful it needs to be sorted and graded to ensure consistency of size. This often requires the rocks to be broken, crushed or ground to an appropriate size. The sorting and grading process takes place in a series of grids, grills, sieves or filters, which allows stone of a particular size to be separated out. This is important to the way in which these rocks are used. For example, if you are using gravel as a pathway, the aggregate needs to be of a generally uniform size. Similarly, it would be difficult to use sand for a particular purpose if there were also large pieces of sandstone in it.

Review
Through discussion and observation, assess the level of understanding of how particles of different sizes can be separated. Assess the children's understanding of the methodology and equipment used and how this skill and process can be used in other ways. Most children should understand this process quite well.

Resources
Examples of suitable non-fiction texts and children's stories that link to the uses of materials; photocopiable page 173 'Building houses'

Speaking scientifically
appropriate, building, material, property, use

Lesson I: Rocky stories

Introduction
Begin by sharing with the children stories and non-fiction texts. For example, you could tell one of the many versions of the story of 'The Three Little Pigs'.

Whole-class work
I. Ask the children to think about, for example, the story of 'The Three Little Pigs'. Ask: *What are the materials that the three little pigs used in building their houses? Why did they choose these materials? Were they good materials to use? Why?*

2. Encourage the children to think about the work they have been doing recently and ask: *Why do we use certain materials for some things and not others?*

Independent work
3. Give out photocopiable page 173 'Building houses'. Ask the children to think about a house and the materials that are used in houses today. They should use their ideas to complete the photocopiable sheet.

4. Give the children time to read and explore some of the non-fiction texts and stories from earlier.

5. Ask them to choose one story and re-write it, but this time the story should feature alternative materials. For example, in the story of 'The Three Little Pigs' what might have happened if the pigs had built a sand house or one made from clay? As an alternative, children could re-write a story to include the ideas at the bottom of the photocopiable sheet. For example, what would happen if Paddington Bear went out walking with an umbrella made of paper?

Whole-class work
6. Bring the children together to share some of their stories.

7. To end the lesson, ask the children to play a game of 'Imagine if'. Ask them to think of a situation similar to those at the bottom of the photocopiable sheet. They should then explore all the positive and negative aspects of this situation. For example, 'Imagine if... umbrellas were made from roof slates', 'Imagine if... door handles were made from chocolate'. Whilst this seems a bit of fun, the ideas and suggestions do lend themselves to further discussion about uses of materials and the choices we make. In addition, there are further investigations that could be carried out to gather evidence to support these ideas.

> **Differentiation**
> ● Some children may need support with the written aspects of this lesson. You may wish to provide this through additional adult support, the use of a word bank, or allowing children to tell their story in pictures as a storyboard.
> ● Challenge confident learners to write more detailed, imaginative responses with scientific justifications clearly evident.

Science in the wider world
Our ability to manipulate the materials around us has played a major part in our development from the Stone Age, through the Iron Age, to the modern age of synthetic and 'man-made' materials. The basic designs of many everyday items today may have changed little since their invention, but the materials they are made from have often been replaced by newer alternatives.

Review
Through scrutiny of the children's work, assess their ability to understand the reasons why we use particular materials to make particular things.

Objectives
● To understand the reasoning behind decisions to use particular materials in particular ways.

Resources
A range of modelling materials and other construction materials (largely determined by the stories written in the previous lesson); children's alternative stories from the previous lesson

Speaking scientifically
appropriate, building, material, property, use

Lesson 2: Make and explain

Introduction
Begin the lesson by asking volunteers to share some of their alternative stories from the previous lesson. Ask the class to listen carefully for how materials have been used in each story. Reinforce ideas about selecting and using materials appropriately depending on their properties. Together, collate some examples from the children's stories.

Group/Paired work
1. Ask the children to use modelling and other materials to build a physical model to represent their story. For example, if they have written about the Three Little Pigs they could build houses using the materials they identified. If they have written about Paddington's umbrellas they could make some models to represent those. You will need to determine how best to group the children so that rather than having several identical buildings, for example, a group could work together to create houses from a range of the materials in their stories, collectively.

2. To ensure that the children are thinking and working scientifically, ask them to devise a test or set of criteria so that their models' use of materials can be tested. For example, those building houses could replicate the huff and puff of the wolf, and those building Paddington's umbrellas could carry out a leak test. Encourage the children to consider the properties of each material when devising the criteria and carrying out their tests.

Whole-class work
3. Bring the children back together and ask them to explain the models they built and the outcomes of their small-scale tests.

4. As they share their models, engage in some questioning and answering to help the children express the reasons for their choices and conclusions about which were the best and worst materials to use. For example: *Was the sand a good material for a house? What might happen when it rains?*

Science in the wider world
Many years ago, people had access to a limited range of natural materials such as stone and wood. Natural raw materials can be traced to several sources: animals, plants or the ground ('animal, vegetable or mineral'). Today, while we still use a number of natural materials, we also use a large number of manufactured materials. These are designed and produced to have quite specific properties. For example, plastic is a strong, light and very versatile material that has replaced many natural products.

Review
Through scrutiny of the children's models and their answers to your questions, assess the children's understanding of the criteria used in selecting materials for particular uses.

Objectives
● To understand how igneous and sedimentary rocks are formed.
● To be able to relate the simple properties of rocks to their formation.

Resources
(Pink) wafer biscuits; honeycomb candy (or Crunchie® bars); sandstone; pumice stone; other igneous and sedimentary rock samples; hand lenses; digital microscopes; laptops

Speaking scientifically
crystal, grain, igneous, layer, sedimentary

Lesson 3: Rock formation

Introduction

Begin the lesson by talking about what the children have learned so far about rocks. Create a class concept map, either on paper or on the interactive board, showing all their knowledge and understanding. This can be added to later. Ask the children if they can recall the names we give to different types of rock. Ensure that they are familiar with the terms *igneous* and *sedimentary*, as these will be the focus of this lesson.

Whole-class work

1. Give each of the children a wafer biscuit and ask them to look at it carefully. Ask: *What can you tell me about the wafer biscuit?* Try to steer answers towards the idea that the wafer biscuit is formed from layers of wafer and cream.

2. Explain to the children that sedimentary rocks are made from tiny pieces of other rock (and the remains of plants and animals). These have sunk to the bottom of the sea where they have formed layers. Sedimentary rock will therefore characteristically have grains making up the sedimentary layers. These layers are squashed by the weight of the layers above them and over millions of years the layers become solid rocks.

3. Ask the children to count the layers in their wafer biscuits. Hand round examples of a sedimentary rock such as sandstone for the children to examine.

4. Next talk about igneous rocks and how they were created from minerals inside the Earth through the intense heat of a volcano. The rock inside a volcano is molten. When the volcano erupts, the molten rock inside it is forced to the surface. As the molten rock flows from the volcano, it cools down and hardens, trapping air inside it. The minerals then became crystallised.

5. Give each child a piece of honeycomb candy (such as a Crunchie® bar) and tell them to look at the bubbles. Show the children a piece of pumice stone, which is a volcanic rock, and ask them to look at the similarities. Some children may have made honeycomb candy at home and will know that bubbles of air are trapped in the liquid. As it cools these form the bubbles in the solid honeycomb.

Paired work

6. Give each pair samples of sandstone and pumice. Ask them to use hand lenses or a digital microscope to look at the rocks and see if they can see the grains and crystals in each.

7. Next, have some more igneous and sedimentary rock samples available for the children to group and classify. They should classify the samples according to whether they contain grains or crystals and therefore whether they are sedimentary or igneous.

8. Let the children record their observations by making some detailed observational drawings of each of the rocks showing the grains and crystals.

Science in the wider world

Examining the structure of a rock can provide us with important insights into how that rock originally formed.

Review

Through discussion with the children and scrutiny of their observational drawings, assess their understanding of igneous and sedimentary rock formation.

SUMMER 1

Objectives

● To consider a range of different rocks.
● To know that igneous rocks are formed from volcanic lava.
● To understand how igneous and sedimentary rocks are formed.
● To be able to relate the simple properties of rocks to their formation.

Resources

Photocopiable page 174 'What type of rock am I?'

Working scientifically

● Asking relevant questions.
● Using straightforward scientific evidence to answer questions or to support their findings.

What type of rock am I?

Revise

● Children should understand that there are three types of rock called metamorphic, igneous and sedimentary.
● They should know some of the characteristics of each of these three types of rock.
● They should understand how igneous and sedimentary rocks were formed.
● They must be able to give examples of each of these different rock types.
● Children should understand how soil is formed and what it is made up of.

Assess

● Use photocopiable page 174 'What type of rock am I?' to assess the children's understanding of rock types. The photocopiable sheet asks them to link each statement with the correct rock type. Most children should be able to make these links correctly by identifying the descriptions of the igneous, metamorphic and sedimentary rocks.
● Through the work in this chapter they should also now be familiar with the names of some different individual rocks. They should be able to give correct examples of igneous, metamorphic and sedimentary rocks.
● Finally, this photocopiable sheet will also assess their understanding of the different layers that lie beneath them. They should be able to identify the components that go into forming soil in terms of rock particles and decaying living matter.

Further practice

● Further understanding of rock types can be gained by extending the range of rocks used and encouraging the children to look at rocks in a different way. Rather than simply seeing a rock, encourage them to begin to broaden their identification base. Try using a branching identification key or branching database to set up an ongoing collection of rocks. This will enable the children to look in more detail at the observable features of the rock samples, to ask very focused questions about these observable features, and then to formulate a question that others can answer as part of the identification process.

Objectives
● To learn about the ways in which humans use rocks.
● To know that rocks are used for particular purposes because of their properties.
● To understand the reasoning behind decisions to use particular materials in particular ways.

Resources
Photocopiable page 175 'Uses of rocks'

Working scientifically
● Asking relevant questions.
● Using straightforward scientific evidence to answer questions or to support their findings.

Uses of rocks

Revise

● Children should have an understanding of the characteristics and properties of different rocks.
● They should be able to describe some of the uses of materials, including rocks.
● They should be able to explain the way in which the properties of a material are linked to its potential uses.
● They should understand that our use of rocks sometimes means that the rock is no longer recognisable as a rock.
● They should know that some materials, such as glass, are made from rocks.

Assess

● Using photocopiable page 175 'Uses of rocks', assess the children's understanding of how rocks are used. Some of the uses are less obvious than others and the children will need to be careful not to simply look for rocks.
● To extend this further and assess the children's understanding more deeply, ask them to write an explanation for each of their choices. Ask: *Why did you identify some items as being made from rocks and not others?*
● The second part of the photocopiable sheet assesses the breadth of the children's understanding of the uses of rocks by asking them to complete three pictures showing their uses. Some children will demonstrate a limited understanding by drawing uses that have observable 'rock' features, whilst others may be able to consider ways in which rock has been used as a raw material in the manufacture of a product.

Further practice

● Further practice might involve looking more widely around school and the local environment at how rocks are used. If you have a local quarry it may be possible to arrange a visit to see the quarry, or perhaps invite the quarry manager to come into school to talk to the children about how the rock is extracted and what uses it is put to. It may also be possible to see that older local buildings have been constructed using rock from this quarry. A local historian or your local library may be able to help, as many will have photographic archives that show buildings being constructed and long-closed local quarries in operation.

Objectives
● To know that soil lies on top of rock.
● To know that there are different kinds of soil.
● To know that different soils have different sized particles and colours.
● To know what fossils are.
● To know how fossils are formed.

Resources
Soil samples; fossils; trays; pots; art materials

Working scientifically
● Asking relevant questions.
● Using straightforward scientific evidence to answer questions or to support their findings.

Soil and fossils

Revise
● Children should have an understanding of soils and the way in which soils are formed.
● They should understand that soil consists of rock particles, water and humus in different quantities, and that these can be seen in soil samples.
● They should be able to identify a fossil and decide if there is evidence that it is from an animal or a plant.
● They should understand that fossils were formed long ago, when living things were trapped within sedimentary rocks.

Assess
● Give the children a pot of soil that you have also added a fossil to. Tell them that this is a miniature archaeological site and that they are going to explore the site.
● Let the children tip the soil sample and fossil out onto a tray and explore the contents of the soil and the fossil. Ask them to draw an annotated picture of the soil and fossil. Then encourage them to use a range of scientific vocabulary to describe the soil and fossil. This description can be written around the annotated picture to form a border.
● Assess their understanding of the components of the soil. Can they identify small rocks, rock particles and decaying living matter (humus)? Is there evidence of water in the soil?
● Can they write something about the fossil? Where might it have come from? How was the fossil formed? Do the children identify that fossils were formed within sedimentary rock?

Further practice
● To develop the children's understanding of soils and soil types further, you could give them further experience linked to gardens and gardening, as this is more likely to be within the breadth of their experience.
● If you have a school garden, use this to explore growing conditions further. You could arrange to visit an allotment or garden centre and get 'experts' to answer the children's questions about soil types.
● Look around the garden centre at how their plants are grouped. Is it possible to see what species of plants prefer to grow in particular soil conditions? A member of the garden centre staff should be able to help you.
● A local gardener might also visit your school and talk to the children about soil types and how soil can be improved and potentially changed to some extent. So can a clay-type soil be improved by adding lots of decaying vegetable matter, for example?

Materials

■ Find examples around school of things that are made from each of the materials below.

Remember: a material is the substance something is made from.

Material	Example of its use
Metal	
Wood	
Plastic	
Glass	
Paper	
Stone	
Brick	

■ Now try to find out what materials these objects in your school are made from. There may be several materials used in making each object.

Object	Materials used
Table	
Chair	
Book	
Pen	
Computer and monitor	
Your classroom	

I can identify which materials objects are made from.

How did you do?

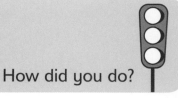

PHOTOCOPIABLE   ■SCHOLASTIC
www.scholastic.co.uk

Rock investigation

■ Plan your investigation and record what you did.

Planning
Our question is...
To find the answer we will...
To carry out our investigation we will need to use...
What we think will happen is...

I can plan and record an investigation.

How did you do?

Rock investigation (continued)

Recording
We carried out our investigation by...
We found out that...
We now know that...

I can plan and record an investigation.

How did you do?

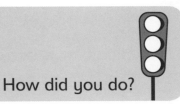

■SCHOLASTIC
www.scholastic.co.uk

The structure of the Earth

1. The picture below shows what the Earth would look like if we took a slice out. Can you identify each of the different layers? Write the names and a sentence about each on the back of this photocopiable sheet.

2. Colour the picture to show the Earth's surface and the different layers.

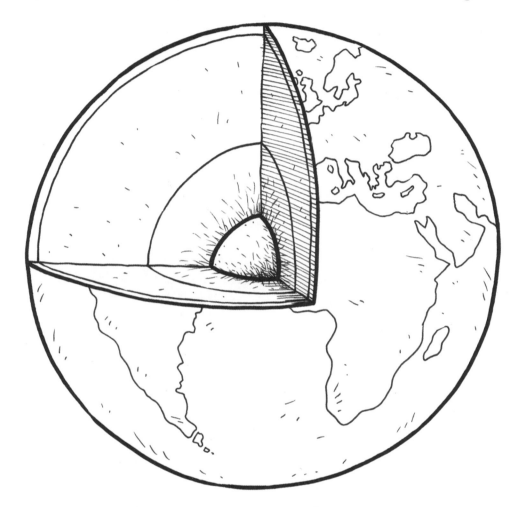

3. Now write a sentence to describe:
■ Igneous rock

_____

■ Sedimentary rock

_____

■ Metamorphic rock

_____

I can begin to describe the structure of the Earth.

How did you do?

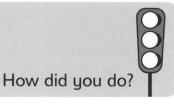

Looking at soil

- Look carefully at the four soil samples you have in front of you.
- Use what you observe to complete the following table.

	Soil sample 1	Soil sample 2	Soil sample 3	Soil sample 4
Draw a picture of your soil, showing as much detail as you can.				
What colour best describes the soil?				
Is it sandy?				
Is it stony?				
Does it look like clay?				
Is there much humus in your soil?				
What type of soil do you think this is? (Choose from sandy, chalky, clay or peat.)				

I can make and record scientific observations.

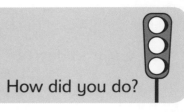

How did you do?

PHOTOCOPIABLE

SCHOLASTIC
www.scholastic.co.uk

Name: _____ Date: _____

Building houses

- Look at this picture of a house.
- Think about the materials that each part listed below is made from. Say why that material is used for that part.

Part of house	Made from	Why?
Window		
Roof		
Door		
Guttering		
Walls		
Door handles		

- Try these questions about what would happen if we used the wrong materials:

1. What would happen if we made an umbrella out of paper?

_____

_____

2. What would happen if we made a hammer out of glass?

_____

_____

I can say why materials are used for specific purposes.

How did you do?

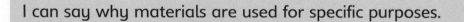 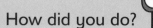

Name: _____ Date: _____

What type of rock am I?

1. What type of rock am I? Match the sentences together.

I was formed from a volcanic eruption.	I am a metamorphic rock.
I was formed gradually from layers that sank to the bottom of the sea.	I am igneous rock.
I don't contain any fossils and didn't come from a volcano.	I am sedimentary rock.

2. Give some examples of these rock types.

Igneous

_____

_____

Metamorphic

_____

_____

Sedimentary

_____

_____

3. Label this diagram to show the layers beneath the ground and how soil is formed.

I can identify different types of rock.

How did you do?

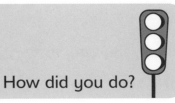

Uses of rocks

1. Circle the objects that are made from rocks.

2. Can you think of some more ways that we use rocks? Draw three pictures.

3. Explain how soil is formed on the back of this sheet. These words will help you.

humus	crushed rock	water

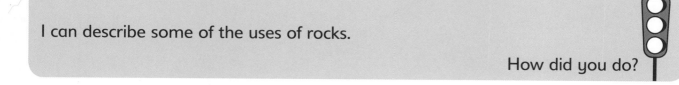

I can describe some of the uses of rocks.

How did you do?

Animals including humans: skeleton, muscles and movement

Expected prior learning
- Know the names of some of the important human body parts.
- Understand the importance of exercise.

Overview of progression
In this chapter children will:
- suggest which body parts we use for common movements
- understand how the skeleton, muscles and joints work and that most animals have similar structures
- know that animals, including humans, grow into adults.

Creative context
- There are several opportunities for children to make simple models as well as illustrating their work for display.

Background knowledge
Like all animals, and unlike plants, humans can move. All our movements depend on our skeletons, muscles and joints working together. It will be important for the children to have some knowledge of the names of simple joints and some of the larger bones in the skeleton.

Movement in living things can vary. For example, some animals fly and some crawl or jump. Their skeletons are often different shapes because of the way that they or parts of their bodies move.

Speaking scientifically
Children should be familiar with the terms: skeleton (including shoulder, arm, leg, jaw, backbone, foot, knee cap and so on), muscle, joint, exoskeleton, growth, exercise.

Preparation
You will need to provide: common classroom resources such as card, paper, coloured pencils, glue, scissors and so on; wall space for frequent displays; pictures of animals, humans, animal skeletons and plants; books about animals and plants; large diagram of human skeleton; paper fasteners; hole punches; paper towels; sterilised animal bones; trowels; gloves; containers; magnifying lenses; art materials; apples; measuring tapes; sticky tape; outline of a baby; string; rulers; graph paper; king prawns; dead insects; trays of damp soil and leaves; timers; secondary information sources; PE kit and apparatus

Some lessons will need more detailed planning in advance and your classroom will need to be organised so that small groups can do practical work using glue, scissors and thicker card.

On the CD-ROM you will find: photocopiable page 'The human body'; interactive activities 'My skeleton', 'Our muscles', 'Animal record breakers', 'Strange skeletons'; media resources 'Skeletons'

■SCHOLASTIC

Chapter at a glance

Week	Lesson	Curriculum objectives	Objectives	Main activity	Working scientifically
1	1	• (Y1) To identify, name, draw and label the basic parts of the human body and say which part of the body is associated with each sense. • To identify that humans and some animals have skeletons.	• To revise the names of the main body parts and how they help us move. • To know that all humans have skeletons. • To understand the link between skeletons and movement.	Reviewing Year 1 and 2 work on animals and the human body. Exploring various movement activities and explaining which part of our bodies we use. Understanding how our movements are similar and/or different to movements of animals and plants.	• Identifying differences, similarities or changes related to simple scientific ideas and processes.
	2	• To identify that humans and some animals have skeletons.	• To recognise that humans have skeletons. • To introduce some of the main bones in our bodies.	Finding and feeling some of the bones in their own bodies. Identifying where some of the bones in the body are on a diagram.	• Gathering, recording, classifying and presenting data in a variety of ways to help in answering questions.
	3	• To identify that humans and some animals have skeletons.	• To identify that many animals have skeletons but that there are certain animals that don't. • To know that animals that are invertebrates don't have a backbone.	Identifying invertebrate and vertebrate animals and looking at their skeletons.	• Gathering, recording, classifying and presenting data in a variety of ways to help in answering questions.
2	1	• To identify that humans and some animals have skeletons and muscles for support, protection and movement.	• To understand that joints allow the skeleton to move. • To identify some of the important joints such as the jaw, knee, elbow and wrist.	Observing how different joints move. Comparing the movements of our joints. Discussing why joints are needed.	• Recording findings using simple scientific language, drawings, labelled diagrams, keys, bar charts, and tables.
	2	• To identify that humans and some animals have skeletons and muscles for support, protection and movement.	• To understand how a joint works. • To use a model to show how a joint works.	Making a model joint. Understanding how one particular joint works.	• Gathering, recording, classifying and presenting data in a variety of ways to help in answering questions.
	3	• To identify that humans and some animals have skeletons and muscles for support, protection and movement.	• To identify some of our muscle systems. • To understand how our skeleton, joints and muscles work together to make movement possible.	Examining arm muscles and how they work together with bones and joints.	• Gathering, recording, classifying and presenting data in a variety of ways to help in answering questions.
3	1	• To identify that humans and some animals have skeletons and muscles for support, protection and movement.	• To understand how our skeleton, joints and muscles work together to make movement possible. • To look at how muscles expand and contract.	Making a model hand. Examining each other's hands to feel how they move.	• Gathering, recording, classifying and presenting data in a variety of ways to help in answering questions.
	2	• To identify that humans and some animals have skeletons and muscles for support, protection and movement.	• To identify that skeletons change in size as we get older.	Recording various measurements from children of different ages and adults.	• Using straightforward scientific evidence to answer questions or to support their findings.
	3	• To identify that humans and some animals have skeletons and muscles for support, protection and movement.	• To identify that bones in the skeleton change and grow in size.	Measuring hands in different ways including area, length and span.	• Using straightforward scientific evidence to answer questions or to support their findings.

Chapter at a glance

Week	Lesson	Curriculum objectives	Objectives	Main activity	Working scientifically
4	1	• To identify that humans and some animals have skeletons and muscles for support, protection and movement.	• To understand that some animals have skeletons on the outside, called exoskeletons.	Observing and investigating crustaceans and insects. Completing closely observed drawings of some creatures with exoskeletons.	• Using straightforward scientific evidence to answer questions or to support their findings.
	2	• To identify that humans and some animals have skeletons and muscles for support, protection and movement.	• To understand the important role of a skeleton in protecting the organs of an animal.	Making a model of a simple rib cage and internal organs.	• Gathering, recording, classifying and presenting data in a variety of ways to help in answering questions.
	3	• To identify that humans and some animals have skeletons and muscles for support, protection and movement.	• To understand how the skeletons of a range of animals vary.	Identifying and describing animals from their skeletons. Drawing outlines of animals using their skeletons as a guide.	• Gathering, recording, classifying and presenting data in a variety of ways to help in answering questions.
5	1	• To identify that humans and some animals have skeletons and muscles for support, protection and movement.	• To understand that we use our bones, muscles and joints when we exercise. • To understand that exercise is important and helps keep our bodies healthy.	Considering the range of different ways we exercise. Keeping an exercise diary.	• Gathering, recording, classifying and presenting data in a variety of ways to help in answering questions.
	2	• To identify that humans and some animals have skeletons and muscles for support, protection and movement.	• To consider the relationship between the skeleton and movement.	Carrying out an investigation to answer the question: 'Do people with short legs take smaller strides than people with long legs?'	• Setting up simple practical enquiries, comparative and fair tests.
	3	• To identify that humans and some animals have skeletons and muscles for support, protection and movement.	• To consider the different ways that minibeasts move.	Collecting minibeasts and recording observations about how they move.	• Gathering, recording, classifying and presenting data in a variety of ways to help in answering questions.
6	1	• To identify that humans and some animals have skeletons and muscles for support, protection and movement.	• To consider the different ways that flying creatures move.	Making a model bird.	• Gathering, recording, classifying and presenting data in a variety of ways to help in answering questions.
	2	• To identify that humans and some animals have skeletons and muscles for support, protection and movement.	• To understand that animals can move in different ways and at different speeds.	Using secondary sources to research the some of the record-breaking ways in which animals move.	• Gathering, recording, classifying and presenting data in a variety of ways to help in answering questions.
	3	• To identify that humans and some animals have skeletons and muscles for support, protection and movement.	• To explore the parts of our bodies that we use during certain exercises.	Using a range of physical activities to explore how our muscles and joints move and work together.	• Using straightforward scientific evidence to answer questions or to support their findings.
Assess and review					

MSCHOLASTIC

Objectives
● To revise the names of the main body parts and how they help us move.
● To know that all humans have skeletons.
● To understand the link between skeletons and movement.

Resources
Pictures and books showing a range of plants and animals doing a variety of things; photocopiable page 201 'What can I do with my body?'

Speaking scientifically
ankle, arm, carnivore, elbow, finger, galloping, head, herbivore, hip, knee, leg, pouncing, neck, shoulder, stalking, wrist

Lesson 1: My body

Previous knowledge
Children should already be familiar with the following:
● the similarities and differences between humans and other animals
● the names of various animals
● the names of various movements
● some of the names of major body parts.

Introduction
Ask the children what kind of movements they made before they came to school this morning. Listen to their examples but make sure that you stop them when they mention cleaning their teeth, for example, and ask a volunteer to mime what they did. What parts of their bodies did they use? Write a list on the board including arms, fingers, legs to stand up, eyes to see, and so on.

Ask the children what movements their pets made this morning – for example, what their dog or cat did. (Like them it should have walked and probably eaten.) What part of its body did it use and was it similar to some of the parts of their own bodies?

Whole-class work
1. Choose a volunteer to complete this short activity. Give each child a piece of paper for their notes and a pencil to write them with. They should write down the numbers 1–10 on their paper.

2. Explain to the children that you are going to tell the volunteer to move about the classroom and that you will number each of the movements. For each number they have to write down which parts of the body are being used.

3. Make sure that the volunteer is sitting down and then get them to go through the following sequence:
● Stand up
● Stretch
● Put their chair under the table
● Walk towards the door
● Stop at a notice or display and read it
● Take hold of the door handle and turn it
● Open the door
● Listen to something in the corridor and then close the door again
● Hop back to their seat
● Sit down and go to sleep

4. Use the activity as the basis for a discussion about the different parts of the body that are used for different movements. For example, during the sequence of movements the legs and arms were used, as well as the toes for balance and small intricate movements of the fingers to open and close the door. They should also know that when we are asleep (number 10) lots of movement still takes place as we breathe and as our heart beats.

5. Ask the children how we stay standing up and how we can move without collapsing. Tell them that our backbones and skeletons keep us rigid and stiff.

6. Tell the children to put both hands on their desks and push themselves up from a sitting to a standing position. Ask them to note how their arm bones keep their arms rigid.

Checkpoint
● How do various animals move and which parts of their bodies do they use?
● Do we move in the same way and use the same parts of our bodies?
● Why do we need to move?
● Describe some simple movements and identify which parts of our bodies we use.

7. Explain that we can't move without also being flexible. Ask a volunteer to walk across the classroom keeping every part of their legs stiff. Point out that it is very difficult – in fact it is impossible, because they have to use their hip joints to move.

8. Talk about joints being important. Ask what joints are used to walk – they should know the names of ankles, knees and hips.

9. Show the class some of the pictures of mammals and other creatures. Make sure they understand that mammals all have skeletons, joints and muscles to help them move. However, different animals move in different ways and their bodies are designed to help them do this.

10. Look at some very specialised animal movements, such as insects and birds flying and kangaroos and frogs jumping. Ask: *Why do they need to move in this way? How do fish and whales move?*

11. Explain that all animals have to eat. They move in certain ways to make sure that they get the food they need, and also to escape from predators that want to eat them. A lion hunts other animals, a deer or a horse eats grass, a giraffe eats leaves from the tops of trees, and so on.

Independent work

12. Hand out photocopiable page 201 'What can I do with my body?' Tell the children that they can talk about what they are going to write for their answers with the person next to them but that they must complete the photocopiable sheet on their own. Encourage them to carefully act out each movement to see what part of their bodies they use.

13. When everyone has finished, ask individual children to say what they have written and discuss what parts of the body are needed for each movement as a class.

Introducing the new area of study

Explain that during the next few weeks the children will be looking at how their skeleton, muscles and joints help them move. They will also investigate other animals' skeletons and whether they are similar or different to ours. They will explore whether the shape of animal skeletons varies because of the way they move.

Differentiation
● Some children can be reluctant to get involved in discussions and this lesson involves a lot of participation in questions and answers. All children should be encouraged to take part.
● Support children who find completing the photocopiable sheet difficult.
● Challenge children to look at snakes or fish and to closely observe how they move.

Science in the wider world

We need to keep our bodies healthy. The more we know about how our bodies work, the easier this becomes. By building up more knowledge about which parts of our bodies we need in order to move, we will become more aware of how to use them carefully.

Review

Children can be assessed on how much previous knowledge they brought to the discussions and how well they could answer the questions during the whole-class work. They can also be assessed on how well they completed the photocopiable sheet.

Objectives
● To recognise that humans have skeletons.
● To introduce some of the main bones in our bodies.

Resources
Large picture of a human skeleton; photocopiable page 202 'The skeleton'; scissors; thin card; paper fasteners; hole punches; interactive activity 'My skeleton' on the CD-ROM

Speaking scientifically
backbone, bone, breast bone, collar bone, finger, foot, hand, hip, jaw, knee cap, pelvis, rib, shin, shoulder blade, skeleton, skull, thigh

Lesson 2: My skeleton

Introduction
Tell the children that we all have skeletons with lots of individual bones. Remind them that these bones hold us together. Ask the children to feel their own bones. (Knuckles, jaws, elbows and knees are easy to find and the hard bones can be easily felt.) Ask them to feel the same bones in the person next to them.

Whole-class work
1. Place the large picture of the human skeleton where all the children can see it. Point to different bones in turn and ask them the names of each of the bones. Make sure that you include the following: skull, backbone, shoulder blade, upper arm, lower arm, hand, ribs, pelvis, upper leg, lower leg and foot.

2. Write the names on the board where the children can see them.

Independent work
3. Give each child photocopiable page 202 'The skeleton' or ask them to complete interactive activity 'My skeleton' on the CD-ROM. Ask them to write the names of the bones in the correct places. Tell them that they can talk to the child sitting next to them, but should complete their own photocopiable sheet.

4. When they have finished, go through the names of the bones and where they are in the body using the large picture of the skeleton.

Paired work
5. The children can work in pairs to make a simple skeleton. Make sure each pair has scissors, card, paper fasteners and access to a hole punch. They should use the skeleton on the photocopiable sheet to help them. Ask the children to try to make the bones the right size, with no bones being too big or too small.

6. They need to draw the following bones on their card: skull, backbone, shoulder blades, upper arm and lower arm bones, hand bones, pelvis, upper leg and lower leg bones, and foot bones.

7. The bones can then be cut out and joined so that they move by punching holes in the bones and using paper fasteners to hold them together.

8. Hanging these skeletons on strings across the classroom will make a good display.

Differentiation
● Support children who need help in identifying the bones and placing the names correctly on the skeleton. Making the skeleton is not easy and many children will need support with punching holes and joining the bones together.
● Challenge children to find out the medical names for the bones that they have marked on their photocopiable sheets.

Science in the wider world
Understanding the body and how it works is important for understanding the kinds of stresses and strains that are placed on the body during exercise or if it is not used properly.

Review
The children can be assessed on how accurately they labelled the skeleton on their photocopiable sheets.

Objectives
● To identify that many animals have skeletons but that there are certain animals that don't.
● To know that animals that are invertebrates don't have a backbone.

Resources
Large picture of human skeleton from previous lesson; the children's completed copies of photocopiable page 202 'The skeleton' from previous lesson; paper towels; collection of clean, sterilised bones; trowels, gloves and containers for collecting worms (or worms that you have collected beforehand); magnifying lenses (preferably one each); art materials; media resource 'Skeletons' on the CD-ROM

Note: Please ensure that you follow your school's health and safety policy with regard to washing hands after this activity. You might also want to refer to the Association for Science Education publication *Be Safe*, http://www.ase.org.uk/resources/health-and-safety-resources/health-and-safety-primary-science/. Ensure that living organisms are safely returned to the same place as they were collected from after the lesson.

Speaking scientifically
invertebrate, jellyfish, vertebrate, worm (and all the names of the bones in our skeleton from the photocopiable sheet)

Lesson 3: Animal skeletons

Introduction
Make sure that the children can see the large human skeleton and that they have their completed copies of photocopiable page 202 'The skeleton' in front of them. Point to various bones on the large skeleton and ask them to say what they are. For example, they need to be able to recognise the ribs, skull and jaw, shoulder blades and leg bones. If some of the children found the scientific/medical names of some of the bones in the last lesson, ask them to tell the class what they are. Tell the children that because we have a backbone (made up of vertebrae), humans are vertebrates – like all other mammals, birds, amphibians, fish and reptiles.

Whole-class work
1. Show the children media resource 'Skeletons' on the CD-ROM. Can the children work out which animal each skeleton belongs to?

2. Pass some of the sterilised bones around so that the children can touch them as well as see them. Ask them to describe the bones. They should understand that they are hard, stiff and solid.

3. Ask the children what bones are for. They should understand that they hold our bodies together and that they do the same for other animals. They are for protection, support and movement.

4. Return to the pictures of other skeletons and ask the children if they can recognise some of the bones. They should understand that the leg bones in animals help them to move, just as our leg bones do.

5. Explain to the children that some animals don't have hard skeletons but are still able to move. Show them the pictures of worms and jellyfish. Tell them that the water in their bodies gives them support just as water in a balloon supports its rubber wall.

Group work
6. Take the children into the school grounds to dig for worms. Bring the worms carefully back into the classroom. You will need enough so that the children can examine them closely.

7. Remind the children that these are creatures without skeletons. Tell the children to look at the worms with their magnifying glasses. Ask them whether they can identify some of the parts of the worms' bodies. They should be able to suggest that worms have skin and that they have a head and a tail.

8. Tell the children to draw a worm as accurately as possible, including as much detail as they can. These drawings can be mounted on display in the classroom near to the skeleton models.

> **Differentiation**
> ● Some children will still need help in recognising the parts of the human body. They may also find the drawings difficult and need extra support and encouragement. Make sure that they use their magnifying lenses to see as much detail as possible.
> ● Challenge children to find out how a worm moves through the soil and how a jellyfish moves through the sea. They could also find out about how poisonous some jellyfish are.

Science in the wider world
Encourage children to learn about the natural world and the creatures that live in it. Understanding more about different animals may help them to make better decisions about the conservation and protection of different species.

Review
The children can be assessed on how well they understand the similarities between human skeletons and those of other creatures, as well as how competently they can complete a closely observed drawing.

Objectives
● To understand that joints allow the skeleton to move.
● To identify some of the important joints such as the jaw, knee, elbow and wrist.

Resources
Photocopiable page 203 'The joints'; large picture of skeleton from previous lesson

Speaking scientifically
ball and socket, elbow, hinge, hip, jaw, joint, knee

Lesson 1: Our joints

Introduction

Ask the children to tell you what our skeletons are for. They should remember that one of the functions of the skeleton is to keep us rigid and support our bodies so we don't collapse like jelly. However, point out to the children that we couldn't move if we were completely rigid and stiff. We have to be able to bend lots of different parts of our bodies.

Whole-class work

1. Ask a volunteer to repeat some of the movements that the children saw in week 1, lesson 1. The volunteer should stand up, walk and bend down to pick something up off the floor.

2. Explain that joints join bones together and are flexible so that we can move. Ask the children which joints were used when the volunteer stood up. Write down the names on the board. (They used knees, hips, ankles and joints between the vertebrae in their backbone.) *How did the volunteer use joints when they walked?* (Again, they used their knees, hips, ankles and joints between the vertebrae in their backbone.) *Which joints did they use to pick something up?* (They used their shoulders, elbows, wrists and finger joints.)

3. Ask the children if anyone knows how their hip joint works. Explain that it is a ball and socket joint. The ball is on the end of their leg bone and the socket is in their pelvis. Show them where this is on the large drawing of the skeleton. Tell all the children to cup one hand for the socket and put the fist of the other hand into it as the ball. They should experiment with this 'joint' and see that it can move in all directions. This is how their hips work and they use this joint to walk and run.

4. Ask someone to open and close the classroom door and ask them how it works. (It uses a hinge.) *Do they know where there are hinge joints in their bodies?* The children should recognise that both their knees and elbows are hinge joints.

Group work

5. Ask the children to look at photocopiable page 203 'The joints'. Show them the ball and socket joint and the hinge joint. (The making of the model skull will be done in the next lesson.)

6. Give each child a piece of paper and ask them to draw themselves moving in three different ways. This could be sitting down, walking, eating and so on. They must label each drawing by drawing a line from each joint that is being used and writing the name of the joint.

> **Differentiation**
> ● Some children will need to spend more time on recognising the names of joints and where they are on the skeleton. They may find labelling the joints on their drawings difficult and need a word bank of appropriate terms.
> ● Challenge children to find out how more complex joints work, such as the ankle, and ask them to explain how their backbone works.

Science in the wider world

The more children know about how their body works, the more likely they are to realise that they need to keep it healthy and to try to find out how to do this.

Review

The children could be assessed on their knowledge of the names of the joints and where they are on the skeleton.

Objectives
● To understand how a joint works.
● To use a model to show how a joint works.

Resources
Photocopiable page 203 'The joints'; card; glue; scissors; paper fasteners; hole punches; pieces of freshly cut apple

Speaking scientifically
ball and socket joint, hinge joint, hip, jaw, skeleton

Lesson 2: A model joint

Introduction

Tell the children to stand up and move to the side of their chairs so that they are in a small space. Ask them to walk two steps without moving their joints. Ask them to pick something up off their desk without moving their joints.

Whole-class work

1. Ask the children what they would look like if they didn't have a skeleton. They should realise that they would be like a jelly or a pile of clothes on the floor, unable to move at all. The skeleton, as they already know, keeps our bodies rigid. They should also realise that our bones will only move in certain directions, even when using large movements such as walking or small, fine movements such as picking up a pencil.

2. Remind them what a ball and socket joint is and ask them to stand up and move their hips. Ask: *How do the hips move? In what directions can you move your hips?* As the ball moves around the socket, it is possible to move it in different directions. The children should practise moving their hip joints slowly and concentrate on how they work. They can stand still and lift up one leg with the knee bent and then with the knee straight. They can move one leg outwards and then back alongside the other leg.

3. Remind the children how a hinge works. Ask them to put their fingers either side of their jaws and then open and shut their mouths. They should be able to feel the hinge joint working as their jaw moves up and down. Give each child a piece of apple and ask them to eat it slowly. Ask them to choose a partner and to feel each other's jaws working as they chew and the hinge joint moves.

Paired work

4. Give each pair another copy of photocopiable page 203 'The joints' (or they can use the one that they already have). They will also need some card, scissors, glue and a paper fastener. In addition they will need access to a paper hole punch, or you could punch the holes yourself when each pair is ready.

5. Tell them that they will be making a working model of the jaw. They will need to cut out the two pieces of the skull and then stick them on to the thin card. They should cut out each of the shapes on the card, punch the holes in the correct places and then join the two parts together with the paper fastener.

6. The children can now see how a hinge joint works. These can be displayed alongside the skeletons and the drawings of worms.

> ### Differentiation
> ● Some children will find creating the model jaw difficult and may need extra help.
> ● Challenge children to find pictures of the human hand with all its joints and bones. They could try to explain how their hand moves in order to pick up small objects like paper clips. Ask them to find out whether apes and monkeys would be able to pick up the same paper clip.

Science in the wider world

If the children understand how important healthy working joints are, they will be more inclined to try to keep their joints healthy. Increasing the weight that joints have to bear increases the likelihood of joint problems as people get older.

Review

The children can be assessed on their understanding of how a ball and socket and a hinge joint work.

Lesson 3: Our muscles

Introduction
Ask the children to do the following activities: smile, pretend to bite something, pick up a pencil, and stand up. They should be able to tell you how they did each action. Elicit the idea that they used their bones and their joints such as their jaw bone, fingers, elbows, thighs and so on. Point out to the children (if they don't mention it themselves) that they couldn't have done any of these activities without using their muscles too.

Whole-class work
1. Explain that muscles attach to bones and hold joints together. We use our muscles to make our bones and joints move.

2. Look at the picture of an athlete running. Ask the children which muscles the athlete is using most. The children should be able to see the arm and leg muscles working hard to make the athlete run quickly. Now share the picture of the body builder. The arm and leg muscles should be exaggerated and easy to see.

3. Tell the children that animals also have muscles. Show the children the pictures of the animals. Ask: *Which muscles is the deer/antelope using most? Why do these muscles have to be strong?* The children should be able to suggest that these animals must be able to run quickly to escape from predators. Look together at the picture of the gorilla. Ask: *Which of its muscles do you think are the most powerful? What about the kangaroo? How do you know which muscles are the most powerful?* (The kangaroo's leg muscles are large and easily seen.)

4. Discuss with the children whether or not most of their muscles can be moved when they want to move them. Do they know a muscle that they can't control? (The heart is a muscle but we don't have to think about making it beat.) Make sure the children understand that most muscles can be controlled.

5. Ask them to straighten and then bend their arms. As they do, they should feel the muscle at the top of their arm changing shape. Write down the names of the arm muscles on the board – biceps and triceps. These are skeletal muscles and are attached to the bones. They can see this happening and feel the movement best in their hands. Ask them to feel their own hand as they flex their fingers and pick things up.

6. Review the names of the main joints and write them on the board.

Independent work
7. Give each child a clean photocopiable page 202 'The skeleton'. This time ask them to label the joints in the correct positions on the skeleton. They can also complete interactive activity 'Our muscles' on the CD-ROM.

8. They should also mark where the arm muscles are in red and label these with their correct names – triceps and biceps.

Differentiation
● Some children will need to be reminded of where the joints are and will need help when completing their photocopiable sheets.
● Challenge children to find out about the muscles of another mammal such as a dog or cat. Are some of the muscles similar to ours?

Science in the wider world
Muscles allow us to move and have to be kept healthy. It is important to know that they can be strained if we try to make them do too much – like lifting something that is too heavy. Good nutrition and eating the right food are also important in keeping the muscles healthy.

Review
The children can be assessed on how well they complete the photocopiable sheet.

Objectives
● To understand how our skeleton, joints and muscles work together to make movement possible.
● To look at how muscles expand and contract.

Resources
Photocopiable page 202 'The skeleton' from the previous lesson; photocopiable page 204 'The muscles'; thick card; scissors; glue; hole punches; paper fasteners; elastic bands; coloured pencils; stethoscopes (if available); extra adult help in the classroom if possible

Speaking scientifically
abdominal, contract, heart, joint, muscle, pectoral, quadriceps, skeleton, stretch

Lesson 1: How muscles work

Introduction
Ask the children to name a muscle that they can't control – they should remember the example of their heart from the previous lesson. Ask them to feel their heart beating. If stethoscopes are available, let them listen to each other's heartbeats. Ask what muscles control arm movements. They should remember triceps and biceps. If they clench their arm they should feel the bump that is their biceps and then the slight movement of their triceps as they relax their arm.

Whole-class work
1. Tell the children that they have over 600 muscles in their bodies. Some are large and some are very small. Smiling and blinking use small muscles. Tell them to smile and try to feel which muscles are moving. They can then do the same when blinking or winking. They could also try very carefully feeling the muscles in a partner's face as their partner blinks or smiles.

2. Ask the children if they know where their quadriceps muscles are. Write the word on the board. These are the large muscles in their thighs. Tell them to stand up, put the palms of their hands on the front of their thighs and then squat down. They should feel the quadriceps stretching and moving.

3. If they stay standing and breathe in and out in an exaggerated way, they should feel their chest muscles, their *pectorals*, moving. If they put their hands on their stomachs and move their stomachs in and out, they will feel their abdominal muscles stretch and contract. Write 'pectorals' and 'abdominals' on the board and tell the children that these muscles help them stand and sit down.

4. Make sure that each child has their own copy of photocopiable page 202 'The skeleton' from the previous lesson. They can now add these new muscles to it. They should add the quadriceps in green, pectorals in blue and abdominals in yellow.

Paired/Group work
5. Explain how the triceps extend the arm and the biceps flex or contract it. It is the biceps they can feel when they flex their arm. Give each group photocopiable page 204 'The muscles' and explain how to make the model hand. (This should show how the muscles stretch and contract.) The difficult part is punching holes in the card, which has to be thicker than usual to take the strain of the elastic bands, and cutting the shapes out of the thick card. Adult volunteers should be able to help do this quickly and easily.

6. The finished model hands can be displayed alongside the skeletons, drawings and hinge joints.

> ### Differentiation
> ● Some children will find identifying where the muscles are difficult and may also need support with reading the names of the muscles.
> ● Challenge children to draw their own scientific diagram of how their arm moves, with a written description and the correct labels.

Science in the wider world
It is important for children to know that we have lots of different muscles. If there are problems with them, particularly the larger ones, then we will have issues with movement. Keeping fit and doing exercise is important to keep all our muscles healthy.

Review
The children can be assessed on how well they have identified and placed the muscles on their 'The skeleton' sheet.

Objectives
● To identify that skeletons change in size as we get older.

Resources
Pictures of human adults (perhaps celebrities) as grown-ups and babies; pictures of other animals as adults and babies; measuring tapes; large sheets of paper; sticky tape; scissors; a volunteer adult who won't object to lying down and being drawn around; an outline of a baby drawn on a piece of paper (this needs forward planning and will depend on knowing someone with a baby)

Speaking scientifically
growth, height, length, size

Lesson 2: Different sizes

Introduction
Show the class the pictures of human babies and adults and ask them to tell you some of the differences. Elicit the idea that babies are small and grow into adults. Show the class the pictures of baby and adult animals and ask: *How are they different?* It will be obvious that baby animals grow into adults.

Whole-class work
1. Look again at the pictures of human babies and adults. Ask the children to tell you what parts of the human body grow as they get older. Elicit the idea that the skeleton grows and the bones get longer and stronger. At the same time the muscles and joints also change in size to support the skeleton and help us move.

2. Place your forearm on the board and ask a child to mark where the elbow is and where the tips of your fingers are. Measure the distance between the two marks and write it down. (This has roughly measured your hand and lower arm bones.)

3. Ask another adult – preferably noticeably shorter or taller than you are – to allow their forearm to be measured and write down the result. Do the same with four volunteer children. Ask: *What do these measurements show you? Do the tallest people have the longest arm bones?* (You should find that taller people do tend to have longer arm bones.)

4. Ask a volunteer child and a volunteer adult to lie down on a large sheet of paper (you will probably need several sheets joined together with tape). Draw around them to give an outline of their bodies. The baby outline you prepared earlier can be mounted alongside the child and adult outlines on the classroom wall to show that humans clearly grow as they get older.

Group work
5. Organise the class into groups of four or five. Each group should write down the names of the children in that group. They should measure each other and record the results so that alongside each name they have the following four measurements: height, arm bone (as it was measured before), leg bone from the ground to the knee, and head circumference measured at the forehead.

6. Find out who is the tallest and shortest in the group. Ask: *Does the shortest child have the shortest leg and arm bones? Is the measurement around their skull also the smallest?* If some other teachers are willing to volunteer, the same measurements can be taken from four adults and the same questions asked.

Differentiation
● Some children will need support with measuring and writing down accurate measurements. If the children work in mixed ability groups they will be able to help each other.
● Challenge children to test the idea that differences in height mean differences in the size of other bones by measuring finger length. They could also use secondary sources to find out about the Egyptian measurement, the cubit. What was it used for?

Science in the wider world
We grow as we develop into adults and it is important that we grow healthily. However, we don't continue to grow after we become adults. Once we have stopped growing we must maintain our bodies to make sure that they stay healthy.

Review
Measuring in centimetres and metres can be difficult and the children can be assessed on how well they can do this.

Objectives
• To identify that bones in the skeleton change and grow in size.

Resources
Results of measurements taken in the previous lesson; photocopiable page 205 'Hands'; string; rulers and measuring tapes; 1cm graph paper

Speaking scientifically
area, finger, height, length, span, thumb

Lesson 3: Hand size

Introduction
Organise the class into groups of four or five, ready for the group work later in the lesson. Make sure each group knows who is the tallest in that group and that everyone knows who the tallest boy and the tallest girl in the class are. Measure them and write their names and heights on the board as reminders for later in the lesson.

Whole-class work
1. Review the work from the previous lesson by asking a series of questions and discussing the answers. The children will need the results of all their measurements. Ask: *Did the adults who were measured have larger bones than the children? Why was that? Will the bones in their skeletons get even bigger?* The children should know that adults stop growing in their late teens so their bones will not get bigger. Adults keep the same shoe size once they have finished growing. This is a good example of bones not continuing to grow.

2. Now ask about the leg and arm bones. *Did the tallest children have the longest bones? Were there any differences between tall boys and tall girls?*

3. Ask the children to hold up their hands, spread out with the palm outwards so that the fingers are splayed. Let them put their hands against a partner's to see if they think there are any differences in size. Ask a volunteer to do this with you so the class can see the difference in size between an adult's and a child's hand.

Group work
4. Organise the children into their groups of four or five. Give each child photocopiable page 205 'Hands'. Tell them they will have to complete it on their own but will need help from others in the group to measure their hands.

5. Make sure each person has a piece of string, some graph paper, a measuring tape, plain paper and a pencil. Explain that they must follow the instructions on the photocopiable sheet to measure their hands in different ways.

Whole-class work
6. The results of the measurements are important. Collect them from the children so that you are able to identify who has the largest span and whose hand has the largest area and longest perimeter.

7. Use these results to ask questions: *Has the tallest person got the largest hand? Are there differences between tall girls and tall boys? Do the tallest people always have the largest bones?*

Differentiation
• Some of the measurements are difficult and it is important to support children when they are trying to measure their hands. Extra adults in the classroom would help.
• Challenge the children to measure some adults. They need only collect span measurements. Do they vary? Do small teachers/parents have smaller hands? Are there differences between men and women?

Science in the wider world
Adults have many similarities in the structure of their bodies but can be different sizes. It is important to understand that most size differences between healthy people are normal.

Review
Children could be assessed on how well they can complete the measurements and interpret their results.

Objectives
● To understand that some animals have skeletons on the outside, called exoskeletons.

Resources
Pictures of a range of animals with exoskeletons including insects, reptiles such as turtles and tortoises, and crustaceans such as crabs and lobsters; clean, cooked whole king prawns (one per table); a collection of dead insects (these can be found on window sills around the school and should include a range of different flies if possible); magnifying lenses; art materials; scissors

Speaking scientifically
crustacean, exoskeleton, insect, moulting

Lesson 1: Skeletons on the outside

Introduction
Ask the children to feel their finger bones and joints. They should be able to feel that there are lots of different ones. Ask them to feel the bones in their wrists. It should be possible to feel them when they are still and as the children flex their wrists. Ask: *What about their thigh bone – is it possible to feel that?* (Probably not.) *Why not?* They should realise that they can't feel it because it is deeper inside their body and not on the surface.

Whole-class work
1. Ask the children what they think their bones are covered by. They should know that there are muscles but also that the whole of their body is covered by a layer of fat and skin. Underneath this are the muscles, joints and bones. Ask: *What is the skin for?* Elicit the idea that it is for protection. It holds everything together and keeps harmful things out. It also helps you keep warm and stay cool.

2. Show the children the pictures of insects and ask them how they are different from us. They should notice the obvious differences such as number of legs, wings and so on, but they should also see that they all have some kind of shell or hard outer covering. Next show them the pictures of lobsters and crabs and ask them to tell you how they are different from us. They should see that they have hard outer shells.

3. Explain that these creatures all have exoskeletons and that their muscles and organs are attached to the inside of their skeletons. Their exoskeletons are usually hard and rigid, not flexible like our skeletons. Remind the children that as we grow bigger and taller our skins grow with us, but tell them that this doesn't happen in most creatures with exoskeletons. These creatures have to moult. They shed their outer layer and grow a new one.

Group work
4. Give each table a king prawn and ask them to examine it, feel it and describe it. They should realise that it is covered in a hard but flexible shell. This is its exoskeleton. Talk about how it moves using its legs.

5. Give out a selection of dead insects and ask the children to again examine and describe them. Many of these insects will have wings but the children should also be able to see the hard outer body parts.

6. Ask the children to draw the king prawn and one insect. Make sure that they use their magnifying lenses to see as much detail as possible. Alongside each drawing, ask them to write a description of how the creature moves and how its exoskeleton protects it.

> **Differentiation**
> ● Some children might find drawing the creatures difficult. Encourage them to put in as much detail as possible.
> ● Challenge children to find out more about some of the sea creatures such as lobsters and crabs – their life cycles, what they eat and how they breathe.

Science in the wider world
It is important for the children to know as much as possible about a wide range of creatures because they live alongside us and they and their habitats need to be protected.

Review
The children can be assessed on how well they can draw from close observation and how observant they were when describing creatures with exoskeletons.

Objectives
● To understand the important role of a skeleton in protecting the organs of an animal.

Resources
Large picture of skeleton from previous lessons; large picture of a skeleton that also shows the heart and lungs; pictures of skeletons of a dog, cat and/or ape; photocopiable page 202 'The skeleton'; thin card; glue; art materials; scissors

Speaking scientifically
backbone, heart, lungs, ribs

Lesson 2: Skeletons for protection

Introduction
Ask the children to use their index fingers to push against their chests and feel their ribs. Tell them to start at the top and work down. Can they count them? (They should be able to count 12 pairs.) Talk about some of their pets such as guinea pigs, dogs, cats or mice. Ask whether the children think these animals have ribs (don't show them the pictures of animal skeletons yet). What do they think their ribs are for?

Whole-class work
1. Talk to the children about what happens when they breathe – their lungs draw in air. Ask them to put their hands on their chests to feel this happening. Explain that oxygen moves around their body in the blood. Tell them that the heart is a pump that pumps the blood around their body. Ask them to feel their heart beating.

2. The heart and lungs are therefore very important organs. Do the children know where they are? Show them the large picture of the skeleton and ask for volunteers to point to where the heart and lungs are. Then show them the picture of the skeleton with the heart and lungs in position to check whether the volunteers were right.

3. Ask the children what they think the ribs are for. They should realise that the ribs are a kind of cage made of hard bones that protects the heart and lungs.

4. Show the children the skeletons of other animals and ask for volunteers to show where they think the heart and lungs will be. They should realise that the ribs are doing exactly the same thing in the animals as in a human skeleton – protecting the heart and lungs.

Independent work
5. Each child needs two sheets of thin card, photocopiable page 202 'The skeleton', a pencil and access to scissors and glue. They should use one piece of thin card to draw a skull and a simple backbone reaching as far as the top of the pelvis. The photocopiable sheet will help them do this.

6. Ask them to draw the lungs on their diagram and colour them blue. Next they should draw the heart and colour it red. They can use the large picture of the skeleton with the lungs and heart in place to help them.

7. Tell them that they will now be making the rib cage to show how it protects the heart and lungs. Ask them to cut out 12 thin strips of card. By gluing each end they should be able to stick these strips in place to give ribs that stand out from the drawing on the card. They should form a kind of cage over the heart and lungs.

> ### Differentiation
> ● This seems like a simple activity but making a model rib cage is not easy. Some children will require adult help to cut out the ribs and stick them on in a suitable 3D shape.
> ● Challenge the children to find out how their ribs are connected to the rest of their skeleton.

Science in the wider world
The children should realise that their heart and lungs are very important organs that need to be kept healthy through a good diet and lots of exercise.

Review
The children can be assessed on their understanding of what their rib cage is for and how it is similar in many other animals.

Objectives
● To understand how the skeletons of a range of animals vary.

Resources
Interactive activity 'Strange skeletons' on the CD-ROM; photocopiable page 206 'Strange skeletons'; an apple

Speaking scientifically
amphibian, mammal, movement, reptile, skeleton

Lesson 3: Strange skeletons

Introduction
Remind the children that they use their bones, joints and muscles when they move. Ask them what moves when they reach out to pick up their pencil from the desk. Tell them to try this. They should realise that they move their arms, elbows and fingers and various bones and muscles inside them. What about when they run? They should know that they need the ball and socket joint in their hip, their knees, leg bones and leg muscles.

Whole-class work
1. Chew a small piece of apple. Ask the children what they see happening as you chew. The jaw will move up and down and from side to side because it is designed to move like that so we can eat.

2. Ask the children to pick up some small object using their thumb and forefinger. What moves? It is this grip that most animals can't do. Only humans, apes and monkeys can pick things up like this. Our bones, muscles and joints make it possible.

3. Why do they think a deer has long, thin legs – can they remember from previous lessons? (It is so it can run quickly.)

4. Show the class the pictures of each of the animal skeletons from the interactive activity 'Strange skeletons' on the CD-ROM. When they have talked about each skeleton, encourage them to match it to the correct animal name.

5. Ask what is strange about the elephant. (Obviously its size and bulk, its tusks and its trunk – though the trunk has no bones and so is not visible within the skeleton.) *What does the elephant do with its trunk?* Remind them that the elephant is a mammal.

6. Look together at the other mammal, the kangaroo. *What looks 'strange' about this skeleton?* (The leg bones and long tail.) Ask: *How do you think a kangaroo moves? Why does it have such large back legs?*

7. The frog is an amphibian. *How do you think it moves? Which part of the skeleton tells us how it moves?*

8. The snake is a reptile and is more difficult. The skeleton is articulated all along its length, which means the snake can curve and slither its body easily.

Group work
9. Give each child photocopiable page 206 'Strange skeletons'. What kind of animal do they think each strange skeleton is from? How do they know? Ask them to write down the name of each animal under its skeleton. They should also write a sentence for each skeleton explaining their answer. For example: *This is a kangaroo because it has huge back legs to hop with and a long tail.*

10. Ask them to draw the outline of each creature around the skeleton.

Differentiation
● This is not a difficult lesson but some children will need help in writing a sentence about each of the creatures on the photocopiable sheet.
● Challenge children to look at the skeletons of other creatures such as a swordfish, a whale or a seal.

Science in the wider world
Once again, it is important for children to understand about a wide range of the creatures that share the Earth and might need protecting in the future.

Review
Children can be assessed on how well they can match the skeletons to the correct animals and how well they understand the relationship between skeleton shape and movement.

Objectives
● To understand that we use our bones, muscles and joints when we exercise.
● To understand that exercise is important and helps keep our bodies healthy.

Resources
Photocopiable page 207 'Exercise diary'

Speaking scientifically
active, bone, exercise, heart, inactive, joint, lungs, muscle

Lesson 1: Exercise

Introduction
Remind the children what happens when they walk and run. Ask a volunteer to walk across the classroom. The class should know that they are using their bones to keep them upright, their muscles to move their bones and joints, and their joints to enable them to bend their bodies (for example, their knees, hips and so on).

Whole-class work
1. Ask the class what else is happening as they walk and run. Elicit the idea that their hearts are beating and that their lungs are drawing in air. Ask them what happens to their heartbeat and breathing when they run. (Their heart beats faster and their breathing gets deeper and faster.)

2. Discuss with the children what happens if muscles aren't used. They should know that the muscles will become weaker and not work so well. Remind them that their heart is a muscle.

3. Ask the children what they think exercise means. List all the different kinds of exercise that they can think of, including walking, running, cycling, PE, playing games and so on. Make a list of any exercise they think they have done already today. Some children will have walked or cycled to school. They might have run around the playground or had a PE lesson.

4. What is their favourite exercise? You could make a simple class 'Favourite Exercise' bar graph using the exercises they have already identified – for example, the bars could include: walking, running, cycling, PE, and any other favourites.

5. Ask the children what the differences are between being active and being inactive. They could list some things they do that are inactive (for example, watching TV, using their computers and so on).

Independent work
6. Give each child photocopiable page 207 'Exercise diary' and ask them to complete their own exercise diary for a week. Keep reminding them to do this throughout the week.

7. At the end of the week, talk about what they have written. Remind them that they must do regular exercise in order to stay healthy. It is important that they keep fit so that their muscles, including their hearts and lungs, continue to work properly.

Differentiation
● Some children might find it easier to draw pictures of their daily exercise in their exercise diary.
● Challenge children to list their activities in their exercise diaries and to write down alongside each activity how long they spent doing this kind of activity. At the end of the week they could add up how long they spent doing exercise in total during that week.

Science in the wider world
Children are becoming less active and their overall health often suffers as a consequence. Muscle tone is lost when there is insufficient use and this includes the heart. Sufficient exercise also helps to burn off excess calories.

Review
Children could be assessed on how well they completed their exercise diary and how well they can explain why exercise is important.

■SCHOLASTIC

Objectives
- To consider the relationship between the skeleton and movement.

Resources
Large picture of the human skeleton; measuring tapes

Speaking scientifically
bone, distance, knee, shin, stride, thigh

Lesson 2: Short legs, short strides?

Introduction
Ask a volunteer to walk quickly across the room and remind the children what parts of their body they use to walk and run. They should be able to remember their thigh bones, knees, feet and ankles, as well as the large thigh muscles called the quadriceps. Ask someone to point to these bones, joints and muscles on the large picture of the skeleton.

Whole-class work
1. Ask the children to tell you what a stride is. Ask for volunteers to show you. Make sure they understand that a stride means taking a normal step. Ask: *Who do you think has the longest stride in the class? Why do you think that? Who do you think has the shortest stride? Why do you think that?* Their answers should suggest that the tallest children will have the longest strides and vice versa.

2. Ask: *Do the children with the shortest legs have the shortest strides? How can we prove whether this is true or not?* Discuss some of their suggestions. These might include measuring the length of people's legs and then measuring their strides – *but how do we measure strides? How do we know that everyone is striding normally and not exaggerating their strides?*

Paired work
3. Organise the class so that the children are working with a partner. Tell them that the first thing to do is to measure everyone's legs as accurately as possible. They can do this for their partner by measuring the distance in centimetres from their partner's hip bone to the floor with a measuring tape. Then their partner should do the same for them.

4. Collect each child's leg measurement, correcting any that are widely inaccurate. Write them on the board in order from the longest to the shortest.

5. Next they need to measure their strides. The best way to do this is over a certain distance. They should count the number of strides it takes them to cover this measured distance. Measure 50 metres on the playground. Each pair can then take it in turns to walk the measured 50 metres and count their number of strides.

6. This number should again be collected and written alongside their leg length on the board. The higher the number of strides, the more strides it took to cover the 50m and so the shorter the stride. Make sure that all the children understand this.

7. Look at the figures and ask the class whether they have managed to prove that the shorter the legs, the shorter the stride.

Differentiation
- Some children will need support when measuring their partner's leg length and may require adult help.
- Challenge children to look closely at how athletes 'stride' as they run, perhaps using a video website. They could also watch dogs run (greyhounds would be particularly good) and see whether their stride gets longer the faster they go.

Science in the wider world
Children should know how their body works and how it moves. The more they know about how complicated these movements are, the more they will begin to understand how important exercise is.

Review
The children can be assessed on how accurately they can record the measurements and how well they can reach a reasoned conclusion.

Objectives
• To consider the different ways that minibeasts move.

Resources
Pictures of common minibeasts, including spiders, slugs, beetles and so on; trowels, gloves and containers for collecting woodlice and snails (or examples that you have collected beforehand); magnifying lenses; trays pre-prepared with damp soil and dead and living leaves
Note: Please ensure that you follow your school's health and safety policy with regard to washing hands after this activity. You might also want to refer to the Association for Science Education publication *Be Safe*, http://www.ase.org.uk/resources/health-and-safety-resources/health-and-safety-primary-science/. Ensure that living organisms are safely returned to the same place as they were collected from after the lesson.

Speaking scientifically
crustacean, mollusc, muscular, segment

Lesson 3: How minibeasts move

Introduction
Talk to the class about how mammals move using a combination of bones, muscles and joints. Ask them to name other creatures that move in this way – frogs (amphibians), birds, fish and reptiles.

Whole-class work
1. Show the children the pictures of common minibeasts. (Avoid talking about flying insects as they will be looked at in another lesson.) Ask them how a spider or a beetle moves. The children should recognise that they use their legs – which is similar to how we move. Make sure the children know that spiders are arachnids, not insects, and have eight legs. Insects like beetles have six legs.

2. Take the class outside to collect woodlice and snails. (Make sure that you have already collected some of these in case the children don't find any.) Tell the children that both these types of creature like damp habitats. Remind the children that they are collecting living things and to be careful when handling them.

3. Bring the snails and woodlice they find into the classroom. Remind the children to wash their hands before doing anything else.

Group work
4. Give each group of four or five children a pre-prepared tray and supervise as they put their woodlice and snails into the trays.

5. Tell the children to use the magnifying lenses to look at the woodlice and describe what they see. Woodlice are crustaceans like lobsters and have 14 flexible body segments, each with a pair of legs. When they use the magnifying lenses to see how the woodlice move, the children should be able to see the legs moving rapidly in perfect sequence.

6. Tell the children to look at the snails and describe how they move. Snails are molluscs and have a shell as an exoskeleton. The first thing the children should notice is that a snail doesn't have legs. They have a single muscular foot that moves in an undulating wave to push it along the surface. Ask: *How is a snail's foot different from ours?* (We have bones and joints and a snail doesn't.) *Why are they slimy?* (The slime helps them to slide their foot across different surfaces.)

7. Tell the children to draw the snail and the woodlouse. Underneath each drawing they should write sentences describing how each minibeast moves.

Differentiation
• Most children will be able to draw the two creatures, but some will need help with writing their sentences. Mixed ability groups should offer support but some children will need adult input.
• Challenge children to explain how spiders move around their webs. They could also look at grasshoppers and consider whether there are similarities between how they move and how frogs and kangaroos move.

Science in the wider world
Minibeasts are a crucial part of many important food chains and most of them need specific habitats in order to survive. The more children know about minibeasts, the better prepared they will be to protect them in the future.

Review
Make sure that the children understand the similarities and differences between how these minibeasts move and can compare their movements to humans and other mammals. The children can be assessed on how well they can describe the movements of their two minibeasts.

Objectives
● To consider the different ways that flying creatures move.

Resources
Pictures of bats, birds and flying insects such as butterflies and dragonflies; pictures of skeletons of bats and birds; thin card; glue; scissors

Speaking scientifically
feather, flight, glide, muscle, wing

Lesson 1: How flying creatures move

Introduction
Ask the children to name of some creatures that move on and underneath the ground; try to get a wide range of suggestions. Next ask the children to suggest some creatures that move through water. They should be able to remember fish, jellyfish and large mammals like whales. They may also mention amphibians again. Mention also birds that move through the water.

Whole-class work
1. Ask the children to name some creatures that move through the air and write their suggestions on the board in three columns. Put flies, butterflies, dragonflies and other insects in one column, bats in another column, and various birds in the third. Ask the children to suggest a title for each column. (They are insects, mammals and birds.)

2. Ask them what flying creatures they have seen in the school grounds or in their own garden or local parks.

3. Ask the children: *What do all of these flying creatures have in common?* (They all have wings that can move.) *What about differences?* (The number of wings can vary. Only birds have feathers and only bats are mammals with fur. Insects have exoskeletons.)

4. Show them the pictures of various flying creatures and their skeletons. Make sure they realise that wings made up of joints and bones push bats and birds through the air using powerful muscles. Birds have light bones and their feathers make their wings more powerful. Bats' wings are like modified arms and hands covered by a thin skin. The children will be able to see this clearly in the pictures of bat skeletons.

5. Insects are more complicated. The wings are a special part of the insect's exoskeleton. There are many different types of insect wings depending on the type of insect.

6. All of these flying creatures move through the air to look for food and to escape from predators.

Independent work
7. Each child should draw the outline of a bird's body (without the wings) on a piece of thin card and colour it carefully so that it looks like a brightly coloured bird. They should then cut the outline out.

8. Next they should draw two separate wings with flaps that can be bent and glued to the bird's body. They can colour these in carefully so that the feathers can be seen, and then cut them out.

9. Finally they should glue a wing to each side of the bird's body so that they can move up and down. These models can be hung on strings in the classroom.

Differentiation
● Some children may need help in making their bird. More adult assistance in the classroom would be useful.
● Insect flight is complicated. Challenge children to use secondary sources to find out more about dragonflies and how their wings actually work.

Science in the wider world
Once again, this topic will help children understand more about the wide range of different living things in the world. Flying insects, for example, are crucial in pollinating the food plants that we eat.

Review
It is important for the children to understand that flight is another way of moving that largely uses the same combination of joints, muscles and bones.

Objectives
● To understand that animals can move in different ways and at different speeds.

Resources
Measuring tapes; timers; secondary sources including books such as *The Guinness Book of Records* and access to the internet; pictures of the animals; art materials; interactive activity 'Animal record breakers' on the CD-ROM

Speaking scientifically
jump, movement, smallest, speed, strongest, tallest

Lesson 2: Animal record breakers

Introduction
Use volunteers to try out some class records. Find out who can jump the furthest, who can run the fastest, and who can stand still the longest. Use the whole class to find out who is the tallest and who has the biggest span. Remind them that we are all different and that in the animal kingdom there all kinds of differences.

Independent/Whole-class work
I. The children can use interactive activity 'Animal record breakers' and a variety of secondary sources to find out about animal record breakers. They can then share their most amazing facts with the whole class. Make sure that each measurement of speed, height, length and so on is put into some kind of context so that the children can understand it better. Here are some examples:

● Blue whales are the longest and loudest animals on Earth – up to 110 feet long and with a song that is louder than a jet engine.
● The giraffe is the tallest animal and can grow to more than 20 feet.
● The smallest reptile is a tiny dwarf gecko. They have lengths of only around 1.6cm when fully grown.
● The peregrine falcon can dive at speeds of over 200mph. The spine-tailed swift can fly across the sky at 70mph at least (some people claim to have recorded them at up to 106mph).
● Cheetahs can run at over 70mph – the speed limit on motorways. The ostrich is the fastest-running bird at about 45mph.
● The North American cougar can leap 20 feet upwards and the southern cricket frog can jump to a height over 60 times its body length. This is the equivalent of a human jumping to the height of a 38 storey building.
● A bird, the Arctic tern, has the longest migration of any animal. It travels around 45,000 miles each year from the North to South Pole and back.
● Rhinoceros beetles can lift 850 times their own weight. If humans could do this they would be able to lift nine fully grown elephants.

2. Ask: *How do these animals do these amazing things?* Remind children that it is because of their skeletons, muscles and joints.

Independent work
3. Ask the children to choose a record breaker – one that they find the most interesting. It could be a mammal, an insect, a bird, or whatever they choose.

4. Tell them to draw their chosen animal carefully and to write a description of why it is a record breaker. If it is the fastest or strongest, what part of its body helps it move like this? These pictures and descriptions can be displayed to show the wide range of different creatures on Earth.

Differentiation
● Some children will find describing their chosen creature difficult and may need adult support with spellings and so on.
● Challenge the children to find out about some human record breakers. For example, who is the fastest ever human being? (This is probably the world 100m record holder.) They could run 100m themselves and see what the time difference is.

Science in the wider world
The world is full of different and spectacular creatures. The children need to be aware of this and should understand that humans have a duty to protect these creatures so they can survive in their own habitats.

Review
The children can be assessed on how well they describe the record breaking creature that they have chosen.

Objectives
● To explore the parts of our bodies that we use during certain exercises.

Resources
Hall/gym and apparatus for PE; PE kit for the children; photocopiable page 'The human body' from the CD-ROM

Speaking scientifically
active, energetic, exercise, joint, muscle

Lesson 3: A PE lesson and our bodies

Introduction
Before the class is taken to the hall/gym, remind them about the lessons on joints, muscles and the skeleton. They should remember that when they move they use a combination of all three. Also remind them about how their lungs take in oxygen from the air and their hearts pump the oxygen round their bodies in the blood.

Whole-class work
1. When the class is in the hall, remind the children that their bodies are designed to be active and that they need to take regular exercise to stay healthy. Tell them that we need to use our muscles in order to keep them strong. Ask them what kind of things they do to exercise their bodies. They will probably suggest things like running, walking and riding bicycles. Find out whether they think they get any exercise at school. They should realise that they play games and do PE.

2. Start the lesson with a vigorous warm-up where the children must change the way they are moving when you tell them to. Call out *run* and after a short time call *walk*, then *hop*, then *skip* and so on.

3. When they have warmed up, tell them to stop and sit on the floor. Ask them which parts of their bodies they used during the warm-up and if their bodies feel different since they started moving. They should feel warmer and realise that they are breathing more heavily. Remind them that they are breathing more deeply because their muscles need more oxygen. Their lungs take it in faster and their heart pumps it around their bodies more quickly.

4. Prepare a circuit using large and small apparatus for the children to move around. Make sure that certain activities are included, such as: forward and backward rolls, pulling themselves up, moving over apparatus, jumping and stretching, throwing a ball to a partner, and so on.

Independent/Paired work
5. When they are changed and back in the classroom, make sure that each child has photocopiable page 'The human body' from the CD-ROM. Ask them to talk with a partner about how they moved during the exercise session, but that they must complete the photocopiable sheet on their own.

6. Write these movements on the board: running, walking, stretching, rolling, bending and throwing. Ask them to look at each movement, for example, 'throwing', and talk about which muscles they used. They should then draw a line from the muscles in various parts of their body that they used to throw a ball and write the label 'throwing'. They should repeat this for each of the movements that have been written on the board.

Differentiation
● Most children should be able to complete this lesson, which is a review of many of the themes of previous lessons. Some children might still need some help in deciding which muscles they used and where they are on the outline of the human body.
● Challenge some children to find out more details about how muscles work and how they are attached to bones. Give them books and internet access so they can do more research and illustrate what they find out.

Science in the wider world
The more the children know about the links between exercise, good food and a healthy body, the better in terms of their future health.

Review
The children can be assessed on how well they can link a movement to the muscles that are used.

Objectives
● To introduce some of the main bones in our bodies.
● To understand that joints allow the skeleton to move.
● To identify some of the important joints such as the jaw, knee, elbow and wrist.
● To identify some of our muscle systems.
● To understand how our skeleton, joints and muscles work together to make movement possible.

Resources
Photocopiable page 202 'The skeleton'; ruler

Working scientifically
● Recording findings using simple scientific language, drawings, labelled diagrams, keys, bar charts, and tables

Bones, muscles and joints

Revise

● First ask the children to tell you what the skeleton is for. They should remember that it is made of hard bones that keep the body rigid.
● Use volunteer children to illustrate the bones of the skeleton, the joints and the muscles. Make this part of the assessment lesson as practical as possible.
● As the first volunteer stands at the front of the class, ask different children to point to each of these bones: shoulder, thigh, backbone, skull, jaw, pelvis, shin, foot and hand. As they do, write the names on the board where the children can see them.
● This can be repeated with a different volunteer and the following joints: hip, knee, elbow, jaw, shoulder and ankle. Finally, repeat with a third volunteer who will help the children remember where the biceps, triceps and quadriceps muscles are.
● Make sure the children understand that the joints can be ball and sockets, like the hips, or hinge-type joints, like the knees and elbows (although this is a simplification).
● They also need to be reminded that it is the muscles that work the joints and move the bones by stretching and contracting.

Assess

● Give each child photocopiable page 202 'The skeleton' and a ruler and pencil. Tell them to write the correct label and draw a line to where it is on the skeleton for each of the following:
   ● Bones: thigh, shoulder, rib, backbone, skull
   ● Joints: jaw, hip, shoulder, elbow, knee
   ● Muscles: biceps, triceps, quadriceps
● Ask them to copy and complete the following sentences:
   ● My hip is a _____ type of joint.
   ● My jaw is a _____ type of joint.
   ● The joint that joins my upper leg bones to my shin bones is called the _____.
   ● _____ are joined to my bones and make my joints move.
   ● My biceps and triceps make my _____ bones move.

Further practice

● If the children have a clean photocopiable sheet they could draw their biceps, triceps and quadriceps muscles on it using different coloured pencils.
● If some children are really interested in how the human skeleton works, they could be encouraged to find out about how two more complicated parts of their bodies move. For example, they could find out about how their hands and wrists work or how their feet and ankles move.

Objectives
● To identify that skeletons change in size as we get older.
● To understand that some animals have skeletons on the outside, called exoskeletons.
● To understand the important role of a skeleton in protecting the organs of an animal.
● To understand how the skeletons of a range of animals vary.

Resources
Pictures of a range of different creatures; photocopiable page 206 'Strange skeletons'; coloured pencils

Working scientifically
● Gathering, recording, classifying and presenting data in a variety of ways to help in answering questions.
● Identifying differences, similarities or changes related to simple scientific ideas and processes.

Different sizes, different shapes

Revise
● Ask the children to look around the classroom and tell you who the tallest person in the class is.
● Remind them that humans grow and that the sizes of bones, muscles and joints change. For example, there are different sizes of handspans. Measure yours and mark it on the board. Measure a volunteer's span and write it alongside yours to show the difference in size.
● Remind them about how some parts of the skeleton in many different creatures protect organs such as the heart and lungs.
● Show them pictures of a range of different creatures including insects, crustaceans, mammals, reptiles, birds and so on. Discuss the shapes of some of these animals. For example, giraffes have very long necks, horses and deer have long, thin legs, and newts and many lizards have long tails.
● As well as these differences in shape and size, there are also similarities. Many mammals such as dogs, cats, lions, tigers and so on have similarly shaped bodies and similarly shaped skeletons, including protective rib cages.
● Show the children pictures of a penguin and a seagull (or other similar birds). Ask: *How do they know these are birds?* (Both have feathers and a beak, and son on.) *What does a penguin use its wings for? What does a seagull use its wings for?*
● Remind the children about exoskeletons and show them pictures of a tortoise, lobster, crab and some different insects.

Assess
● Make sure that each child has photocopiable page 206 'Strange skeletons'. Ask them to write sentences under each skeleton on the photocopiable sheet to describe how it is different from our human skeleton and how it is similar.
● Ask them to draw a human skeleton from the waist up. On their skeleton they must label the rib cage and draw their heart and lungs in the correct position. Ask them to write a sentence describing what the rib cage does.
● Tell them to read all the following sentences and answer 'yes' or 'no' to each one:
  ● A rat has an exoskeleton. _____
  ● Exoskeletons are always soft. _____
  ● Frogs and kangaroos have similar-shaped back legs. _____
  ● All mammals have four legs. _____
  ● My leg bones will always stay the same size. _____
  ● A lobster's skeleton is similar to mine. _____
  ● A gorilla's skeleton is similar to mine. _____

Further practice
● The children could explore the differences and similarities in the size and shape of a range of mammals, such as blue whales and mice, humans and gorillas, lions and domestic cats.
● Reptiles come in all sorts of shapes and sizes. The children could compare the similarities and differences between a giant iguana and the tiniest gecko.
● Insects and crustaceans such as crabs and lobsters have all kinds of fascinating body shapes. Many insect heads look like aliens from another world. They could be the inspiration for some imaginative writing, art work or model making.

Objectives
● To consider the relationship between the skeleton and movement.
● To consider the different ways that minibeasts move.
● To consider the different ways that flying creatures move.
● To understand that animals can move in different ways and at different speeds.

Resources
Pictures of a range of creatures including humans, other mammals, reptiles, birds and insects; pictures of skeletons of some of these creatures; photocopiable page 206 'Strange skeletons'; coloured pencils

Working scientifically
● Identifying differences, similarities or changes related to simple scientific ideas and processes.
● Asking relevant questions and using different types of scientific enquiries to answer them.

How different creatures move

Revise
● Remind the children that creatures may live mostly in the air, on the ground, under the ground, in plants, or in water.
● Humans live on the ground. Ask: *How do we move around from place to place?* (We mainly use our legs.) Ask how our legs work. The children should know that they use a combination of the bones in our skeleton, joints and muscles.
● Show the children pictures of various other ground-living mammals. Talk about how they run, walk or jump. Discuss how some are large and some small, some hunt and some are hunted.
● Some creatures live underground, such as moles (mammals) and worms. Talk about how they move in different ways and how their bodies are shaped to help them move. Moles, for example, have large front legs for digging.
● Creatures that mainly live in plants (usually trees) can climb using their hands, feet and tails. They include mammals such as monkeys, reptiles such as lizards and all kinds of insects.
● Flying creatures such as insects, bats and birds are very different animals but they all have wings. There are similarities in how their wings push them through the air.
● Most creatures that live in water, like fish and whales, have streamlined bodies that can cut through the water. Others float, like jellyfish.
● Show the children a selection of skeletons and ask them to look at the bones and say how the creature moves. For example, you could use a bird, a bat, a cat and a fish. The children should be able to identify legs, tails and wings.

Assess
● Give each child photocopiable page 206 'Strange skeletons'. Tell them to look at each of the skeletons and to write sentences about how each of the creatures moves. They should say which part of their skeleton each creature uses most to help them move.
● Ask them to answer each of these questions:
  ● How does a mole move through the ground?
  ● What part of its body does a bat use to move through the air?
  ● What part of its body does an elephant use to get its food?
● Tell them to answer 'yes' or 'no' to these statements:
  ● Bats have feathers on their wings like birds do. _____
  ● Whales and fish move through the water in similar ways._____
  ● All insects move mainly by flying. _____
  ● All birds move mainly by flying. _____
  ● All reptiles move by slithering along like snakes. _____

Further practice
● The children could look more closely at differences in how animals move by considering birds that don't fly. For example, how does an ostrich move? How are its wings different from those of a blackbird? How does a penguin move? What parts of its body does it use?
● Alternatively, they could explore differences between how mammals move. For example, how do elephants and bats move? What about whales or seals?
● Reptiles can be very different in terms of how they move. For example, snakes crawl and slither, lizards use their legs and turtles swim.

What can I do with my body?

■ Look at these pictures. Say which parts of your body you use for each of these activities. Choose from: legs, head, eyes, ears and your whole body.

I can identify which parts of my body I use when I exercise.

How did you do?

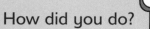

The skeleton

■ Look at the wordlist in the box. Can you use these names to label the correct bones on the diagram? Use reference books to help you and write your answers in the correct spaces.

breast bone	shoulder blade	jaw	pelvis	lower arm	hip bone
backbone	collar bone	rib	upper arm	skull	finger bones	lower leg
	knee cap	foot bones	thigh bone		

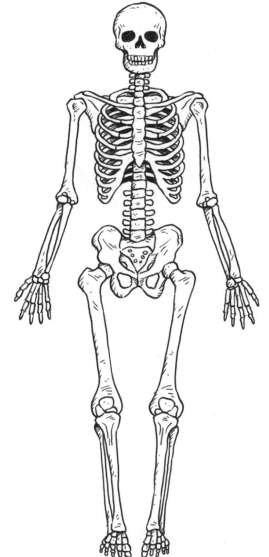

■ Can you find out the medical names for these bones?
■ Find out how many bones there are in your body.

I can name some of the bones in the human body.

How did you do?

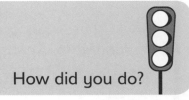

PHOTOCOPIABLE   ■SCHOLASTIC
www.scholastic.co.uk

The joints

You will need: card; a pencil; a paper-fastener; scissors and glue.

Joints are where one bone joins another bone. Most joints allow bones to move. There are two main types of joint:

Ball and socket	Hinge

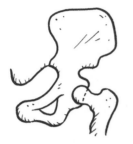

■ Make a model skull showing a hinge joint.

1. Trace the shapes of the skull below or cut them out and glue them on to card.

2. Fix a paper-fastener through the "X" on each piece to join to the skull.

■ Does it move like your jaw?
■ Can you name other bones which have a ball and socket or hinge joint?

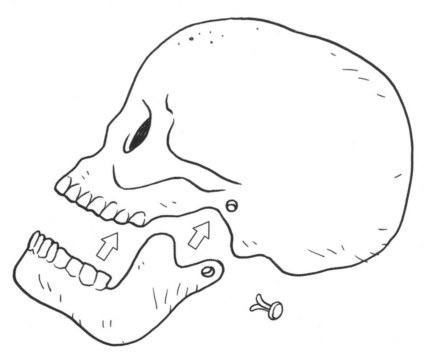

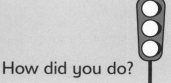

I can identify different types of joint.

How did you do?

The muscles

You will need: strong card; scissors; three elastic bands and a paper-fastener.

Muscles help our bodies move. There are over 600 muscles in our bodies and they are joined to our bones with tendons. They work in pairs so that each movement can be reversed. For example: the biceps in your arm flex your arm and the triceps extend it.

■ Make a model hand.

1. Cut out shapes A and B below. Glue them on to thick card and cut them out again.

2. Join the two pieces of card together with the paper-fastener and elastic bands.

3. When you move the handles together, the "fingers" open. Watch how the bands stretch and contract like your muscles. Try to pick up objects with your "hand".

■ Can you design a model arm or leg that moves?

I can show how muscles work in pairs.

How did you do?

PHOTOCOPIABLE    **SCHOLASTIC**
www.scholastic.co.uk

Name: _____   Date: _____

Hands

■ You will need: a ruler; 1cm squared paper; string; measuring tape; plain paper and a pencil.

■ Carry out these activities to discover all you can about your hands.

Area

■ Trace your hand on to squared paper.

■ Put an "X" in all the whole squares and count the total.

■ Now count up all the halves to make whole squares. Add the two totals together to find the area.

Perimeters

■ Carefully place a length of string around the outline of your hand on the squared paper.

■ Stretch the string along the measuring tape to find the total length.

Joints

■ Count the number of joints in your fingers and thumb.

Handspans

■ Stretch your hand out as wide as it will go. Measure the distance between the tip of the little finger and the thumb. This is your handspan.

■ Now record your results for all of the above.

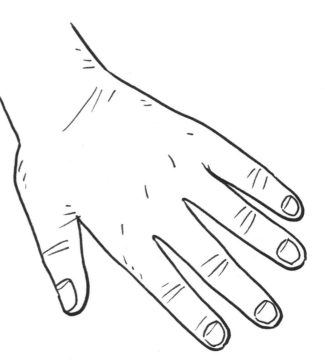

I can make scientific observations and record the results.

How did you do?

Strange skeletons

■ Look at the strange skeletons below. Write the name of the animal below its skeleton.

■ Write a sentence for each skeleton to explain your answer.

■ Draw the outline of each creature around its skeleton.

_____   _____

_____   _____

_____   _____

_____   _____

_____   _____

_____   _____

_____   _____

_____   _____

I can identify some animals from the shapes of their skeletons.

How did you do?

PHOTOCOPIABLE

SCHOLASTIC
www.scholastic.co.uk

Exercise diary

■ Fill in the exercise diary below every day for a week. Show all the different types of exercise you do, both at school and outside school.

Day	Exercise done		
		At school	Outside school
Monday	1		
	2		
	3		
Tuesday	1		
	2		
	3		
Wednesday	1		
	2		
	3		
Thursday	1		
	2		
	3		
Friday	1		
	2		
	3		
Saturday	1		
	2		
	3		
Sunday	1		
	2		
	3		

My favourite sort of exercise is _____.

Exercise is important because _____

_____

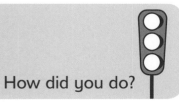

I can identify different types of excercise and say why it is important.

How did you do?

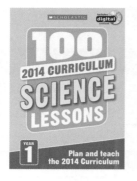

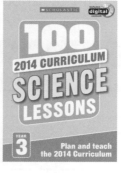
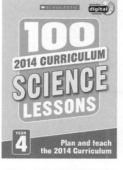

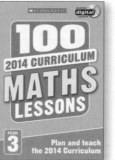
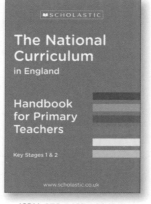